GREAT LIVES

Martin Luther

KING JR.

First edition for the United States, Canada, and the Philippines
published in 2019 by B.E.S. Publishing

All inquiries should be addressed to:
B.E.S. Publishing
250 Wireless Boulevard
Hauppauge, NY 11788
www.bes-publishing.com

ISBN: 978-1-4380-1205-6

Library of Congress Control No.: 2018963806

Conceived, designed, and produced by The Bright Press,
an imprint of The Quarto Group.
The Old Brewery, 6 Blundell Street,
London, N7 9BH, United Kingdom
T (0) 20 7700 6700 F (0) 20 7700 8066
www.QuartoKnows.com

Publisher: Mark Searle
Creative Director: James Evans
Managing Editor: Jacqui Sayers
Editor: Judith Chamberlain
Project Editors: Anna Southgate, Lucy York
Art Director: Katherine Radcliffe
Design: Lyndsey Harwood and Geoff Borin
Storyboard: Jess Taylor
Pencils: Dave Shephard
Inks: Fiona W. Dunn
Color: Sarah Skeate

Date of Manufacture: May 2019
Manufactured by: Transcontinental, Quebec, Canada

Printed in Canada

MIX
Paper from responsible sources
FSC® C011825
FSC www.fsc.org

9 8 7 6 5 4 3 2 1

GREAT LIVES
MARTIN LUTHER
KING JR.

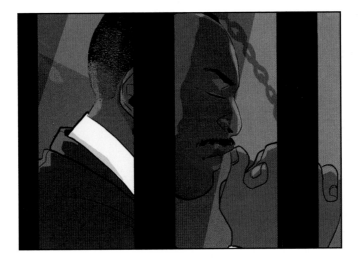

By Rachel Ruiz with illustrations by
Fiona W. Dunn and Sarah Skeate

B.E.S.
PUBLISHING

CONTENTS

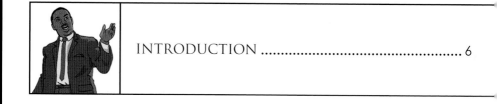

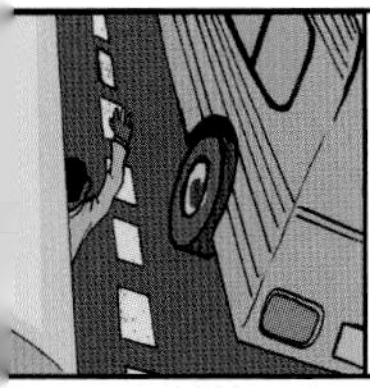

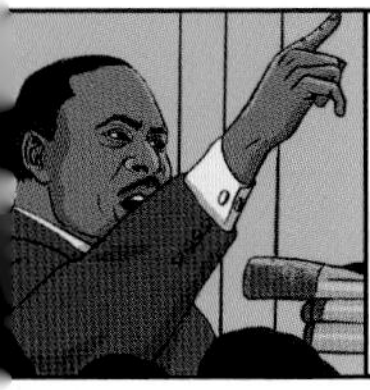

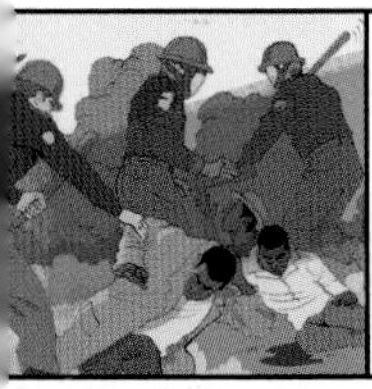

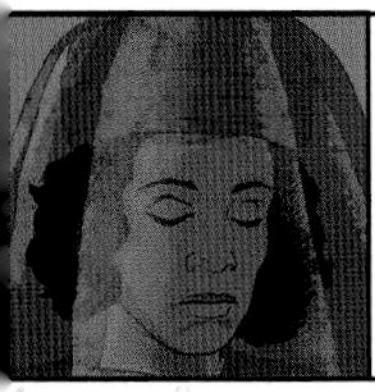

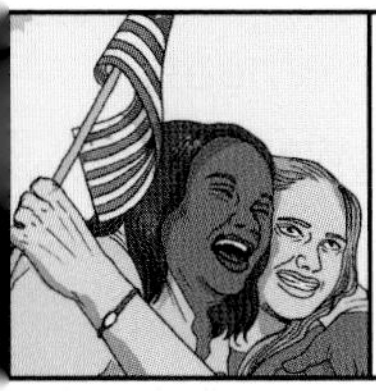

INTRODUCTION

On August 28, 2013, President Barack Hussein Obama, the first African-American president in U.S. history, stood on the steps of the Lincoln Memorial in Washington, D.C. He was there to mark the 50th Anniversary of the March on Washington, which Dr. Martin Luther King Jr. had been so instrumental in planning, and he spoke to the crowds of people who had assembled there:

"Dr. King explained that the goals of African Americans were identical to those of working people of all races: decent wages, fair working conditions, livable housing, old age security, health and welfare measures—conditions in which families can grow, have education for their children, and respect in the community. What King was describing has been the dream of every American." Fifty years earlier, Martin stood on those same steps and delivered his "I Have A Dream" speech.

Martin was born in Atlanta, Georgia, in 1929 when racism was rampant and segregation was legal—and would remain so for another three decades. The son, grandson, and great-grandson of Baptist ministers, Martin grew up to become a minister himself. He graduated from high school early and went on to study at Morehouse College and Crozer Theological Seminary, before earning a doctorate at Boston University. When Martin became the leader of America's modern civil rights movement in the late 1950s and 1960s, he often said it was a role he did not ask for, but he could not turn away from it either. Martin used both his education and his Christian faith to guide him as he led thousands to fight for, and achieve, legal equality for African Americans in the United States.

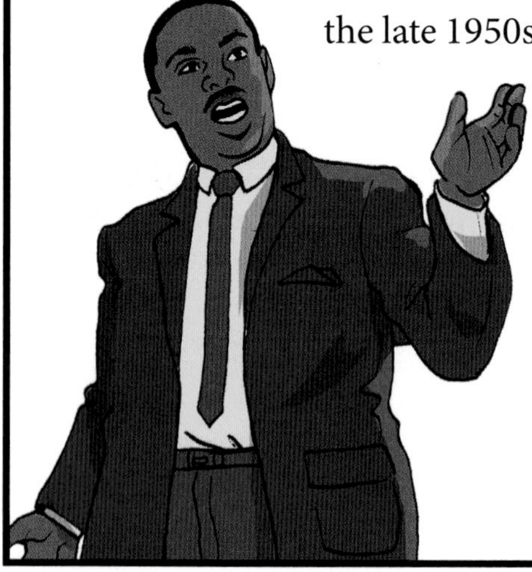

What is remarkable about the fight, is that it was peaceful. Martin was inspired by Mahatma Gandhi, who led India to freedom from British rule using nonviolent protest. Martin instructed civil rights marchers not to strike back— no matter what. "Nonviolent resistance is the most potent weapon available to oppressed people in their struggle for freedom," he once said. In 1964, at the age of 35, Martin became the youngest person to win the Nobel Peace Prize.

On April 4, 1968, Martin made the ultimate sacrifice in the name of equality when he was struck down by a sniper's bullet. He was in Memphis, Tennessee, to support striking African-American sanitation workers who had organized a strike for equal pay and safe working conditions. Martin was 39 years old. In less than 13 years, he had accomplished what many had previously thought impossible. Thanks to the hard work, dedication, and sacrifice of Martin and many other civil rights activists that fought alongside him, racial segregation was outlawed, and the Civil Rights Act and Voting Rights Act were passed. Their achievements didn't stop there:

"Because they marched, America became more free and more fair, not just for African Americans but for women and Latinos, Asians and Native Americans, for Catholics, Jews, and Muslims, for gays, for Americans with disabilities. America changed for you and for me." --Barack Obama, August 28, 2013, 50th Anniversary of the March on Washington.

CHAPTER 1

A KING IS BORN

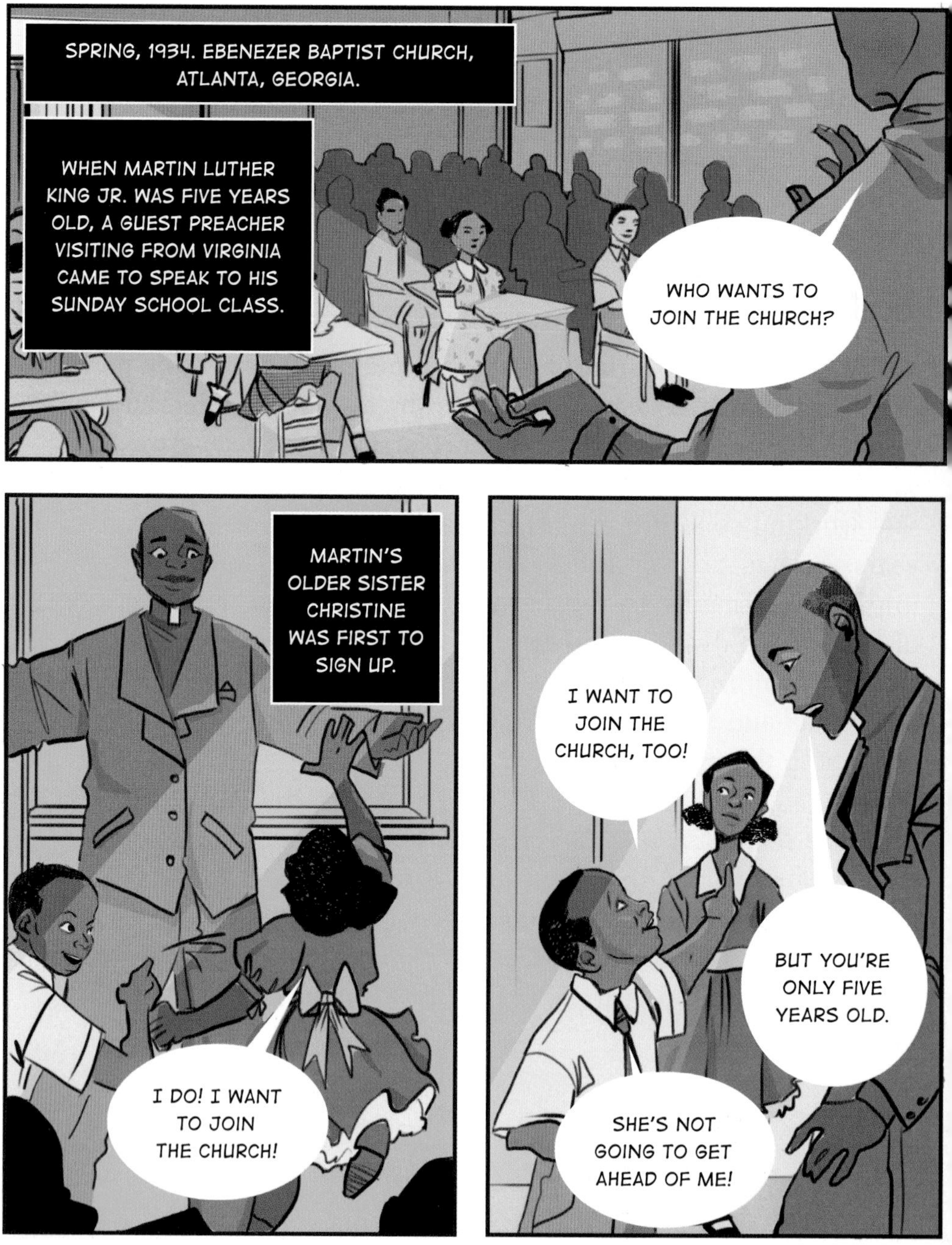
SPRING, 1934. EBENEZER BAPTIST CHURCH, ATLANTA, GEORGIA.
WHEN MARTIN LUTHER KING JR. WAS FIVE YEARS OLD, A GUEST PREACHER VISITING FROM VIRGINIA CAME TO SPEAK TO HIS SUNDAY SCHOOL CLASS.
WHO WANTS TO JOIN THE CHURCH?
MARTIN'S OLDER SISTER CHRISTINE WAS FIRST TO SIGN UP.
I DO! I WANT TO JOIN THE CHURCH!
I WANT TO JOIN THE CHURCH, TOO!
BUT YOU'RE ONLY FIVE YEARS OLD.
SHE'S NOT GOING TO GET AHEAD OF ME!

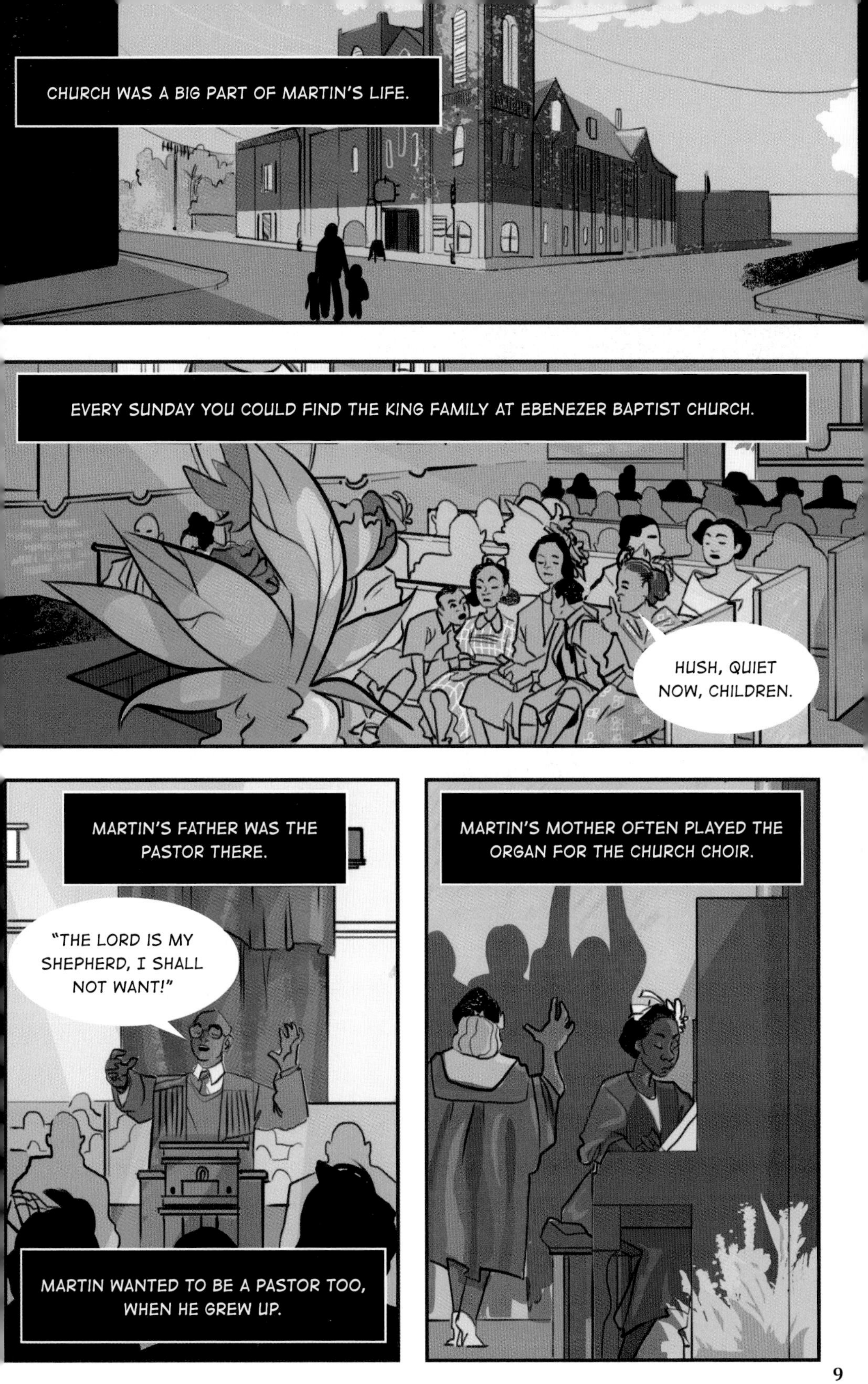
CHURCH WAS A BIG PART OF MARTIN'S LIFE.
EVERY SUNDAY YOU COULD FIND THE KING FAMILY AT EBENEZER BAPTIST CHURCH.
HUSH, QUIET NOW, CHILDREN.
MARTIN'S FATHER WAS THE PASTOR THERE.
"THE LORD IS MY SHEPHERD, I SHALL NOT WANT!"
MARTIN WANTED TO BE A PASTOR TOO, WHEN HE GREW UP.
MARTIN'S MOTHER OFTEN PLAYED THE ORGAN FOR THE CHURCH CHOIR.

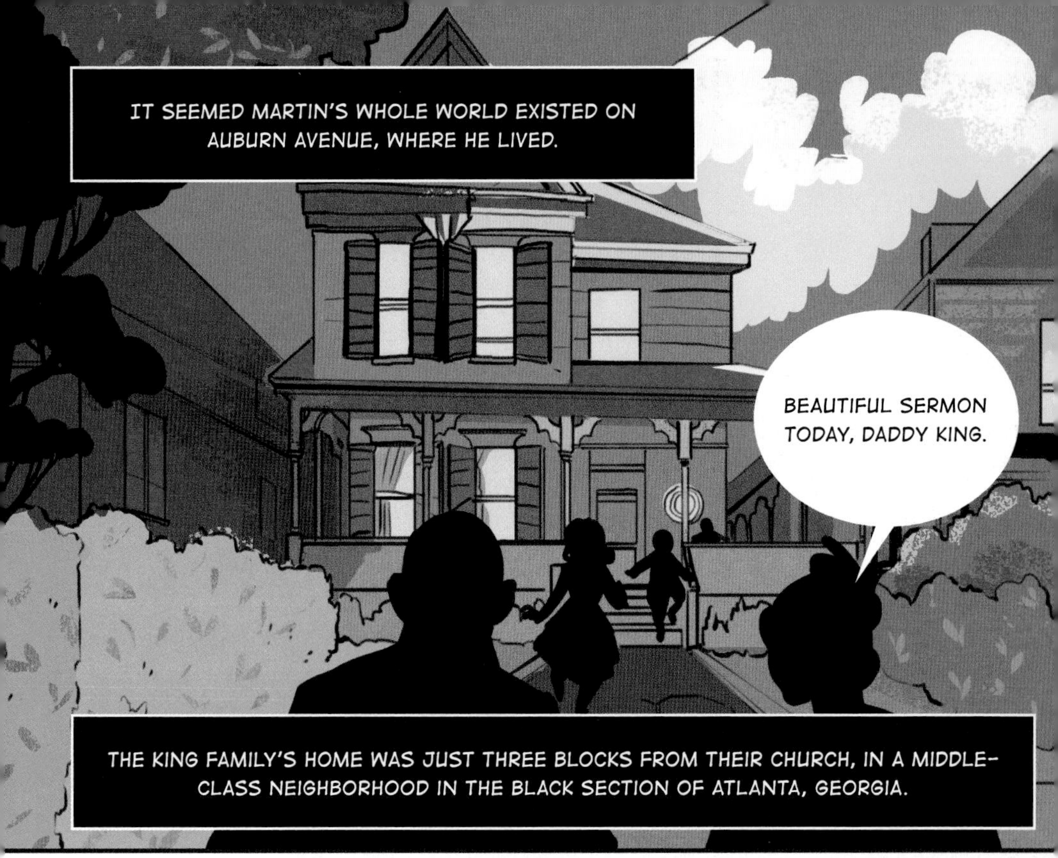
IT SEEMED MARTIN'S WHOLE WORLD EXISTED ON AUBURN AVENUE, WHERE HE LIVED.
BEAUTIFUL SERMON TODAY, DADDY KING.
THE KING FAMILY'S HOME WAS JUST THREE BLOCKS FROM THEIR CHURCH, IN A MIDDLE-CLASS NEIGHBORHOOD IN THE BLACK SECTION OF ATLANTA, GEORGIA.

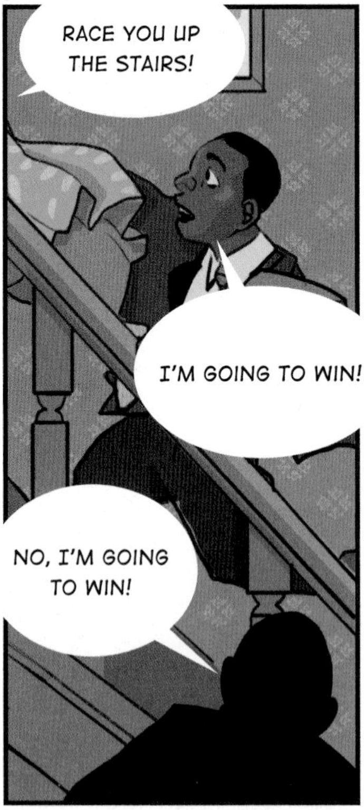
RACE YOU UP THE STAIRS!
I'M GOING TO WIN!
NO, I'M GOING TO WIN!

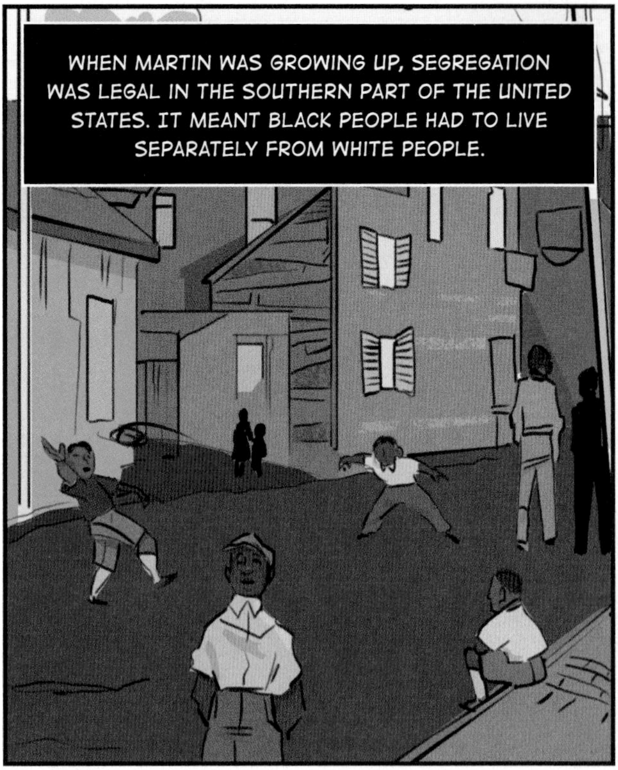
WHEN MARTIN WAS GROWING UP, SEGREGATION WAS LEGAL IN THE SOUTHERN PART OF THE UNITED STATES. IT MEANT BLACK PEOPLE HAD TO LIVE SEPARATELY FROM WHITE PEOPLE.

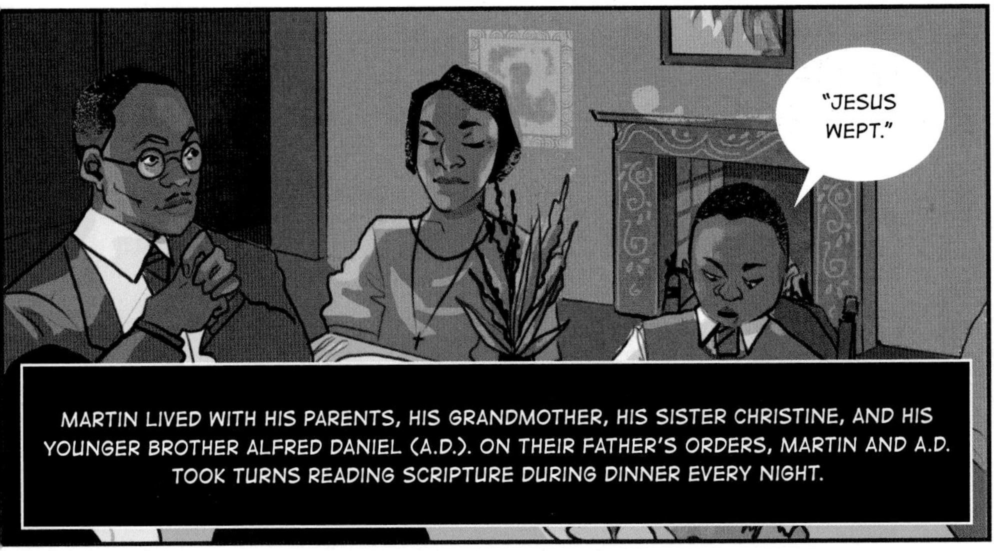
"JESUS WEPT."
MARTIN LIVED WITH HIS PARENTS, HIS GRANDMOTHER, HIS SISTER CHRISTINE, AND HIS YOUNGER BROTHER ALFRED DANIEL (A.D.). ON THEIR FATHER'S ORDERS, MARTIN AND A.D. TOOK TURNS READING SCRIPTURE DURING DINNER EVERY NIGHT.

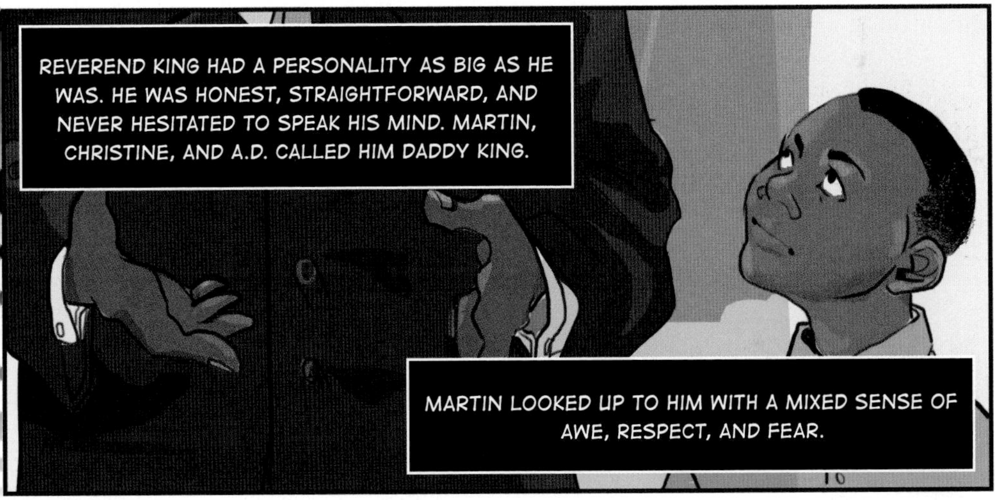
REVEREND KING HAD A PERSONALITY AS BIG AS HE WAS. HE WAS HONEST, STRAIGHTFORWARD, AND NEVER HESITATED TO SPEAK HIS MIND. MARTIN, CHRISTINE, AND A.D. CALLED HIM DADDY KING.
MARTIN LOOKED UP TO HIM WITH A MIXED SENSE OF AWE, RESPECT, AND FEAR.

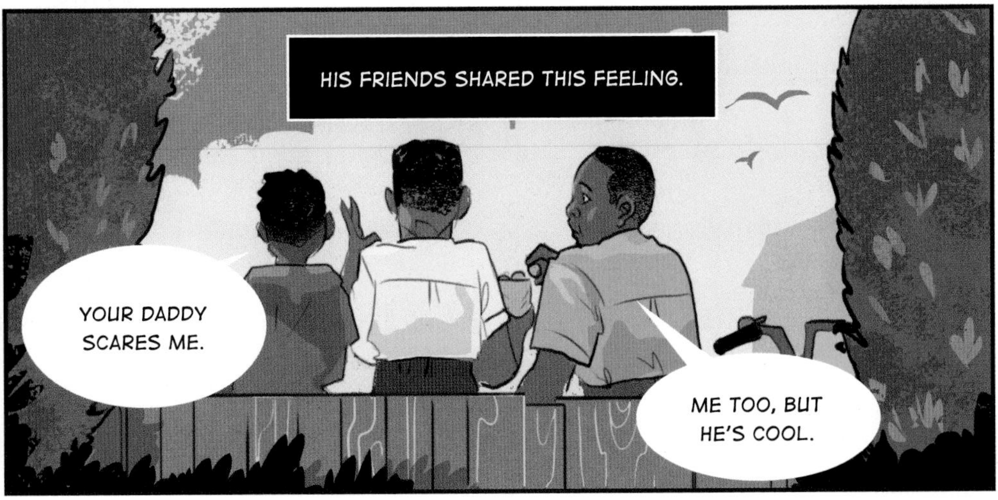
HIS FRIENDS SHARED THIS FEELING.
YOUR DADDY SCARES ME.
ME TOO, BUT HE'S COOL.

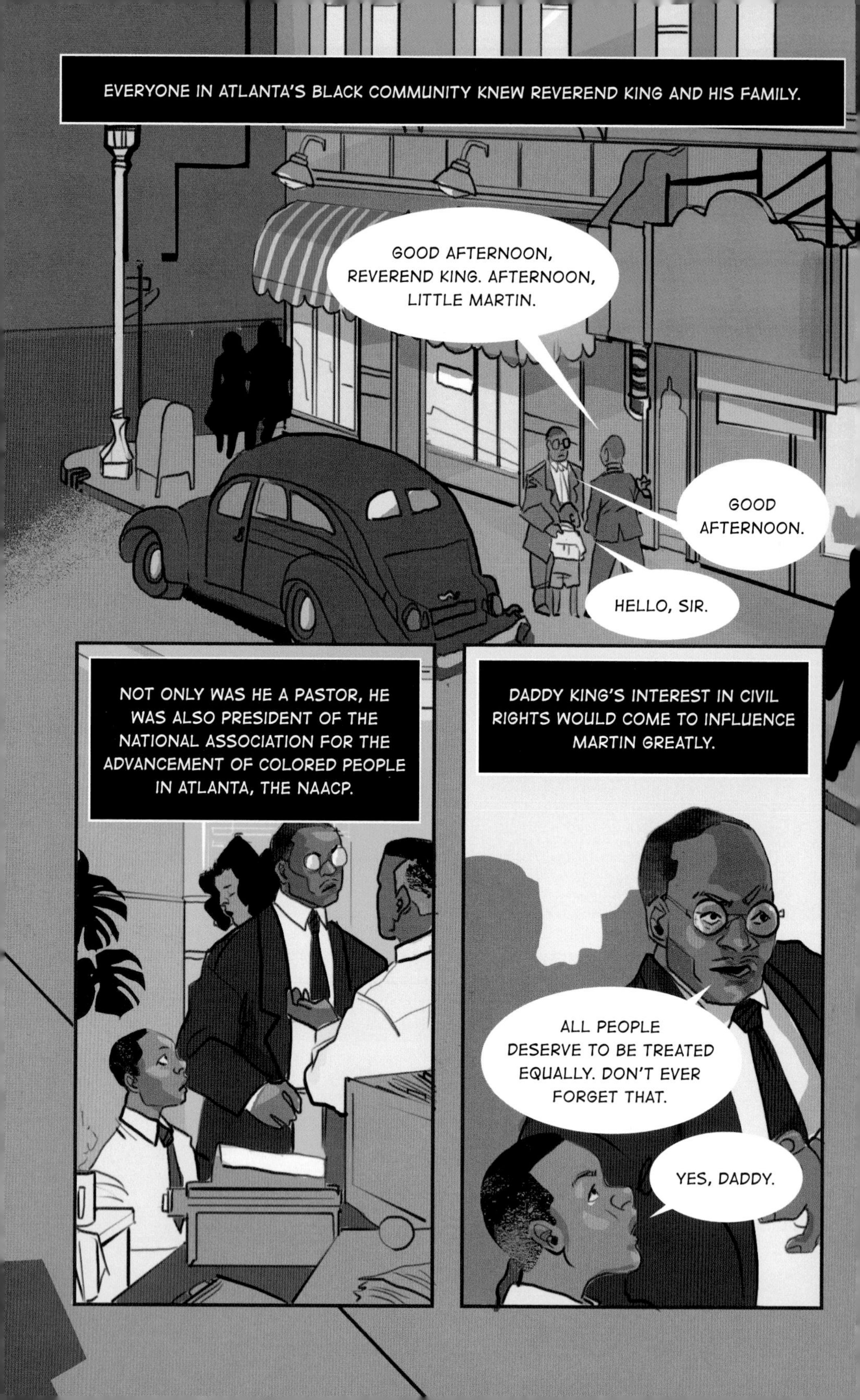
EVERYONE IN ATLANTA'S BLACK COMMUNITY KNEW REVEREND KING AND HIS FAMILY.
GOOD AFTERNOON, REVEREND KING. AFTERNOON, LITTLE MARTIN.
GOOD AFTERNOON.
HELLO, SIR.
NOT ONLY WAS HE A PASTOR, HE WAS ALSO PRESIDENT OF THE NATIONAL ASSOCIATION FOR THE ADVANCEMENT OF COLORED PEOPLE IN ATLANTA, THE NAACP.
DADDY KING'S INTEREST IN CIVIL RIGHTS WOULD COME TO INFLUENCE MARTIN GREATLY.
ALL PEOPLE DESERVE TO BE TREATED EQUALLY. DON'T EVER FORGET THAT.
YES, DADDY.

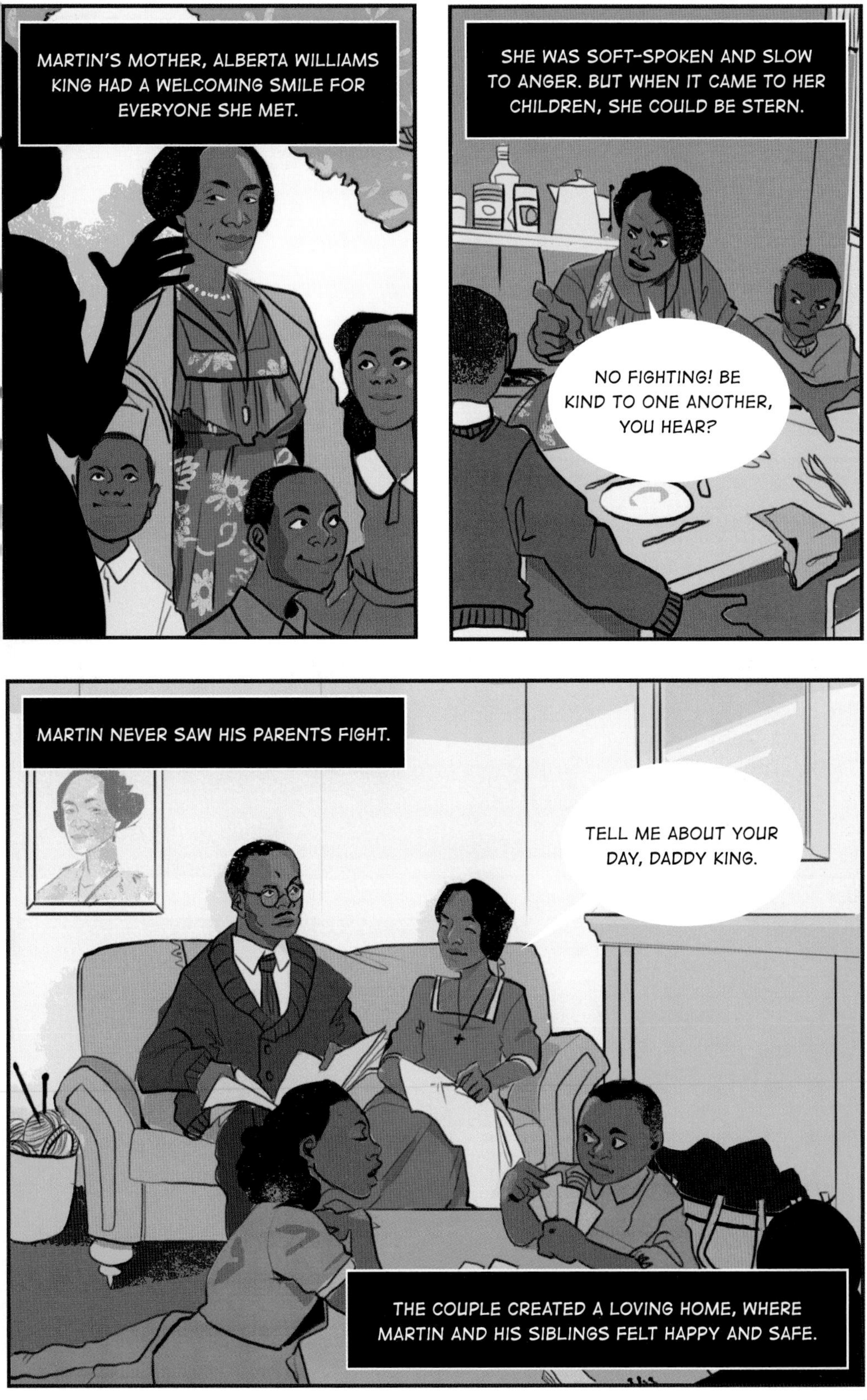
MARTIN'S MOTHER, ALBERTA WILLIAMS KING HAD A WELCOMING SMILE FOR EVERYONE SHE MET.
SHE WAS SOFT-SPOKEN AND SLOW TO ANGER. BUT WHEN IT CAME TO HER CHILDREN, SHE COULD BE STERN.
NO FIGHTING! BE KIND TO ONE ANOTHER, YOU HEAR?
MARTIN NEVER SAW HIS PARENTS FIGHT.
TELL ME ABOUT YOUR DAY, DADDY KING.
THE COUPLE CREATED A LOVING HOME, WHERE MARTIN AND HIS SIBLINGS FELT HAPPY AND SAFE.

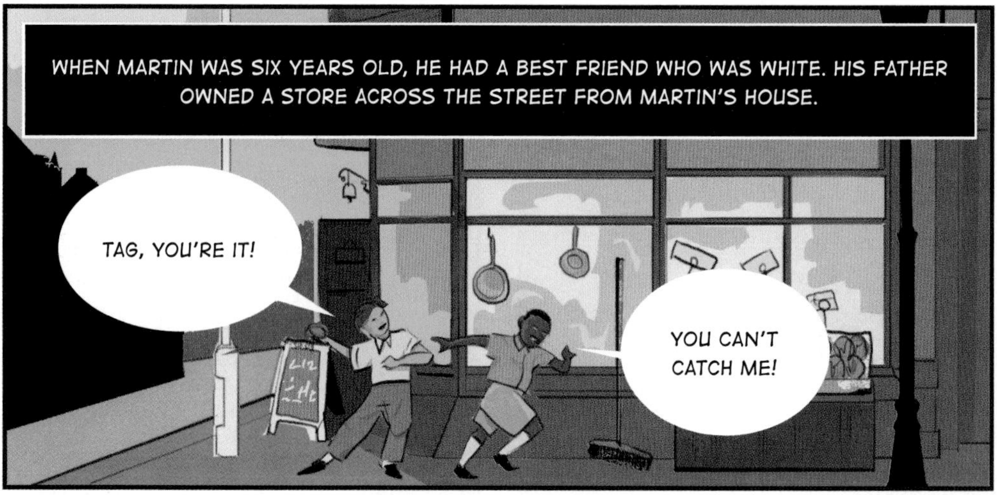
WHEN MARTIN WAS SIX YEARS OLD, HE HAD A BEST FRIEND WHO WAS WHITE. HIS FATHER OWNED A STORE ACROSS THE STREET FROM MARTIN'S HOUSE.
TAG, YOU'RE IT!
YOU CAN'T CATCH ME!

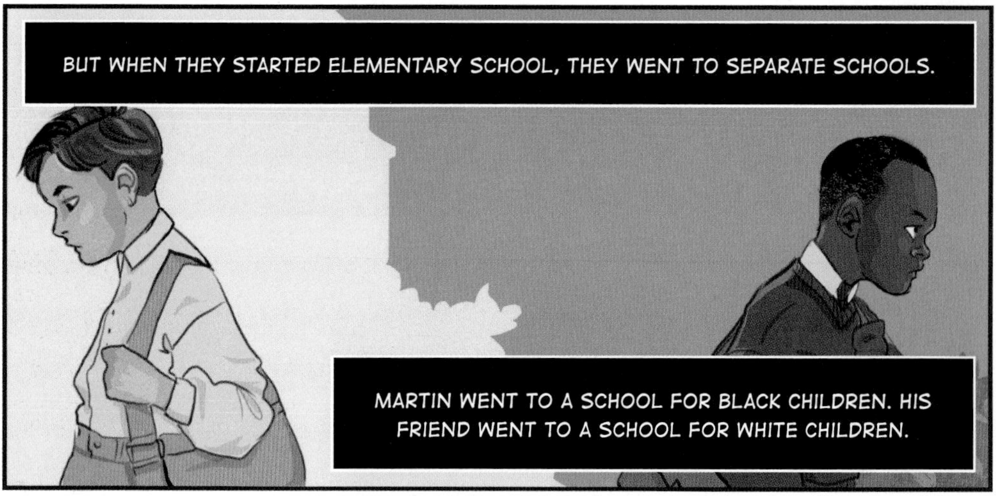
BUT WHEN THEY STARTED ELEMENTARY SCHOOL, THEY WENT TO SEPARATE SCHOOLS.
MARTIN WENT TO A SCHOOL FOR BLACK CHILDREN. HIS FRIEND WENT TO A SCHOOL FOR WHITE CHILDREN.

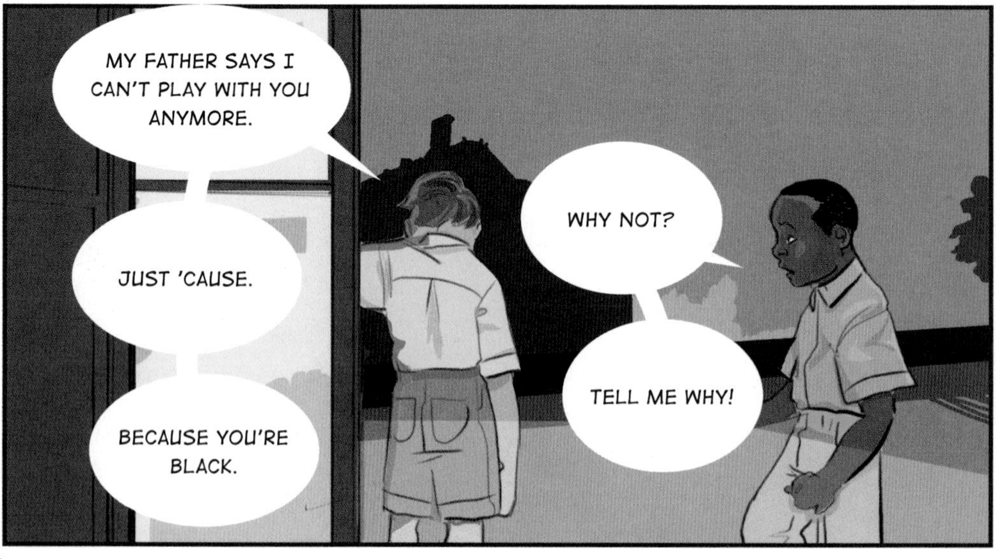
MY FATHER SAYS I CAN'T PLAY WITH YOU ANYMORE.
WHY NOT?
JUST 'CAUSE.
TELL ME WHY!
BECAUSE YOU'RE BLACK.

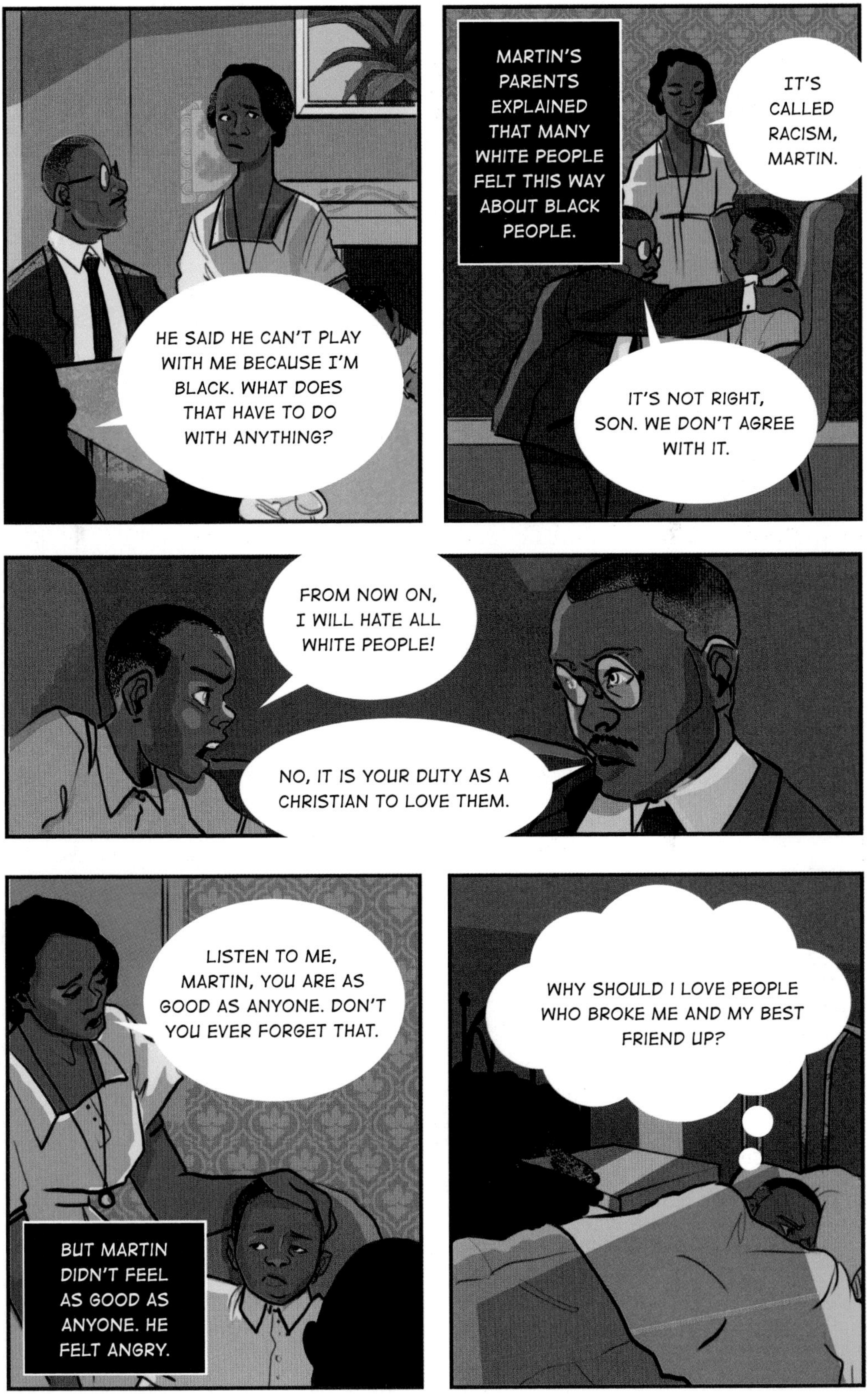
HE SAID HE CAN'T PLAY WITH ME BECAUSE I'M BLACK. WHAT DOES THAT HAVE TO DO WITH ANYTHING?
MARTIN'S PARENTS EXPLAINED THAT MANY WHITE PEOPLE FELT THIS WAY ABOUT BLACK PEOPLE.
IT'S CALLED RACISM, MARTIN.
IT'S NOT RIGHT, SON. WE DON'T AGREE WITH IT.
FROM NOW ON, I WILL HATE ALL WHITE PEOPLE!
NO, IT IS YOUR DUTY AS A CHRISTIAN TO LOVE THEM.
LISTEN TO ME, MARTIN, YOU ARE AS GOOD AS ANYONE. DON'T YOU EVER FORGET THAT.
BUT MARTIN DIDN'T FEEL AS GOOD AS ANYONE. HE FELT ANGRY.
WHY SHOULD I LOVE PEOPLE WHO BROKE ME AND MY BEST FRIEND UP?

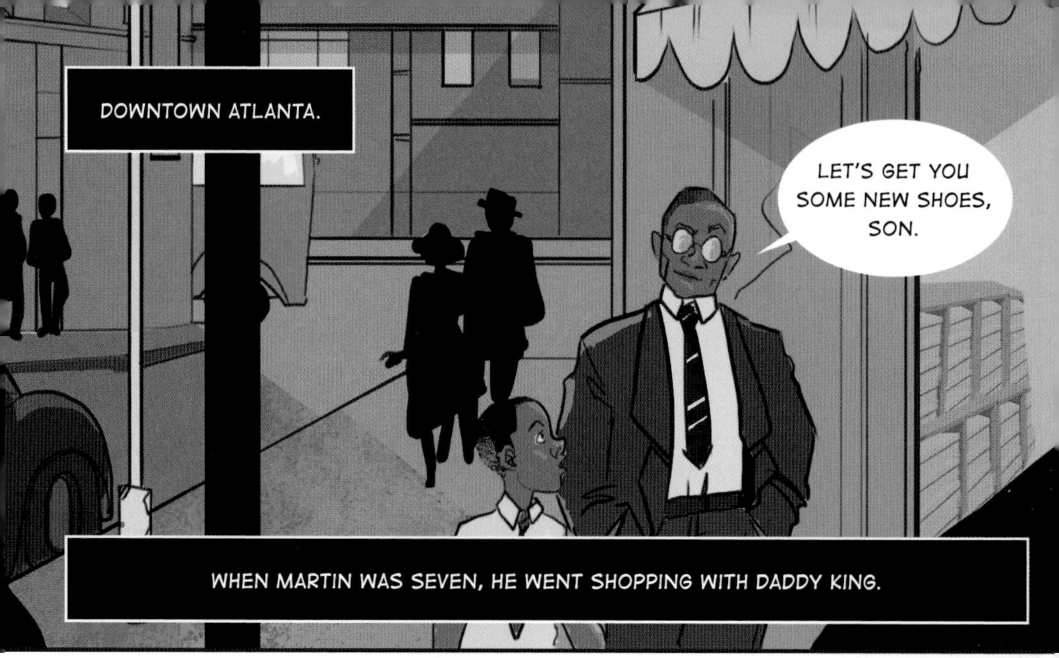
DOWNTOWN ATLANTA.
LET'S GET YOU SOME NEW SHOES, SON.
WHEN MARTIN WAS SEVEN, HE WENT SHOPPING WITH DADDY KING.

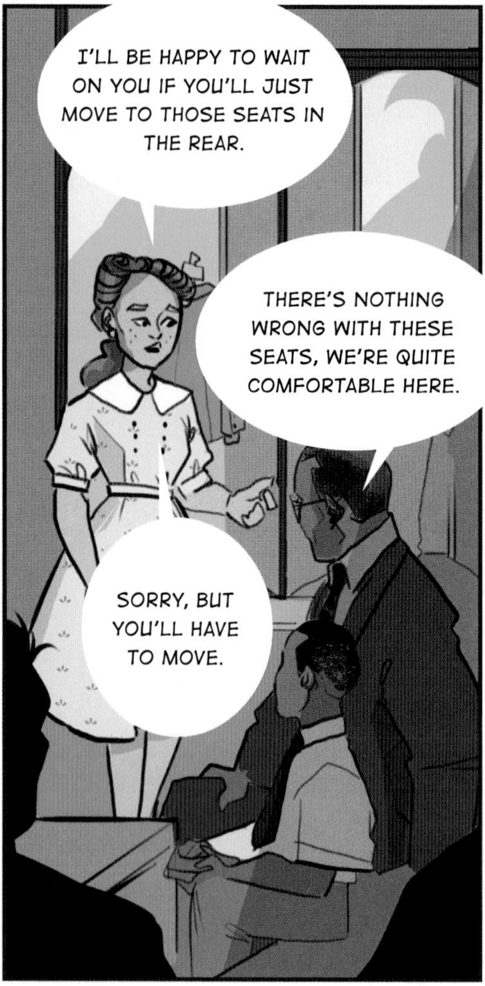
I'LL BE HAPPY TO WAIT ON YOU IF YOU'LL JUST MOVE TO THOSE SEATS IN THE REAR.
THERE'S NOTHING WRONG WITH THESE SEATS, WE'RE QUITE COMFORTABLE HERE.
SORRY, BUT YOU'LL HAVE TO MOVE.

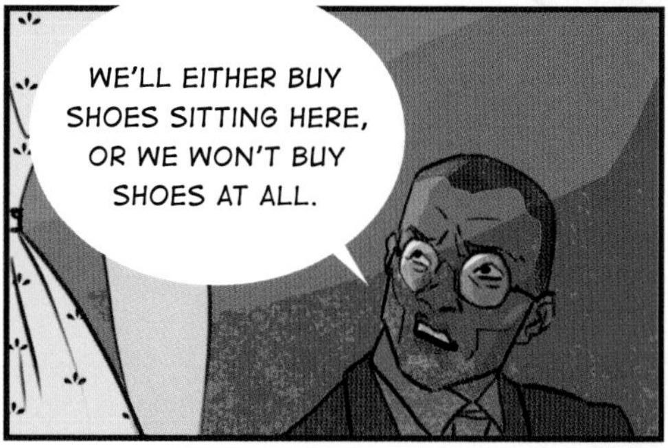
WE'LL EITHER BUY SHOES SITTING HERE, OR WE WON'T BUY SHOES AT ALL.

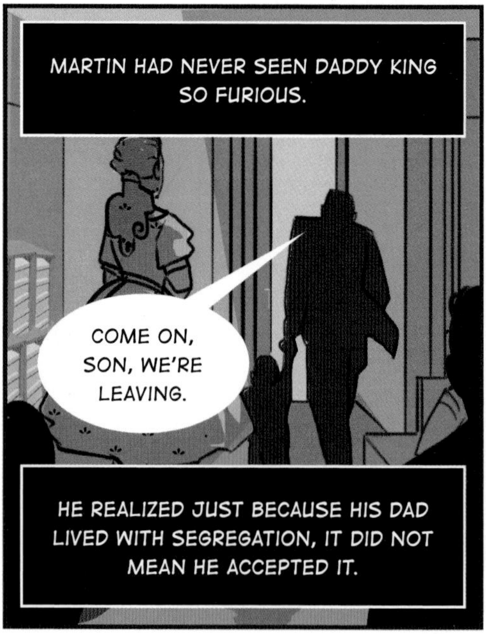
MARTIN HAD NEVER SEEN DADDY KING SO FURIOUS.
COME ON, SON, WE'RE LEAVING.
HE REALIZED JUST BECAUSE HIS DAD LIVED WITH SEGREGATION, IT DID NOT MEAN HE ACCEPTED IT.

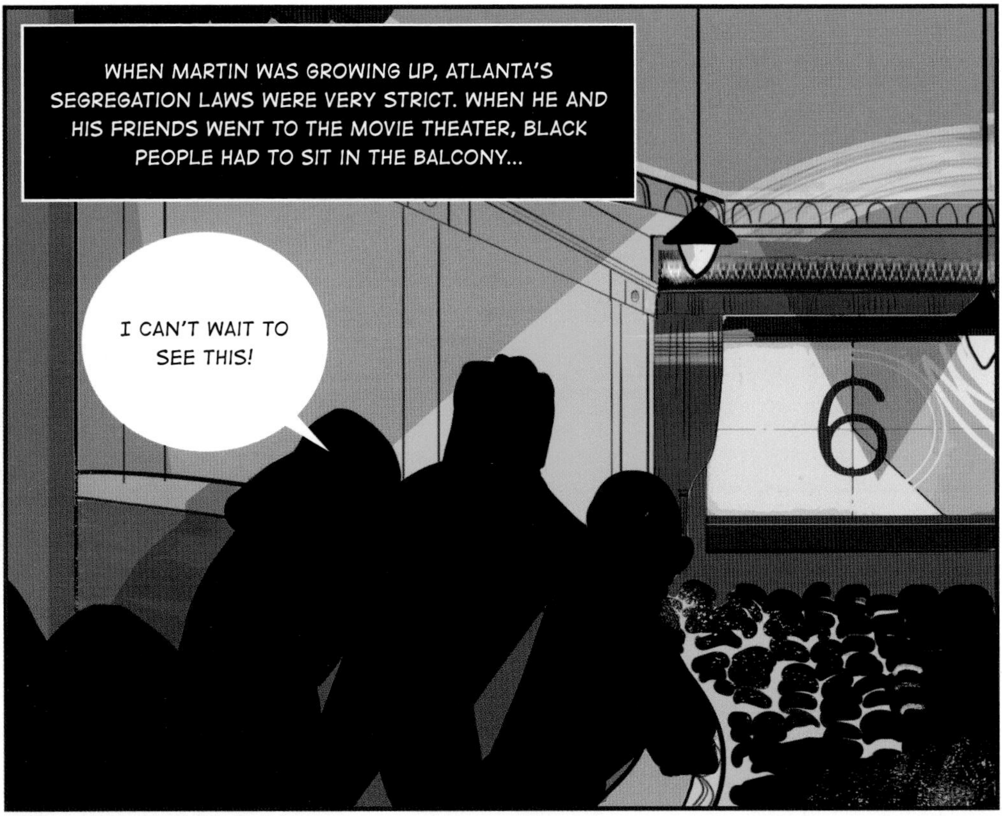
WHEN MARTIN WAS GROWING UP, ATLANTA'S SEGREGATION LAWS WERE VERY STRICT. WHEN HE AND HIS FRIENDS WENT TO THE MOVIE THEATER, BLACK PEOPLE HAD TO SIT IN THE BALCONY...
I CAN'T WAIT TO SEE THIS!
6

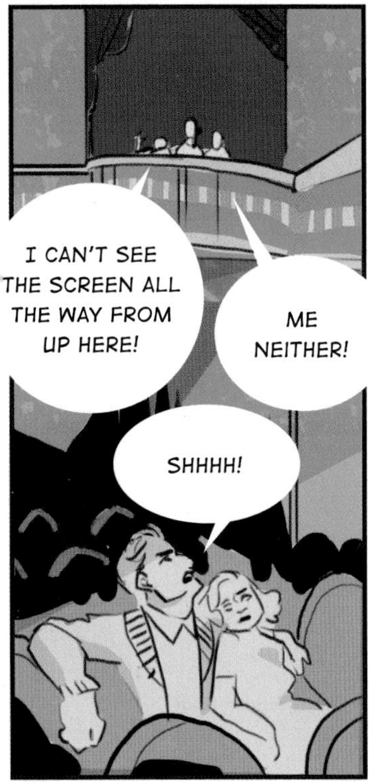
I CAN'T SEE THE SCREEN ALL THE WAY FROM UP HERE!
ME NEITHER!
SHHHH!

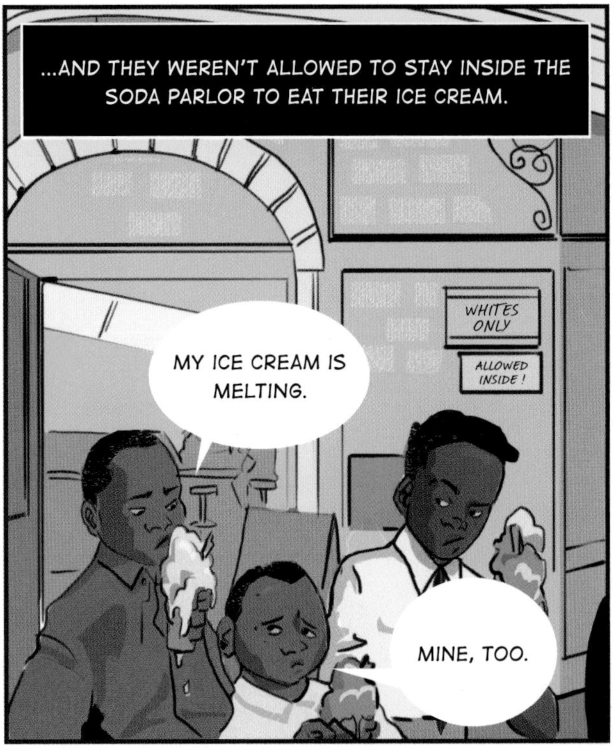
...AND THEY WEREN'T ALLOWED TO STAY INSIDE THE SODA PARLOR TO EAT THEIR ICE CREAM.
WHITES ONLY
ALLOWED INSIDE!
MY ICE CREAM IS MELTING.
MINE, TOO.

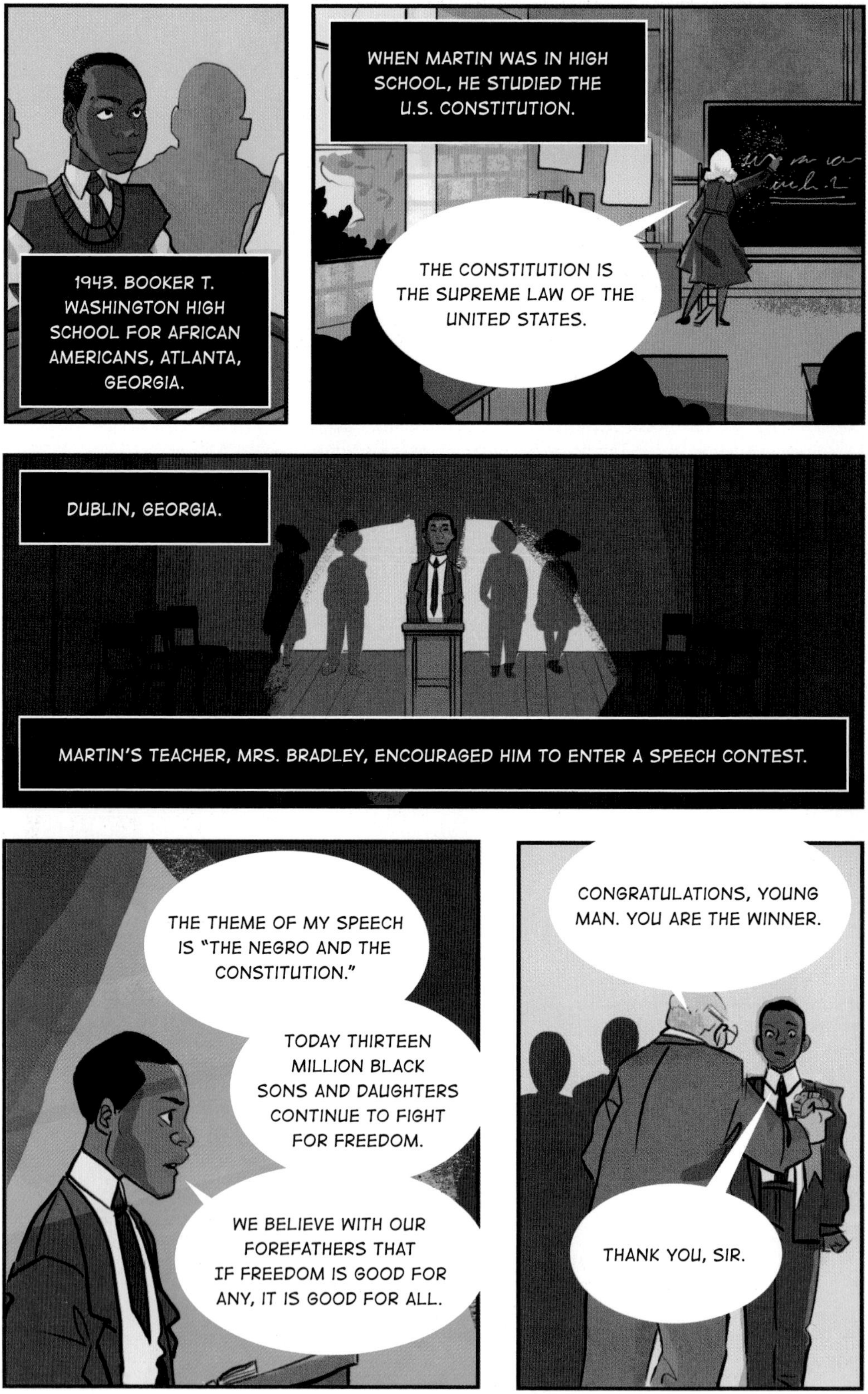
1943. BOOKER T. WASHINGTON HIGH SCHOOL FOR AFRICAN AMERICANS, ATLANTA, GEORGIA.
WHEN MARTIN WAS IN HIGH SCHOOL, HE STUDIED THE U.S. CONSTITUTION.
THE CONSTITUTION IS THE SUPREME LAW OF THE UNITED STATES.
DUBLIN, GEORGIA.
MARTIN'S TEACHER, MRS. BRADLEY, ENCOURAGED HIM TO ENTER A SPEECH CONTEST.
THE THEME OF MY SPEECH IS "THE NEGRO AND THE CONSTITUTION."
TODAY THIRTEEN MILLION BLACK SONS AND DAUGHTERS CONTINUE TO FIGHT FOR FREEDOM.
WE BELIEVE WITH OUR FOREFATHERS THAT IF FREEDOM IS GOOD FOR ANY, IT IS GOOD FOR ALL.
CONGRATULATIONS, YOUNG MAN. YOU ARE THE WINNER.
THANK YOU, SIR.

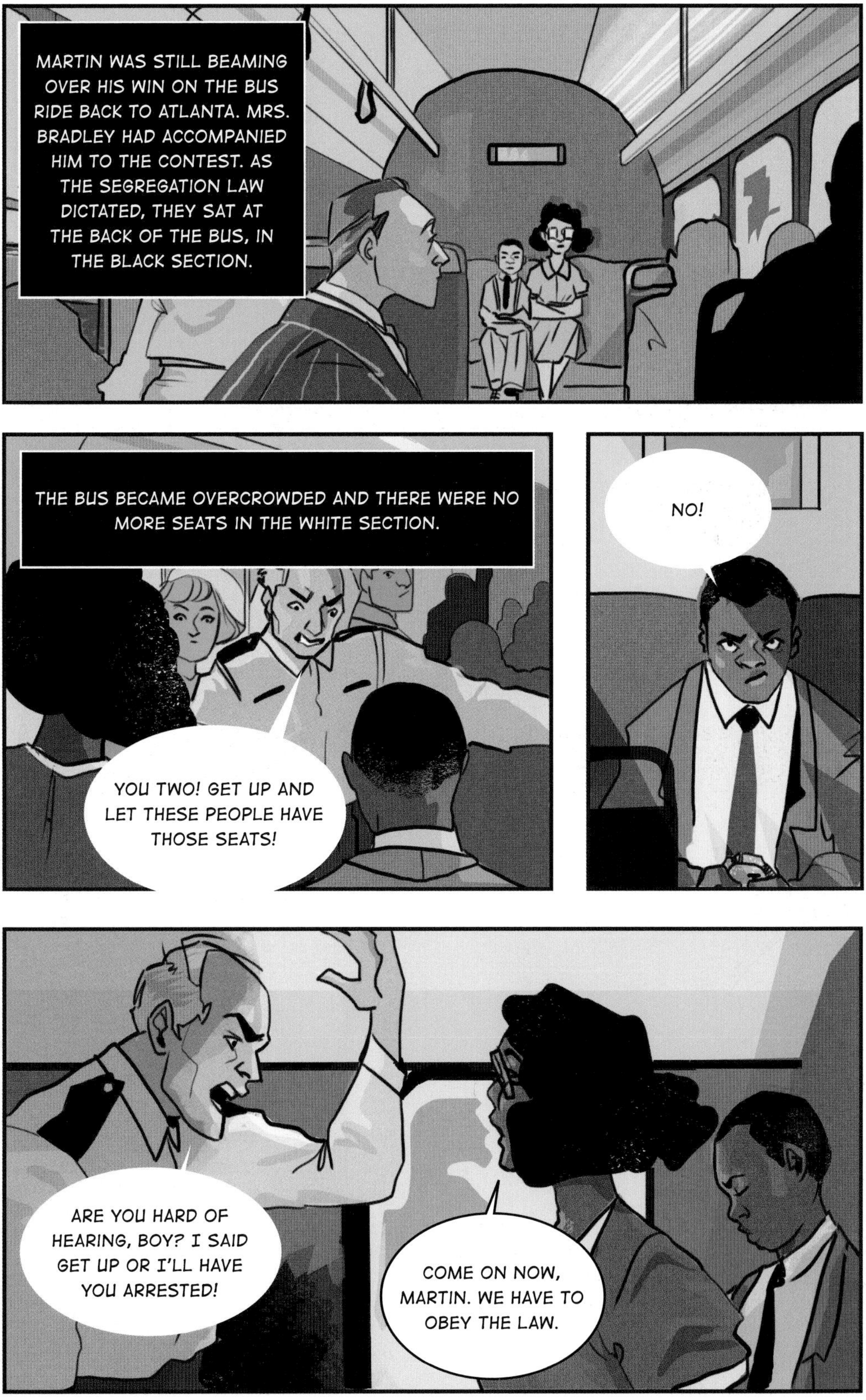
MARTIN WAS STILL BEAMING OVER HIS WIN ON THE BUS RIDE BACK TO ATLANTA. MRS. BRADLEY HAD ACCOMPANIED HIM TO THE CONTEST. AS THE SEGREGATION LAW DICTATED, THEY SAT AT THE BACK OF THE BUS, IN THE BLACK SECTION.
THE BUS BECAME OVERCROWDED AND THERE WERE NO MORE SEATS IN THE WHITE SECTION.
YOU TWO! GET UP AND LET THESE PEOPLE HAVE THOSE SEATS!
NO!
ARE YOU HARD OF HEARING, BOY? I SAID GET UP OR I'LL HAVE YOU ARRESTED!
COME ON NOW, MARTIN. WE HAVE TO OBEY THE LAW.

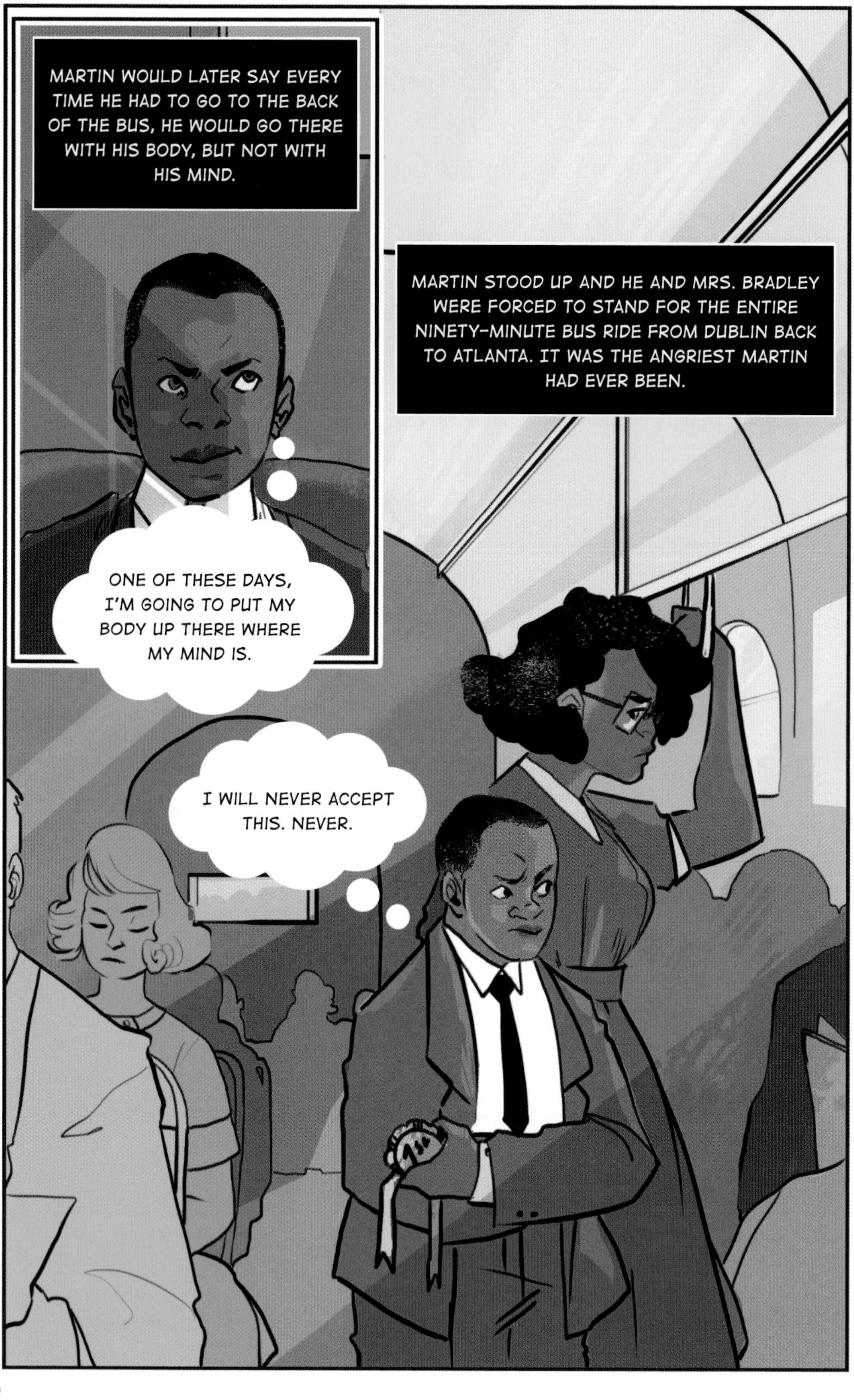
MARTIN WOULD LATER SAY EVERY TIME HE HAD TO GO TO THE BACK OF THE BUS, HE WOULD GO THERE WITH HIS BODY, BUT NOT WITH HIS MIND.
ONE OF THESE DAYS, I'M GOING TO PUT MY BODY UP THERE WHERE MY MIND IS.
MARTIN STOOD UP AND HE AND MRS. BRADLEY WERE FORCED TO STAND FOR THE ENTIRE NINETY-MINUTE BUS RIDE FROM DUBLIN BACK TO ATLANTA. IT WAS THE ANGRIEST MARTIN HAD EVER BEEN.
I WILL NEVER ACCEPT THIS. NEVER.

CHAPTER 2

THE YOUNG COLLEGE STUDENT

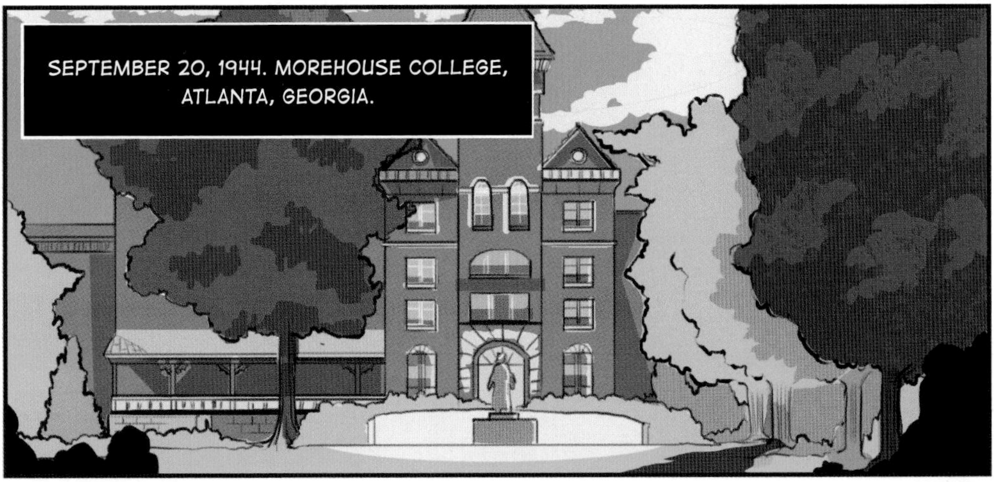
SEPTEMBER 20, 1944. MOREHOUSE COLLEGE, ATLANTA, GEORGIA.

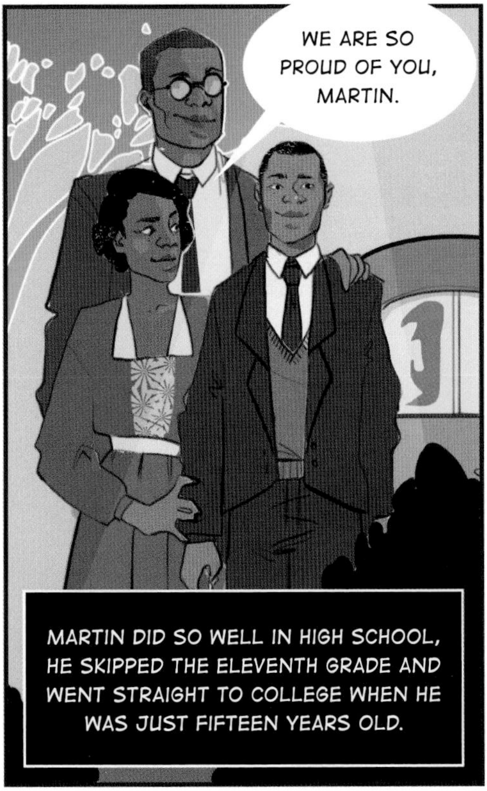
WE ARE SO PROUD OF YOU, MARTIN.
MARTIN DID SO WELL IN HIGH SCHOOL, HE SKIPPED THE ELEVENTH GRADE AND WENT STRAIGHT TO COLLEGE WHEN HE WAS JUST FIFTEEN YEARS OLD.

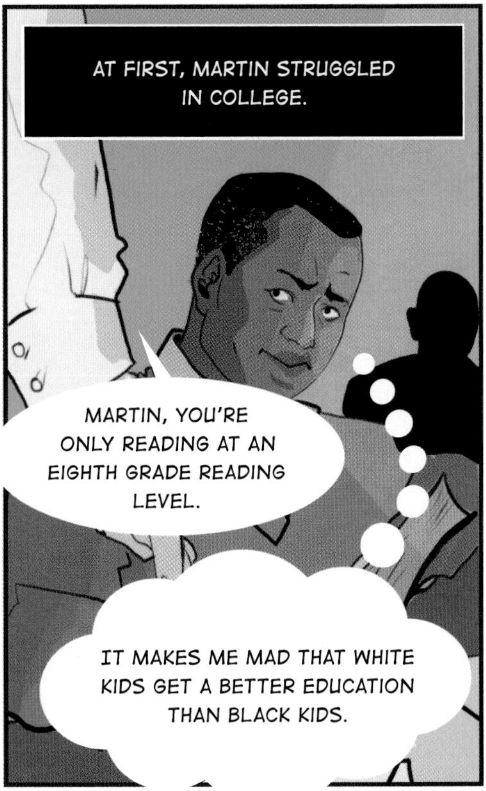
AT FIRST, MARTIN STRUGGLED IN COLLEGE.
MARTIN, YOU'RE ONLY READING AT AN EIGHTH GRADE READING LEVEL.
IT MAKES ME MAD THAT WHITE KIDS GET A BETTER EDUCATION THAN BLACK KIDS.

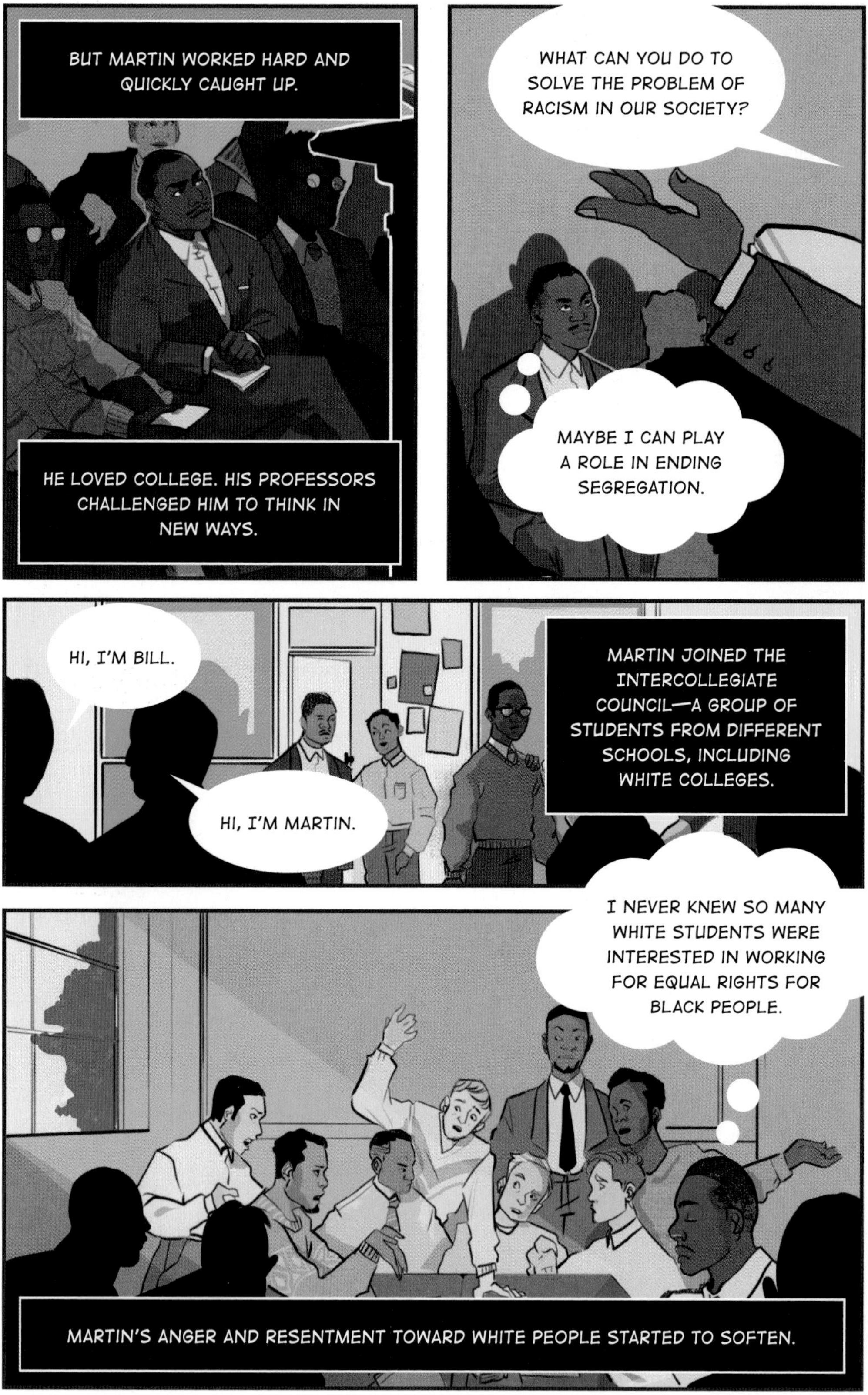
BUT MARTIN WORKED HARD AND QUICKLY CAUGHT UP.
HE LOVED COLLEGE. HIS PROFESSORS CHALLENGED HIM TO THINK IN NEW WAYS.
WHAT CAN YOU DO TO SOLVE THE PROBLEM OF RACISM IN OUR SOCIETY?
MAYBE I CAN PLAY A ROLE IN ENDING SEGREGATION.
HI, I'M BILL.
HI, I'M MARTIN.
MARTIN JOINED THE INTERCOLLEGIATE COUNCIL—A GROUP OF STUDENTS FROM DIFFERENT SCHOOLS, INCLUDING WHITE COLLEGES.
I NEVER KNEW SO MANY WHITE STUDENTS WERE INTERESTED IN WORKING FOR EQUAL RIGHTS FOR BLACK PEOPLE.
MARTIN'S ANGER AND RESENTMENT TOWARD WHITE PEOPLE STARTED TO SOFTEN.

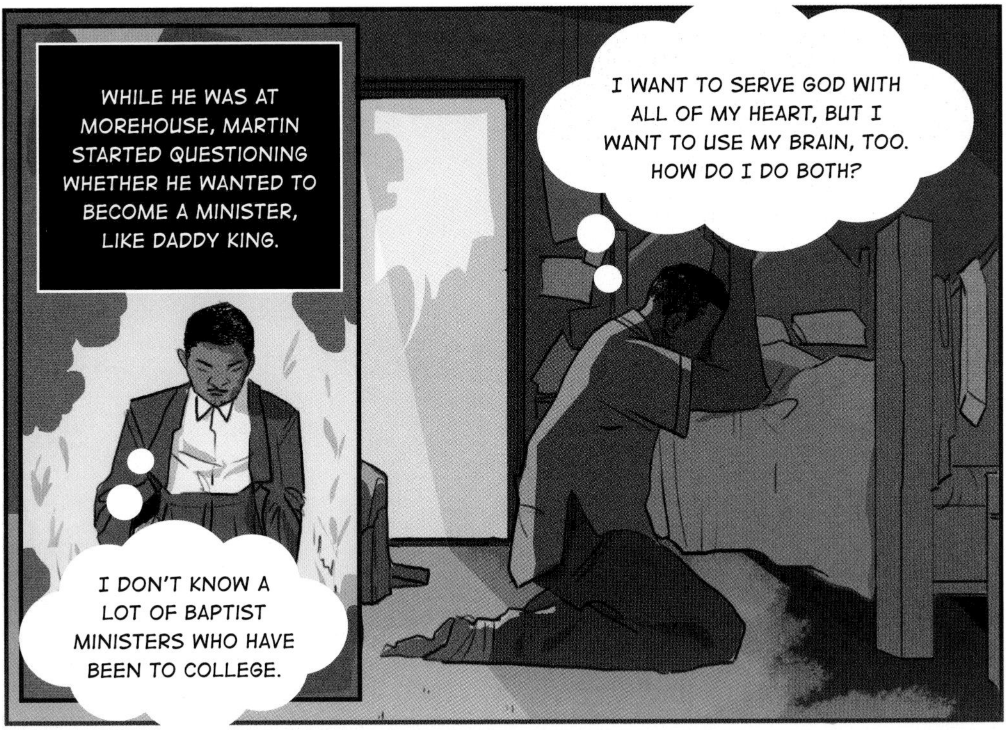
WHILE HE WAS AT MOREHOUSE, MARTIN STARTED QUESTIONING WHETHER HE WANTED TO BECOME A MINISTER, LIKE DADDY KING.
I DON'T KNOW A LOT OF BAPTIST MINISTERS WHO HAVE BEEN TO COLLEGE.
I WANT TO SERVE GOD WITH ALL OF MY HEART, BUT I WANT TO USE MY BRAIN, TOO. HOW DO I DO BOTH?

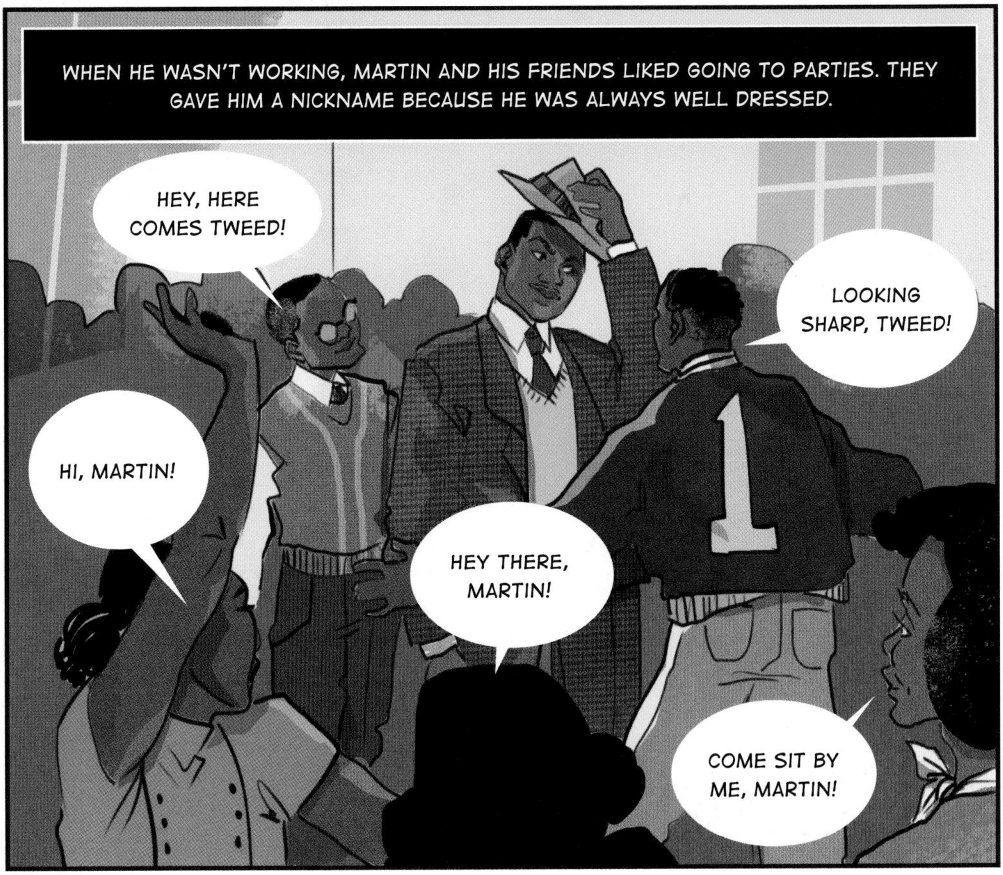
WHEN HE WASN'T WORKING, MARTIN AND HIS FRIENDS LIKED GOING TO PARTIES. THEY GAVE HIM A NICKNAME BECAUSE HE WAS ALWAYS WELL DRESSED.
HEY, HERE COMES TWEED!
LOOKING SHARP, TWEED!
HI, MARTIN!
HEY THERE, MARTIN!
COME SIT BY ME, MARTIN!

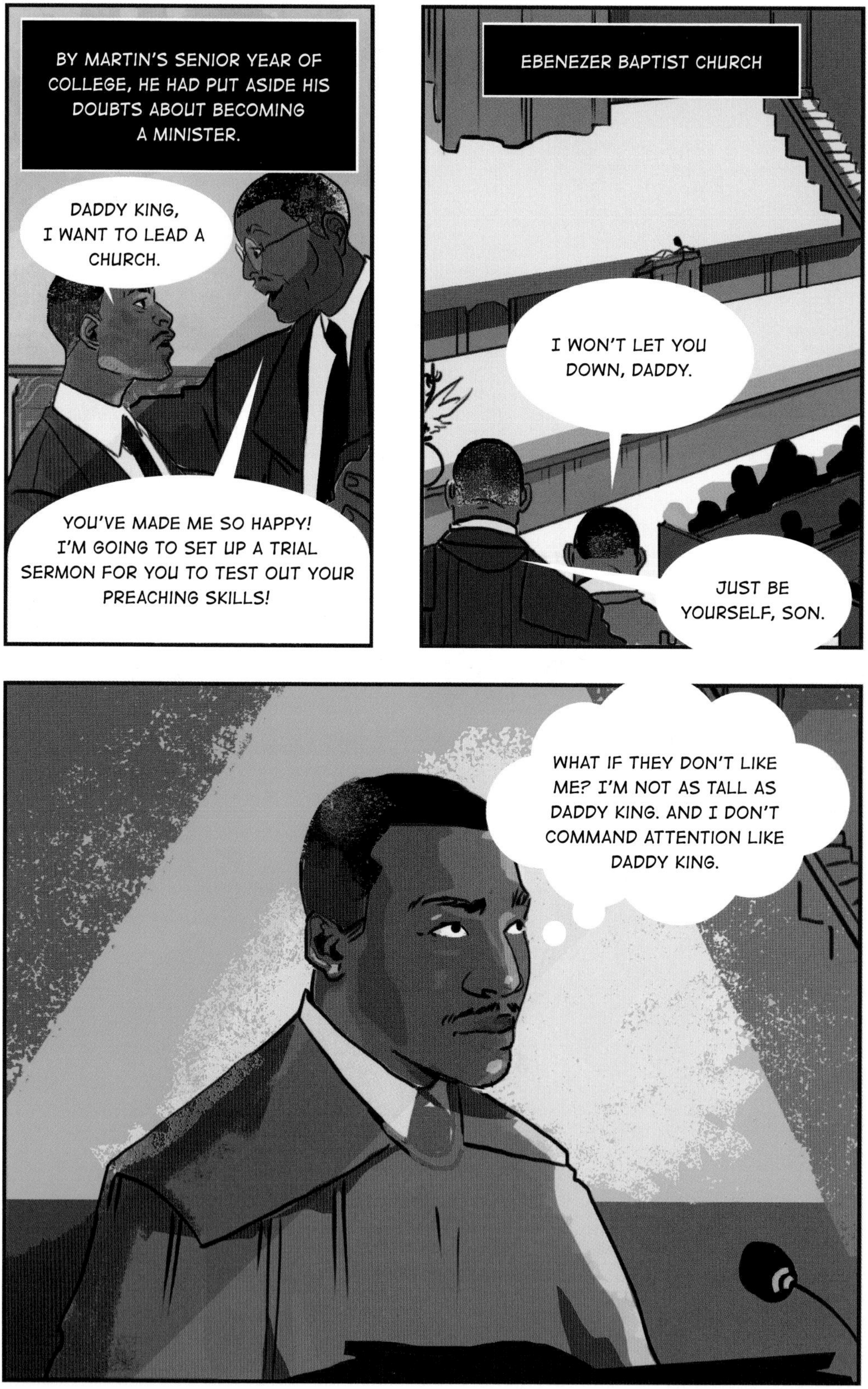
BY MARTIN'S SENIOR YEAR OF COLLEGE, HE HAD PUT ASIDE HIS DOUBTS ABOUT BECOMING A MINISTER.
DADDY KING, I WANT TO LEAD A CHURCH.
YOU'VE MADE ME SO HAPPY! I'M GOING TO SET UP A TRIAL SERMON FOR YOU TO TEST OUT YOUR PREACHING SKILLS!
EBENEZER BAPTIST CHURCH
I WON'T LET YOU DOWN, DADDY.
JUST BE YOURSELF, SON.
WHAT IF THEY DON'T LIKE ME? I'M NOT AS TALL AS DADDY KING. AND I DON'T COMMAND ATTENTION LIKE DADDY KING.

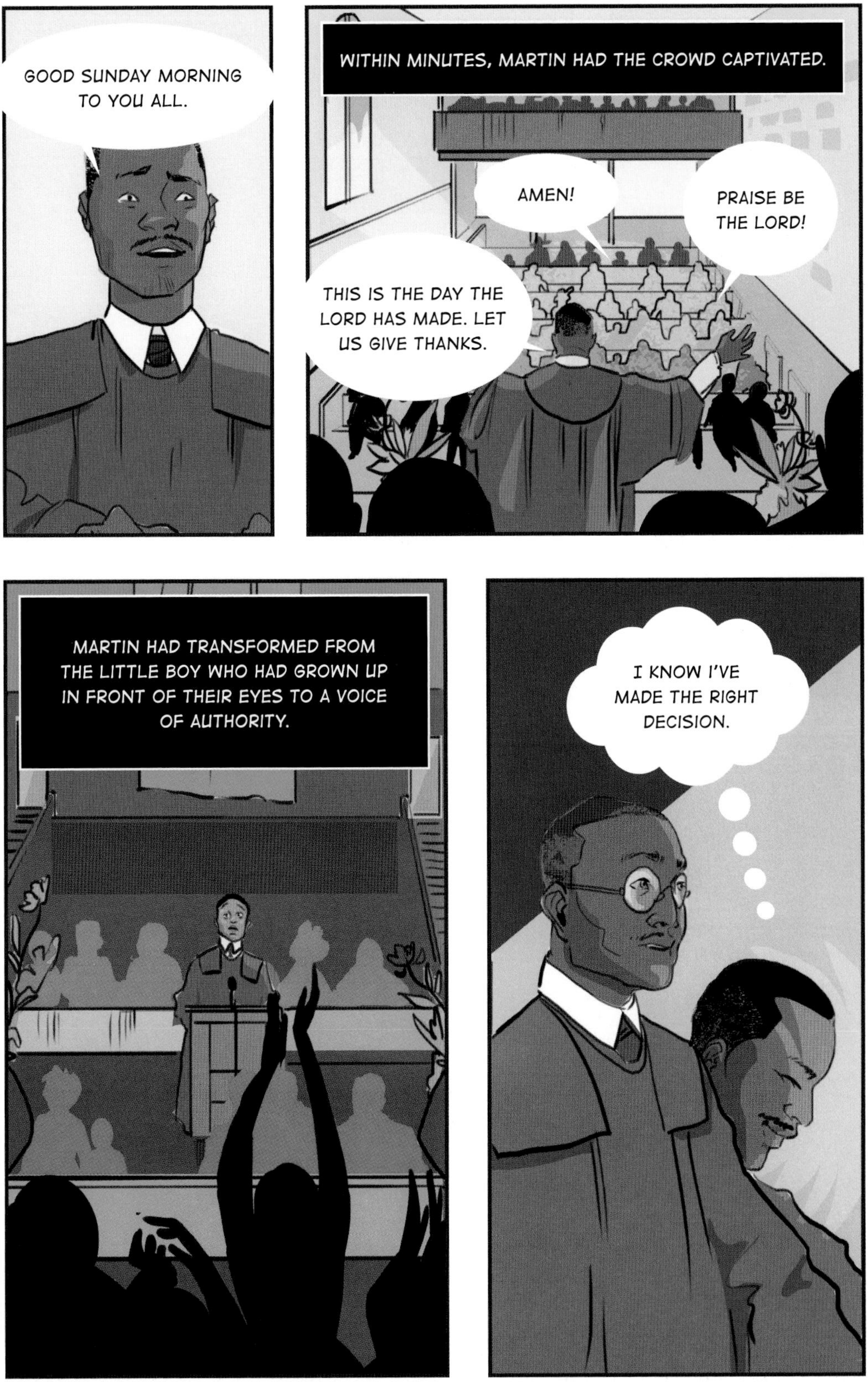
GOOD SUNDAY MORNING TO YOU ALL.
WITHIN MINUTES, MARTIN HAD THE CROWD CAPTIVATED.
AMEN!
PRAISE BE THE LORD!
THIS IS THE DAY THE LORD HAS MADE. LET US GIVE THANKS.
MARTIN HAD TRANSFORMED FROM THE LITTLE BOY WHO HAD GROWN UP IN FRONT OF THEIR EYES TO A VOICE OF AUTHORITY.
I KNOW I'VE MADE THE RIGHT DECISION.

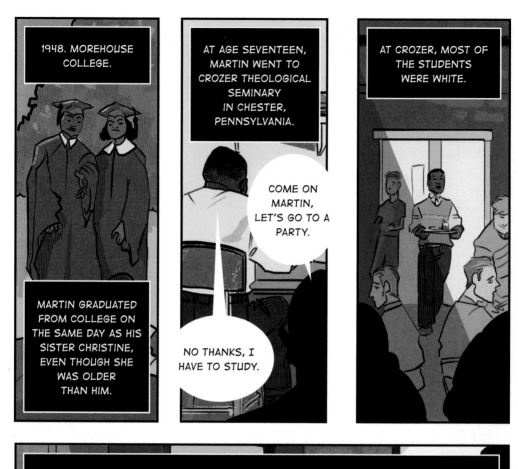

1948. MOREHOUSE COLLEGE.

MARTIN GRADUATED FROM COLLEGE ON THE SAME DAY AS HIS SISTER CHRISTINE, EVEN THOUGH SHE WAS OLDER THAN HIM.

AT AGE SEVENTEEN, MARTIN WENT TO CROZER THEOLOGICAL SEMINARY IN CHESTER, PENNSYLVANIA.

COME ON MARTIN, LET'S GO TO A PARTY.

NO THANKS, I HAVE TO STUDY.

AT CROZER, MOST OF THE STUDENTS WERE WHITE.

IT WAS ANOTHER OPPORTUNITY FOR MARTIN TO DO SOMETHING HE DID NOT GET TO DO BACK HOME IN ATLANTA: GET ALONG WITH WHITE PEOPLE.

HEY, MARTIN, WANT TO JOIN US?

SURE, THANK YOU.

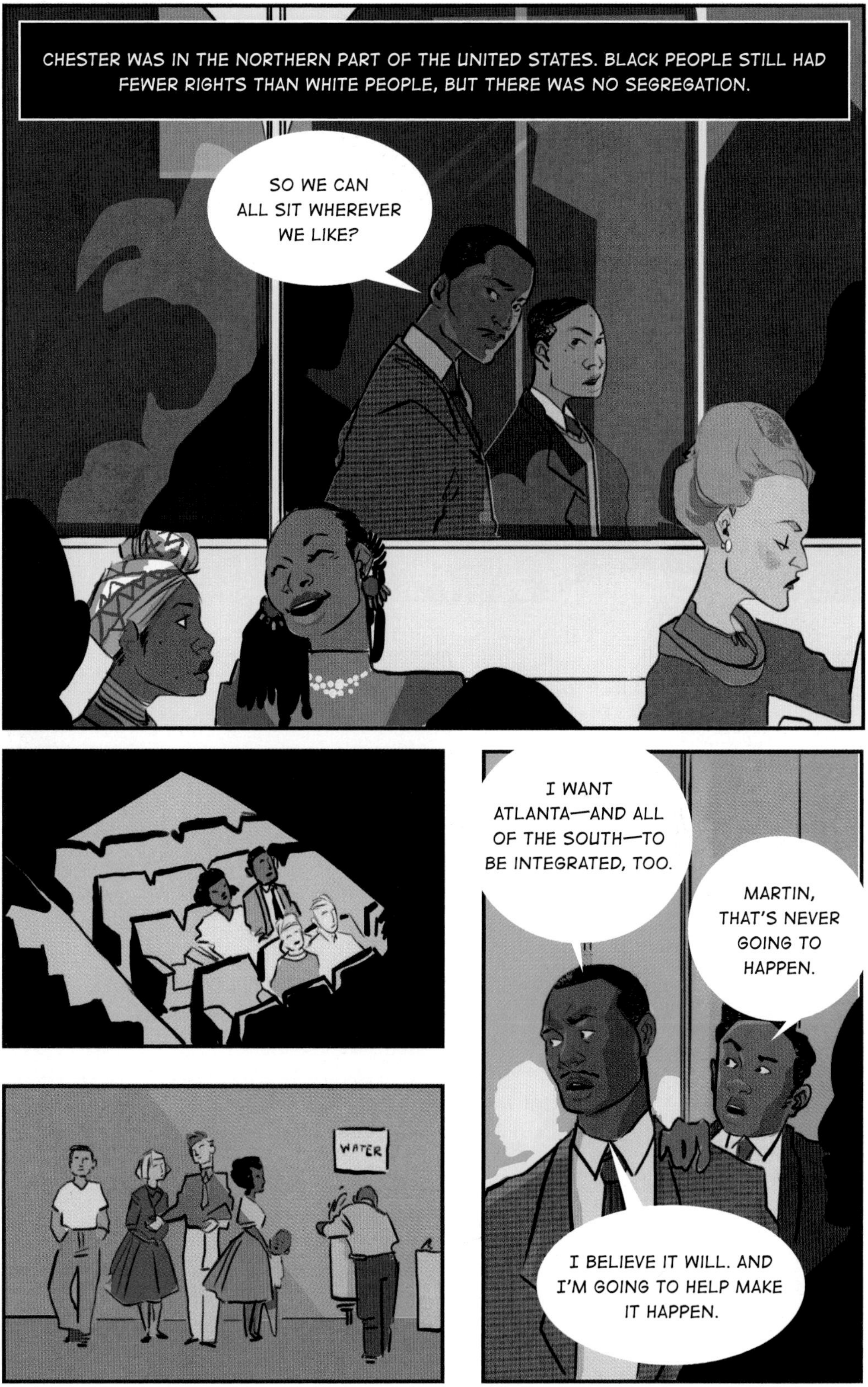
CHESTER WAS IN THE NORTHERN PART OF THE UNITED STATES. BLACK PEOPLE STILL HAD FEWER RIGHTS THAN WHITE PEOPLE, BUT THERE WAS NO SEGREGATION.
SO WE CAN ALL SIT WHEREVER WE LIKE?
WATER
I WANT ATLANTA—AND ALL OF THE SOUTH—TO BE INTEGRATED, TOO.
MARTIN, THAT'S NEVER GOING TO HAPPEN.
I BELIEVE IT WILL. AND I'M GOING TO HELP MAKE IT HAPPEN.

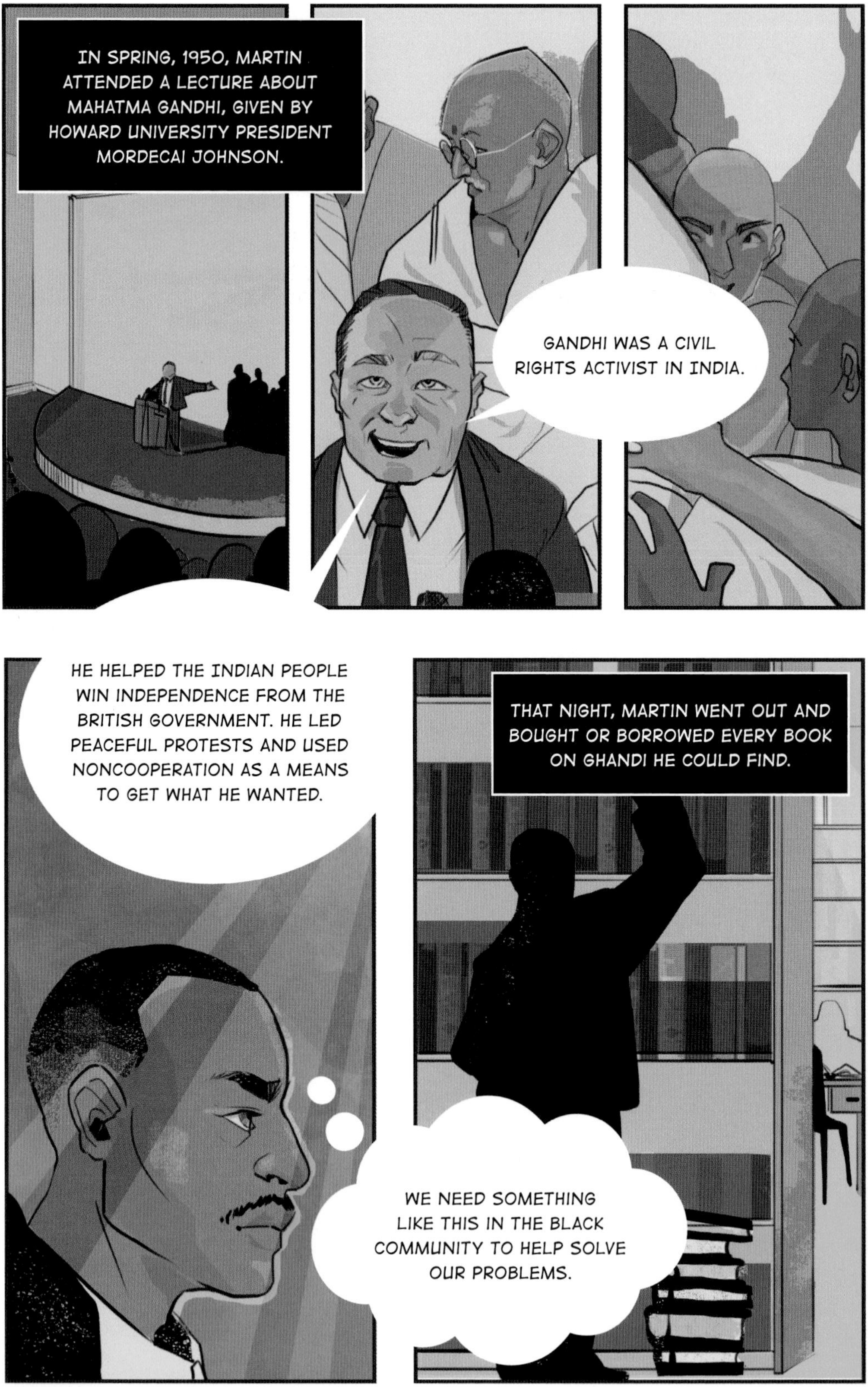
IN SPRING, 1950, MARTIN ATTENDED A LECTURE ABOUT MAHATMA GANDHI, GIVEN BY HOWARD UNIVERSITY PRESIDENT MORDECAI JOHNSON.
GANDHI WAS A CIVIL RIGHTS ACTIVIST IN INDIA.
HE HELPED THE INDIAN PEOPLE WIN INDEPENDENCE FROM THE BRITISH GOVERNMENT. HE LED PEACEFUL PROTESTS AND USED NONCOOPERATION AS A MEANS TO GET WHAT HE WANTED.
THAT NIGHT, MARTIN WENT OUT AND BOUGHT OR BORROWED EVERY BOOK ON GHANDI HE COULD FIND.
WE NEED SOMETHING LIKE THIS IN THE BLACK COMMUNITY TO HELP SOLVE OUR PROBLEMS.

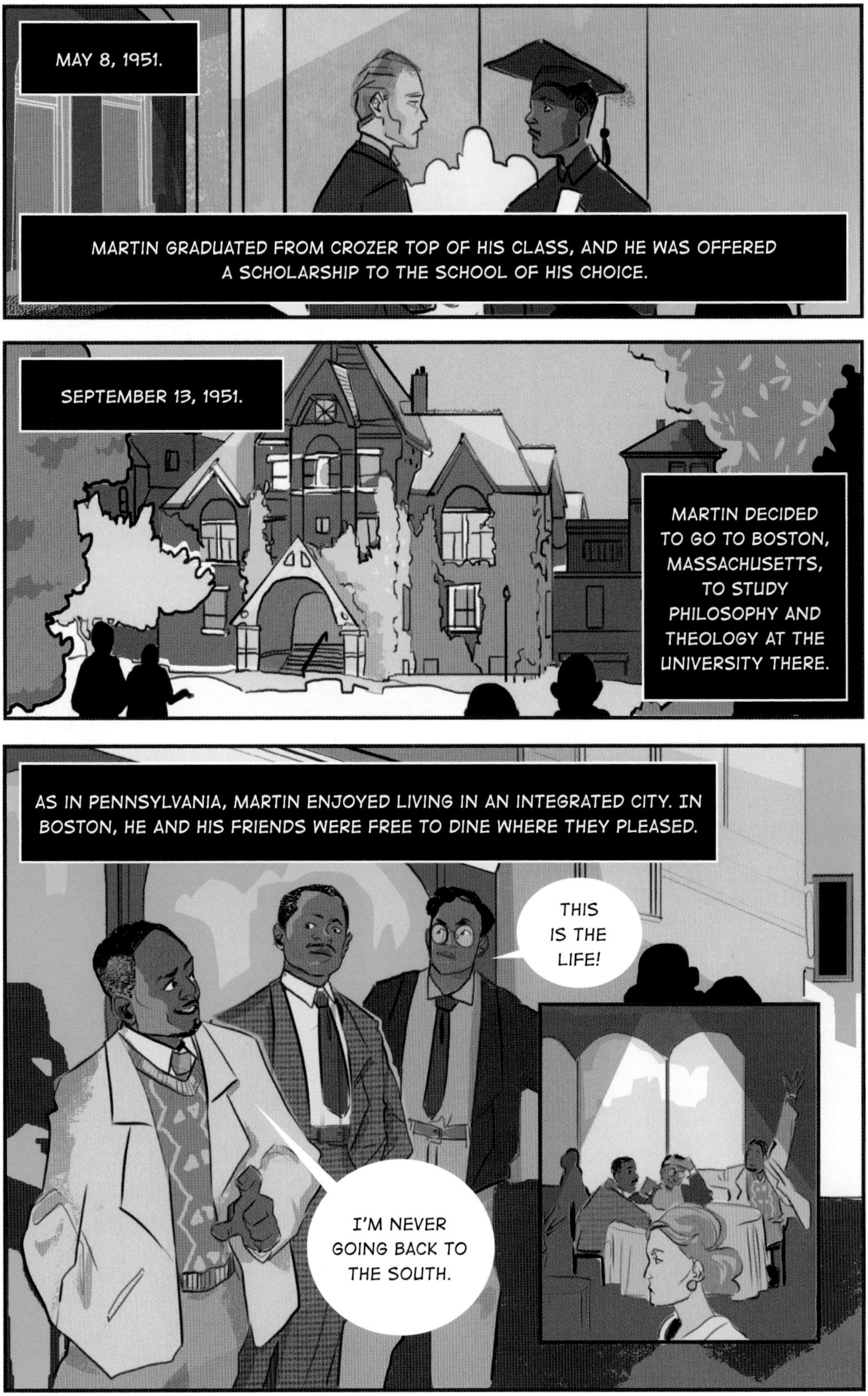
MAY 8, 1951.
MARTIN GRADUATED FROM CROZER TOP OF HIS CLASS, AND HE WAS OFFERED A SCHOLARSHIP TO THE SCHOOL OF HIS CHOICE.
SEPTEMBER 13, 1951.
MARTIN DECIDED TO GO TO BOSTON, MASSACHUSETTS, TO STUDY PHILOSOPHY AND THEOLOGY AT THE UNIVERSITY THERE.
AS IN PENNSYLVANIA, MARTIN ENJOYED LIVING IN AN INTEGRATED CITY. IN BOSTON, HE AND HIS FRIENDS WERE FREE TO DINE WHERE THEY PLEASED.
THIS IS THE LIFE!
I'M NEVER GOING BACK TO THE SOUTH.

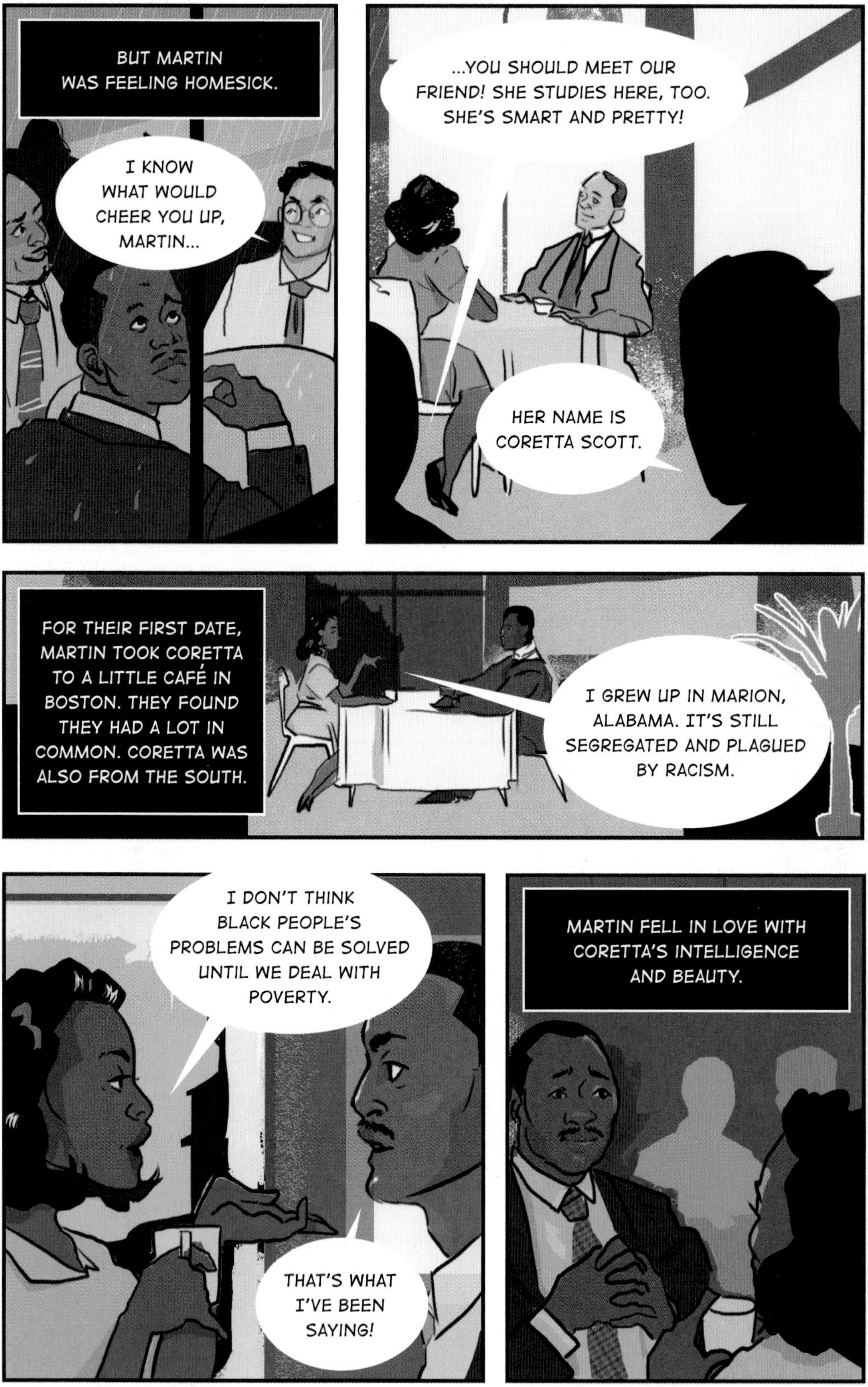
BUT MARTIN WAS FEELING HOMESICK.
I KNOW WHAT WOULD CHEER YOU UP, MARTIN...
...YOU SHOULD MEET OUR FRIEND! SHE STUDIES HERE, TOO. SHE'S SMART AND PRETTY!
HER NAME IS CORETTA SCOTT.
FOR THEIR FIRST DATE, MARTIN TOOK CORETTA TO A LITTLE CAFÉ IN BOSTON. THEY FOUND THEY HAD A LOT IN COMMON. CORETTA WAS ALSO FROM THE SOUTH.
I GREW UP IN MARION, ALABAMA. IT'S STILL SEGREGATED AND PLAGUED BY RACISM.
I DON'T THINK BLACK PEOPLE'S PROBLEMS CAN BE SOLVED UNTIL WE DEAL WITH POVERTY.
THAT'S WHAT I'VE BEEN SAYING!
MARTIN FELL IN LOVE WITH CORETTA'S INTELLIGENCE AND BEAUTY.

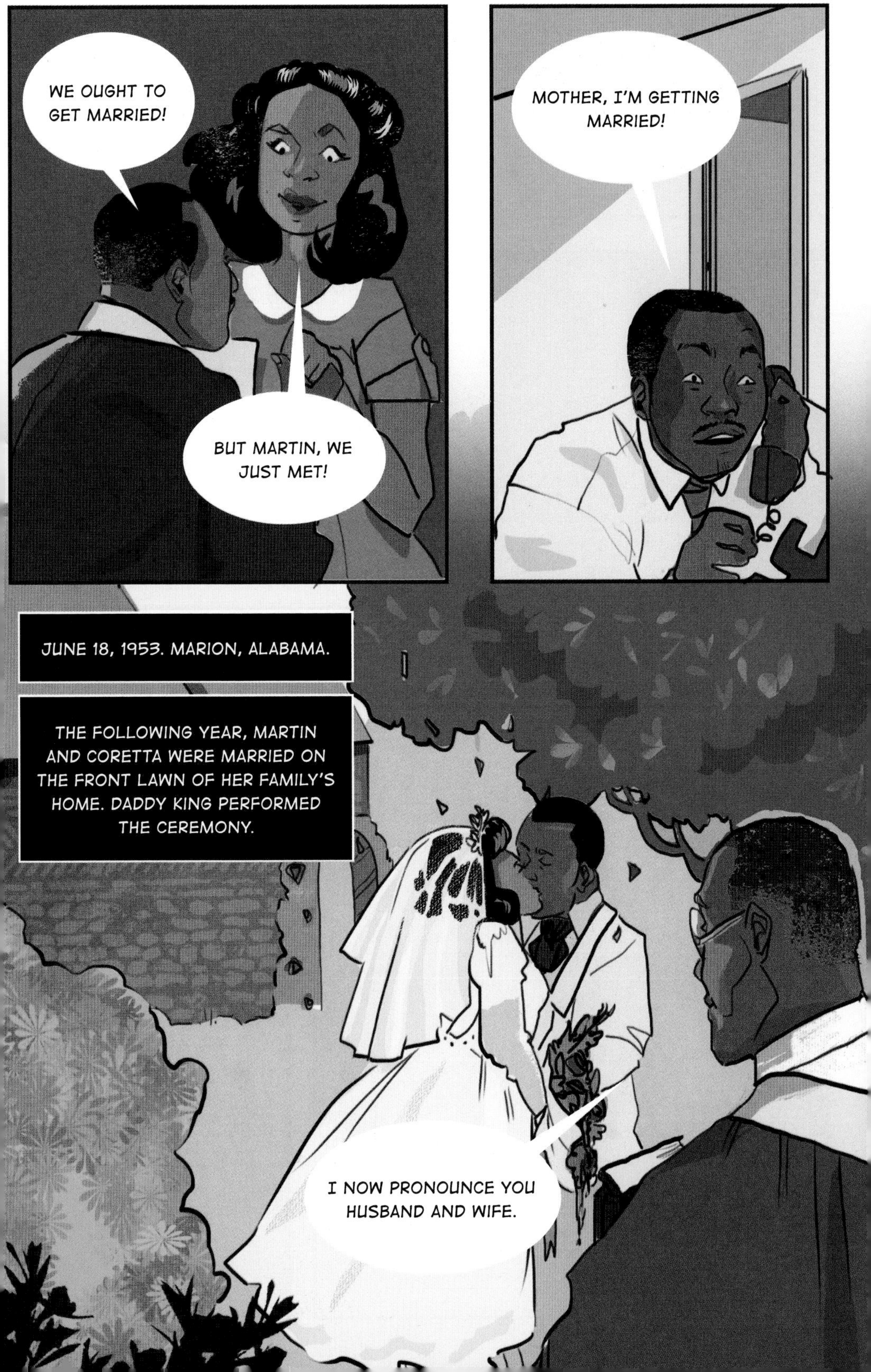
WE OUGHT TO GET MARRIED!
BUT MARTIN, WE JUST MET!
MOTHER, I'M GETTING MARRIED!
JUNE 18, 1953. MARION, ALABAMA.
THE FOLLOWING YEAR, MARTIN AND CORETTA WERE MARRIED ON THE FRONT LAWN OF HER FAMILY'S HOME. DADDY KING PERFORMED THE CEREMONY.
I NOW PRONOUNCE YOU HUSBAND AND WIFE.

CHAPTER 3

MAN OF THE CHURCH

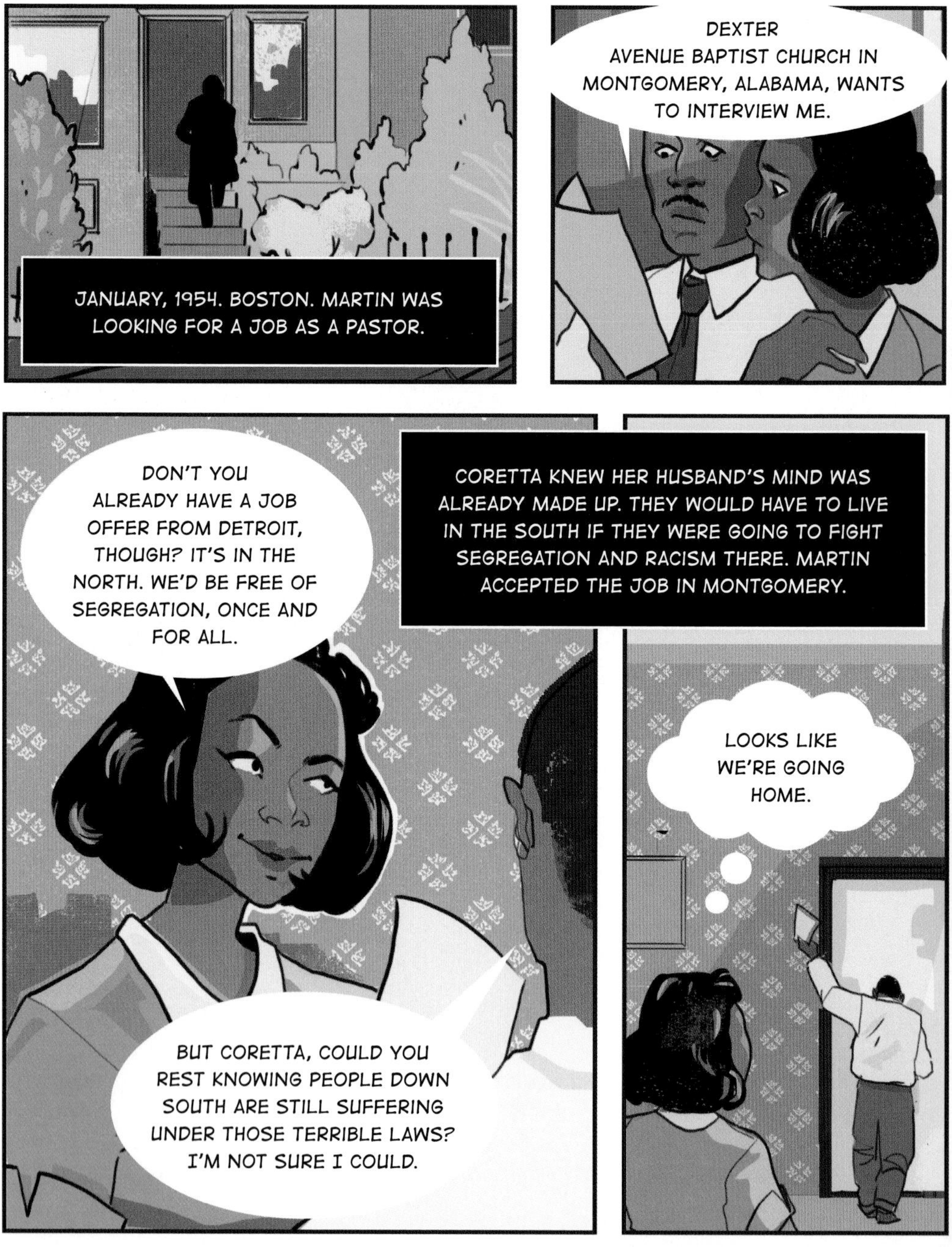
JANUARY, 1954. BOSTON. MARTIN WAS LOOKING FOR A JOB AS A PASTOR.
DEXTER AVENUE BAPTIST CHURCH IN MONTGOMERY, ALABAMA, WANTS TO INTERVIEW ME.
DON'T YOU ALREADY HAVE A JOB OFFER FROM DETROIT, THOUGH? IT'S IN THE NORTH. WE'D BE FREE OF SEGREGATION, ONCE AND FOR ALL.
BUT CORETTA, COULD YOU REST KNOWING PEOPLE DOWN SOUTH ARE STILL SUFFERING UNDER THOSE TERRIBLE LAWS? I'M NOT SURE I COULD.
CORETTA KNEW HER HUSBAND'S MIND WAS ALREADY MADE UP. THEY WOULD HAVE TO LIVE IN THE SOUTH IF THEY WERE GOING TO FIGHT SEGREGATION AND RACISM THERE. MARTIN ACCEPTED THE JOB IN MONTGOMERY.
LOOKS LIKE WE'RE GOING HOME.

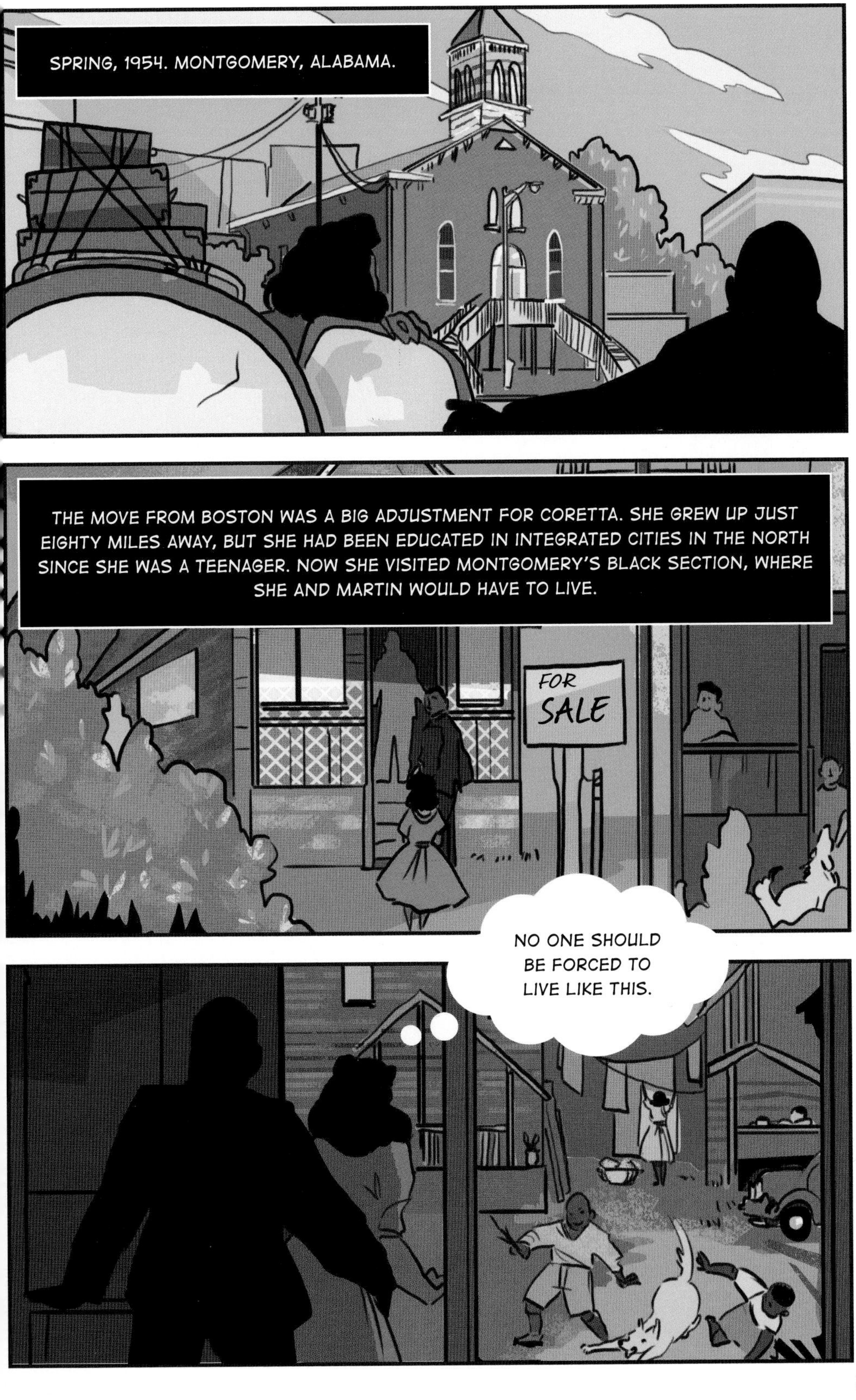
SPRING, 1954. MONTGOMERY, ALABAMA.
THE MOVE FROM BOSTON WAS A BIG ADJUSTMENT FOR CORETTA. SHE GREW UP JUST EIGHTY MILES AWAY, BUT SHE HAD BEEN EDUCATED IN INTEGRATED CITIES IN THE NORTH SINCE SHE WAS A TEENAGER. NOW SHE VISITED MONTGOMERY'S BLACK SECTION, WHERE SHE AND MARTIN WOULD HAVE TO LIVE.
FOR SALE
NO ONE SHOULD BE FORCED TO LIVE LIKE THIS.

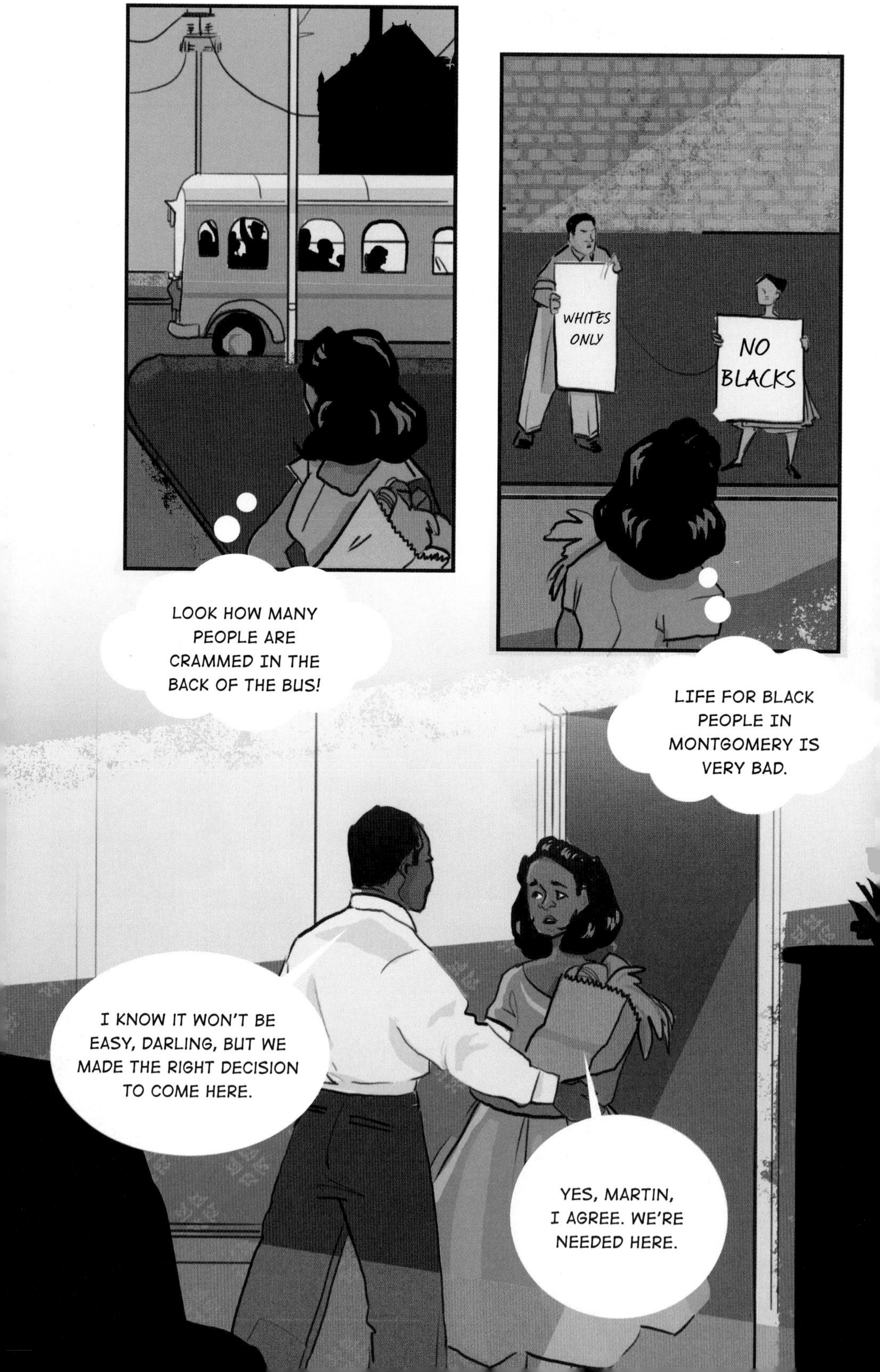
WHITES ONLY
NO BLACKS
LOOK HOW MANY PEOPLE ARE CRAMMED IN THE BACK OF THE BUS!
LIFE FOR BLACK PEOPLE IN MONTGOMERY IS VERY BAD.
I KNOW IT WON'T BE EASY, DARLING, BUT WE MADE THE RIGHT DECISION TO COME HERE.
YES, MARTIN, I AGREE. WE'RE NEEDED HERE.

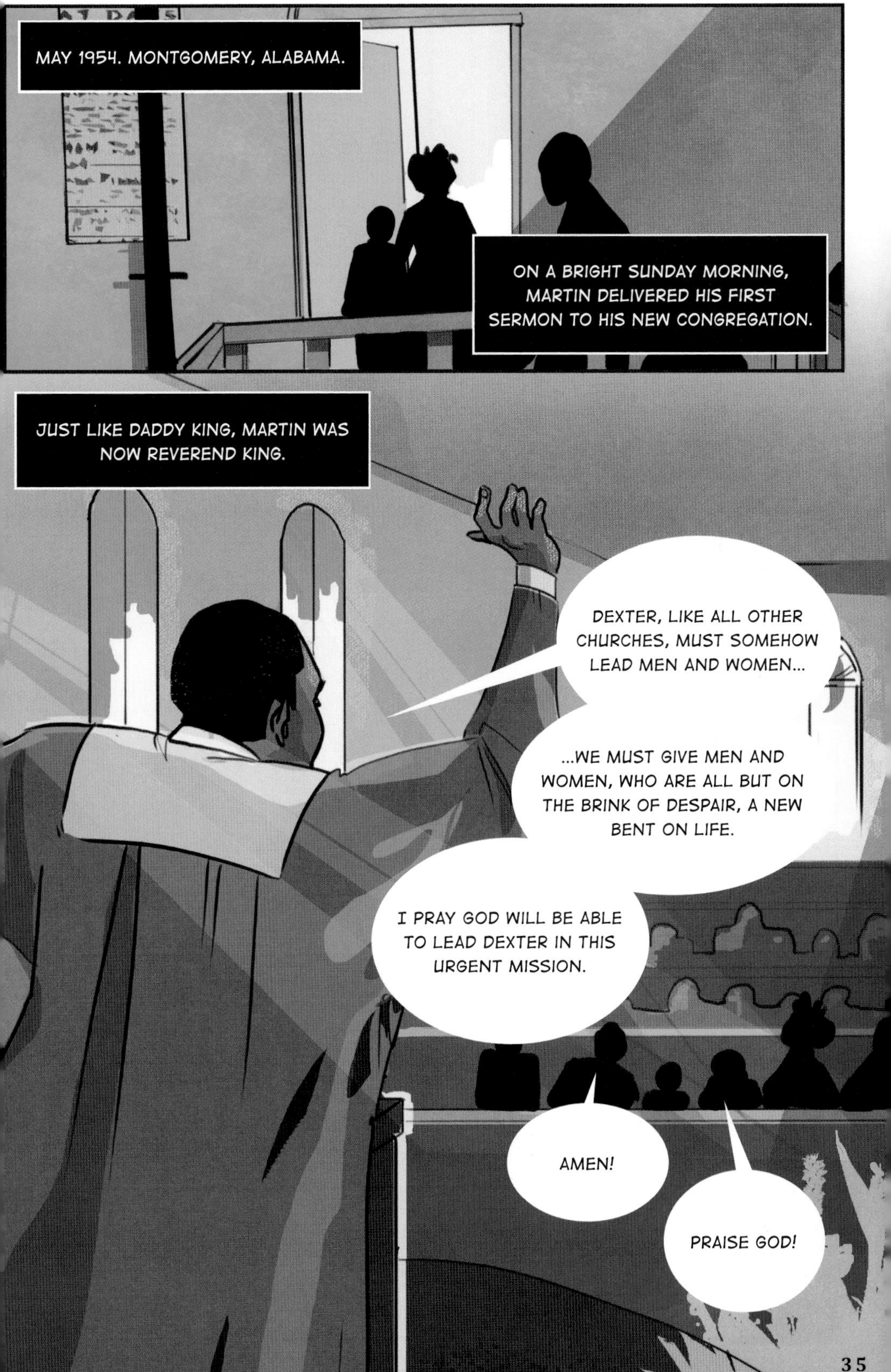
MAY 1954. MONTGOMERY, ALABAMA.
ON A BRIGHT SUNDAY MORNING, MARTIN DELIVERED HIS FIRST SERMON TO HIS NEW CONGREGATION.
JUST LIKE DADDY KING, MARTIN WAS NOW REVEREND KING.
DEXTER, LIKE ALL OTHER CHURCHES, MUST SOMEHOW LEAD MEN AND WOMEN...
...WE MUST GIVE MEN AND WOMEN, WHO ARE ALL BUT ON THE BRINK OF DESPAIR, A NEW BENT ON LIFE.
I PRAY GOD WILL BE ABLE TO LEAD DEXTER IN THIS URGENT MISSION.
AMEN!
PRAISE GOD!

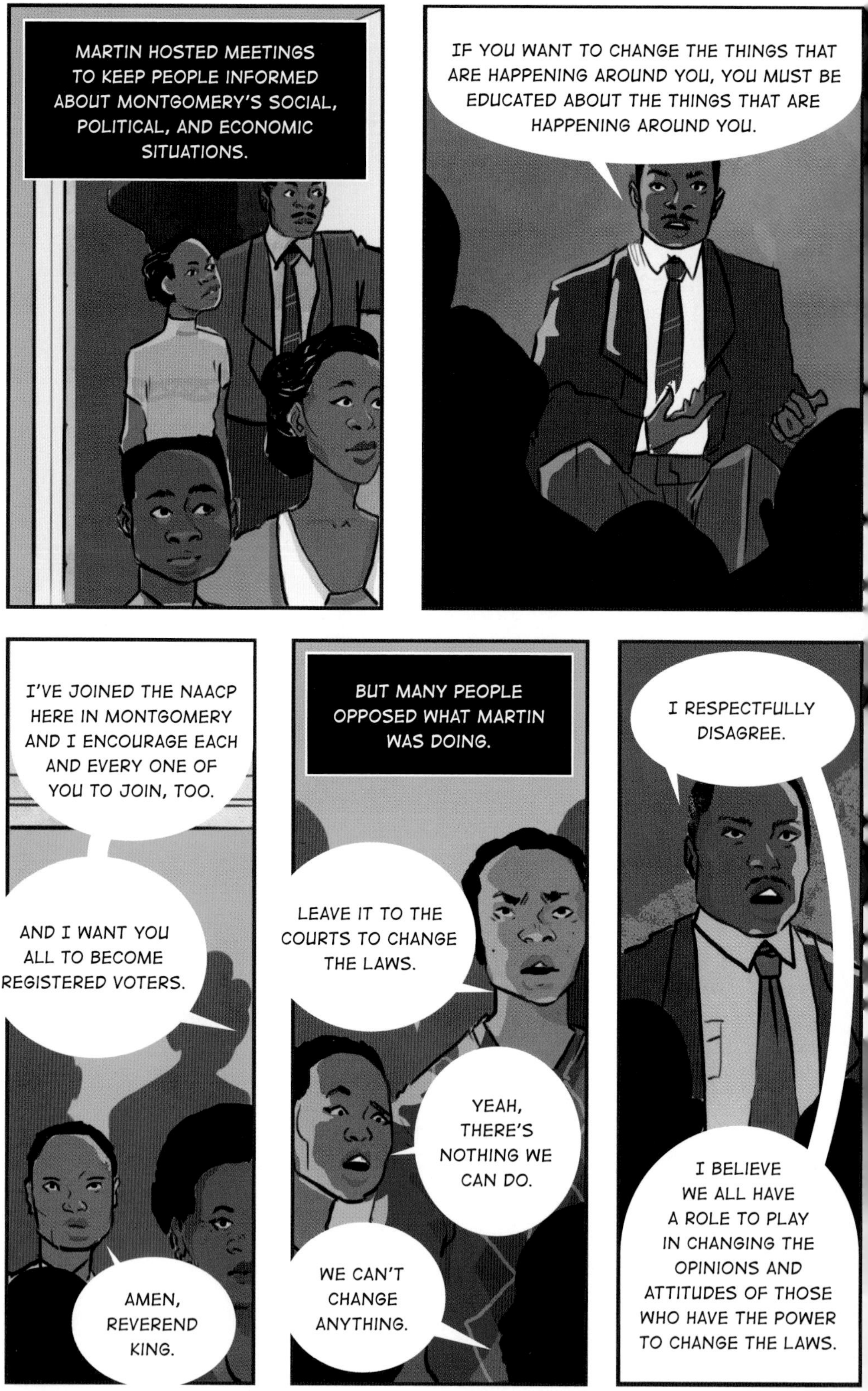
MARTIN HOSTED MEETINGS TO KEEP PEOPLE INFORMED ABOUT MONTGOMERY'S SOCIAL, POLITICAL, AND ECONOMIC SITUATIONS.
IF YOU WANT TO CHANGE THE THINGS THAT ARE HAPPENING AROUND YOU, YOU MUST BE EDUCATED ABOUT THE THINGS THAT ARE HAPPENING AROUND YOU.
I'VE JOINED THE NAACP HERE IN MONTGOMERY AND I ENCOURAGE EACH AND EVERY ONE OF YOU TO JOIN, TOO.
AND I WANT YOU ALL TO BECOME REGISTERED VOTERS.
AMEN, REVEREND KING.
BUT MANY PEOPLE OPPOSED WHAT MARTIN WAS DOING.
LEAVE IT TO THE COURTS TO CHANGE THE LAWS.
YEAH, THERE'S NOTHING WE CAN DO.
WE CAN'T CHANGE ANYTHING.
I RESPECTFULLY DISAGREE.
I BELIEVE WE ALL HAVE A ROLE TO PLAY IN CHANGING THE OPINIONS AND ATTITUDES OF THOSE WHO HAVE THE POWER TO CHANGE THE LAWS.

ON NOVEMBER 17, 1955, MARTIN AND CORETTA WELCOMED THEIR FIRST CHILD INTO THE WORLD.

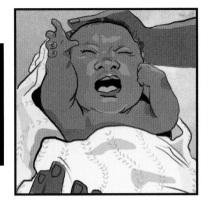

A DAUGHTER THEY NAMED YOLANDA DENISE.

WE'LL CALL HER YOKI.

WE LOVE YOU ALREADY, YOKI.

ONCE BABY YOLANDA CAME ALONG, THE KINGS DID NOT GET MUCH SLEEP.

YOU KEEP ME BUSY WALKING THE FLOORS, LITTLE ONE.

JUST TWO WEEKS AFTER YOKI'S BIRTH, AN INCIDENT OCCURRED ON A MONTGOMERY CITY BUS THAT WOULD PUT MARTIN IN THE MIDDLE OF A FIRESTORM AND CHANGE HIS LIFE FOREVER.

CHAPTER 4

MONTGOMERY BUS BOYCOTT

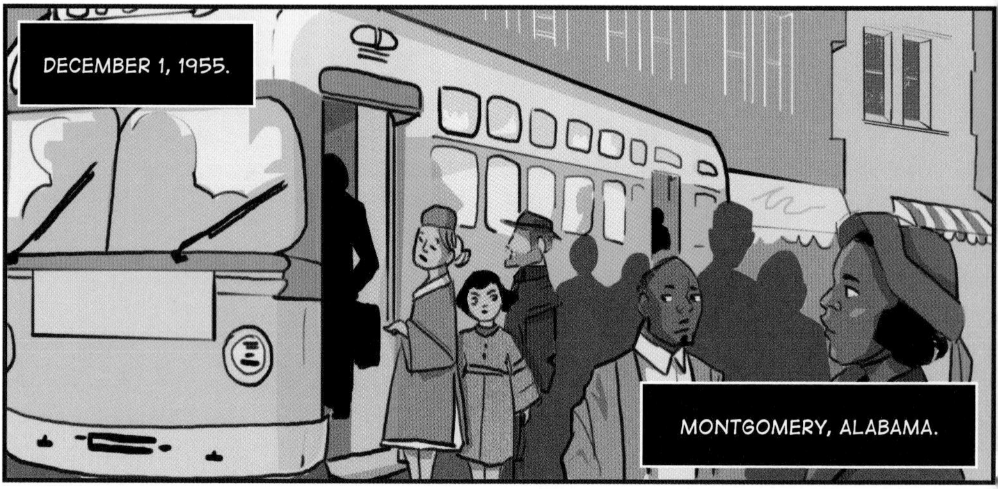

DECEMBER 1, 1955.
MONTGOMERY, ALABAMA.

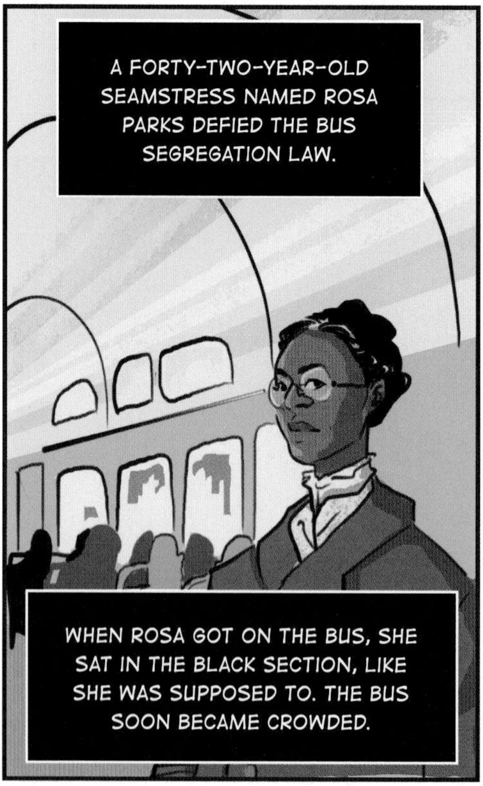

A FORTY-TWO-YEAR-OLD SEAMSTRESS NAMED ROSA PARKS DEFIED THE BUS SEGREGATION LAW.
WHEN ROSA GOT ON THE BUS, SHE SAT IN THE BLACK SECTION, LIKE SHE WAS SUPPOSED TO. THE BUS SOON BECAME CROWDED.

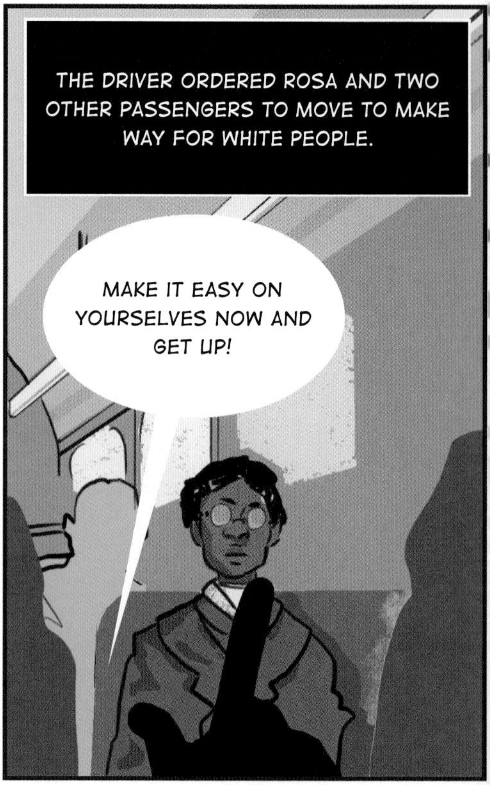

THE DRIVER ORDERED ROSA AND TWO OTHER PASSENGERS TO MOVE TO MAKE WAY FOR WHITE PEOPLE.
MAKE IT EASY ON YOURSELVES NOW AND GET UP!

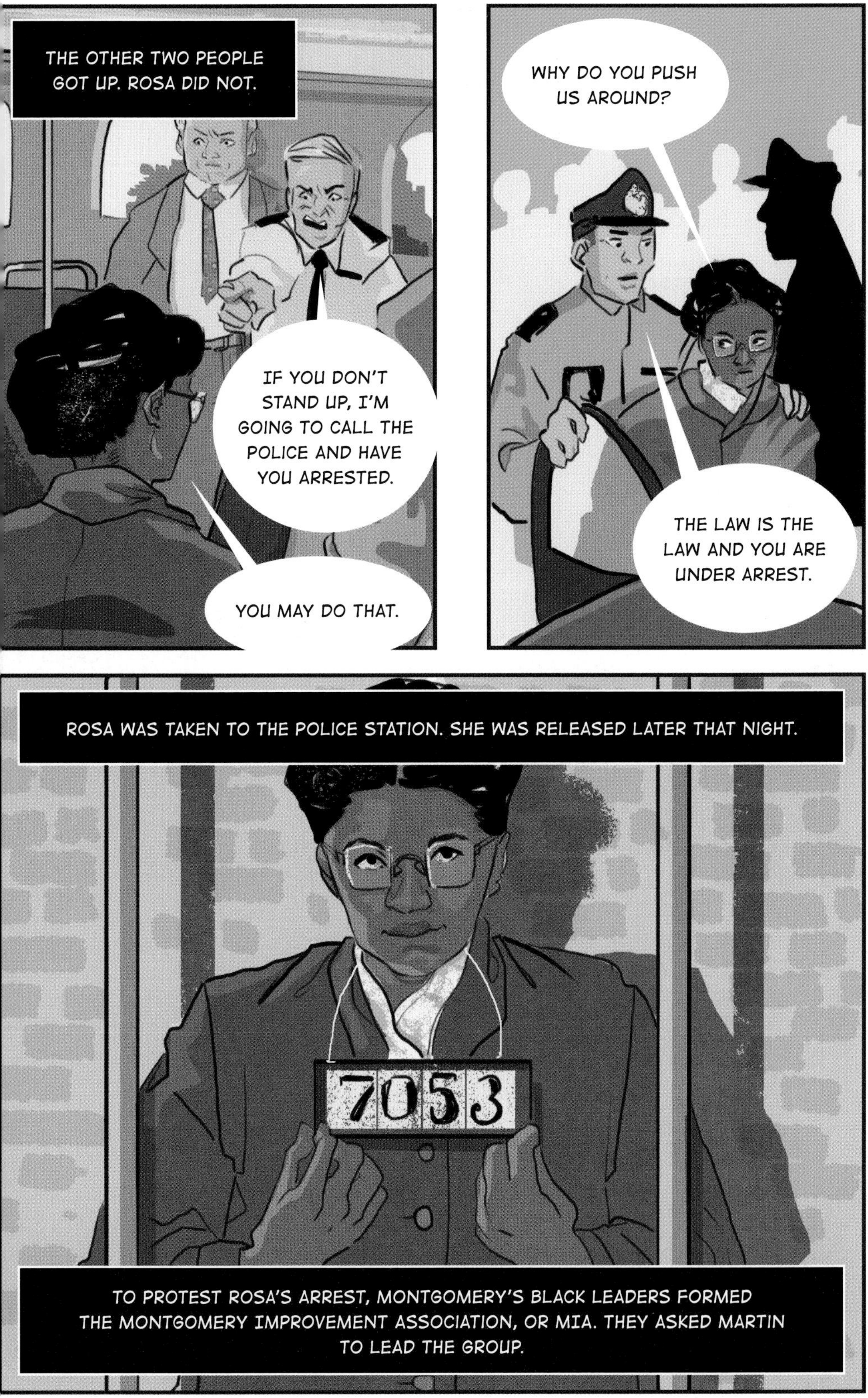
THE OTHER TWO PEOPLE GOT UP. ROSA DID NOT.
IF YOU DON'T STAND UP, I'M GOING TO CALL THE POLICE AND HAVE YOU ARRESTED.
YOU MAY DO THAT.
WHY DO YOU PUSH US AROUND?
THE LAW IS THE LAW AND YOU ARE UNDER ARREST.
ROSA WAS TAKEN TO THE POLICE STATION. SHE WAS RELEASED LATER THAT NIGHT.
7053
TO PROTEST ROSA'S ARREST, MONTGOMERY'S BLACK LEADERS FORMED THE MONTGOMERY IMPROVEMENT ASSOCIATION, OR MIA. THEY ASKED MARTIN TO LEAD THE GROUP.

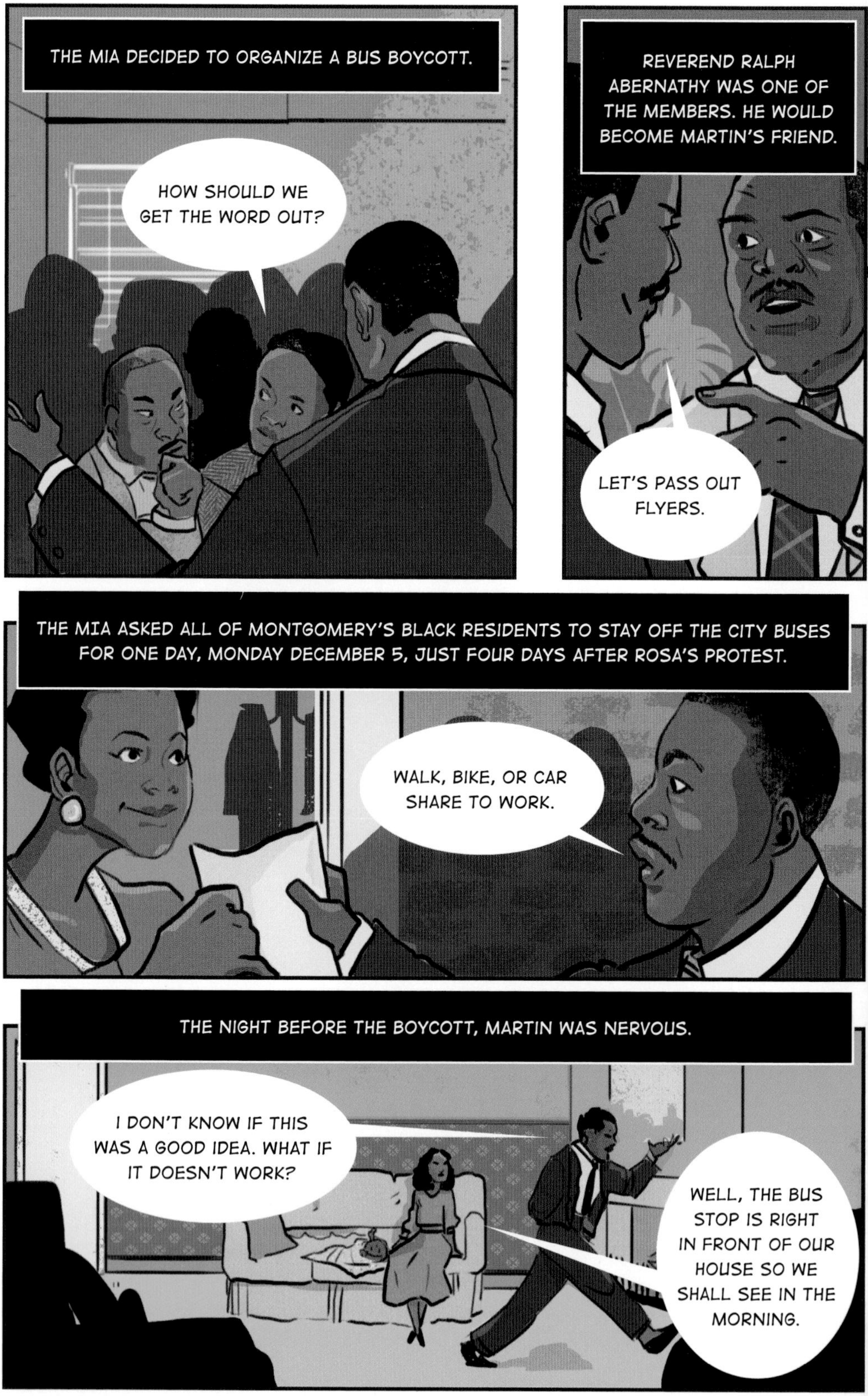
THE MIA DECIDED TO ORGANIZE A BUS BOYCOTT.
HOW SHOULD WE GET THE WORD OUT?
REVEREND RALPH ABERNATHY WAS ONE OF THE MEMBERS. HE WOULD BECOME MARTIN'S FRIEND.
LET'S PASS OUT FLYERS.
THE MIA ASKED ALL OF MONTGOMERY'S BLACK RESIDENTS TO STAY OFF THE CITY BUSES FOR ONE DAY, MONDAY DECEMBER 5, JUST FOUR DAYS AFTER ROSA'S PROTEST.
WALK, BIKE, OR CAR SHARE TO WORK.
THE NIGHT BEFORE THE BOYCOTT, MARTIN WAS NERVOUS.
I DON'T KNOW IF THIS WAS A GOOD IDEA. WHAT IF IT DOESN'T WORK?
WELL, THE BUS STOP IS RIGHT IN FRONT OF OUR HOUSE SO WE SHALL SEE IN THE MORNING.

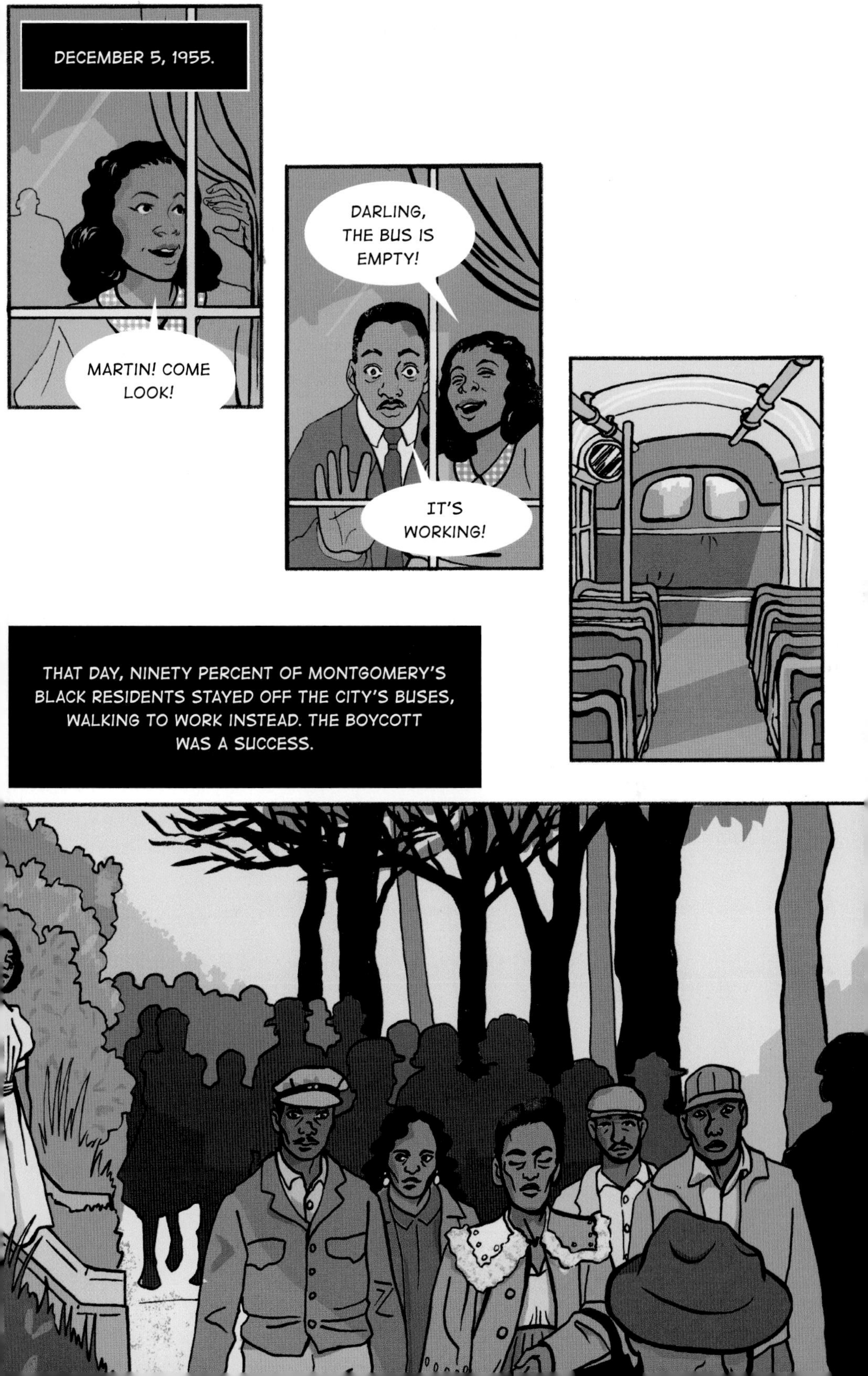
DECEMBER 5, 1955.
MARTIN! COME LOOK!
DARLING, THE BUS IS EMPTY!
IT'S WORKING!
THAT DAY, NINETY PERCENT OF MONTGOMERY'S BLACK RESIDENTS STAYED OFF THE CITY'S BUSES, WALKING TO WORK INSTEAD. THE BOYCOTT WAS A SUCCESS.

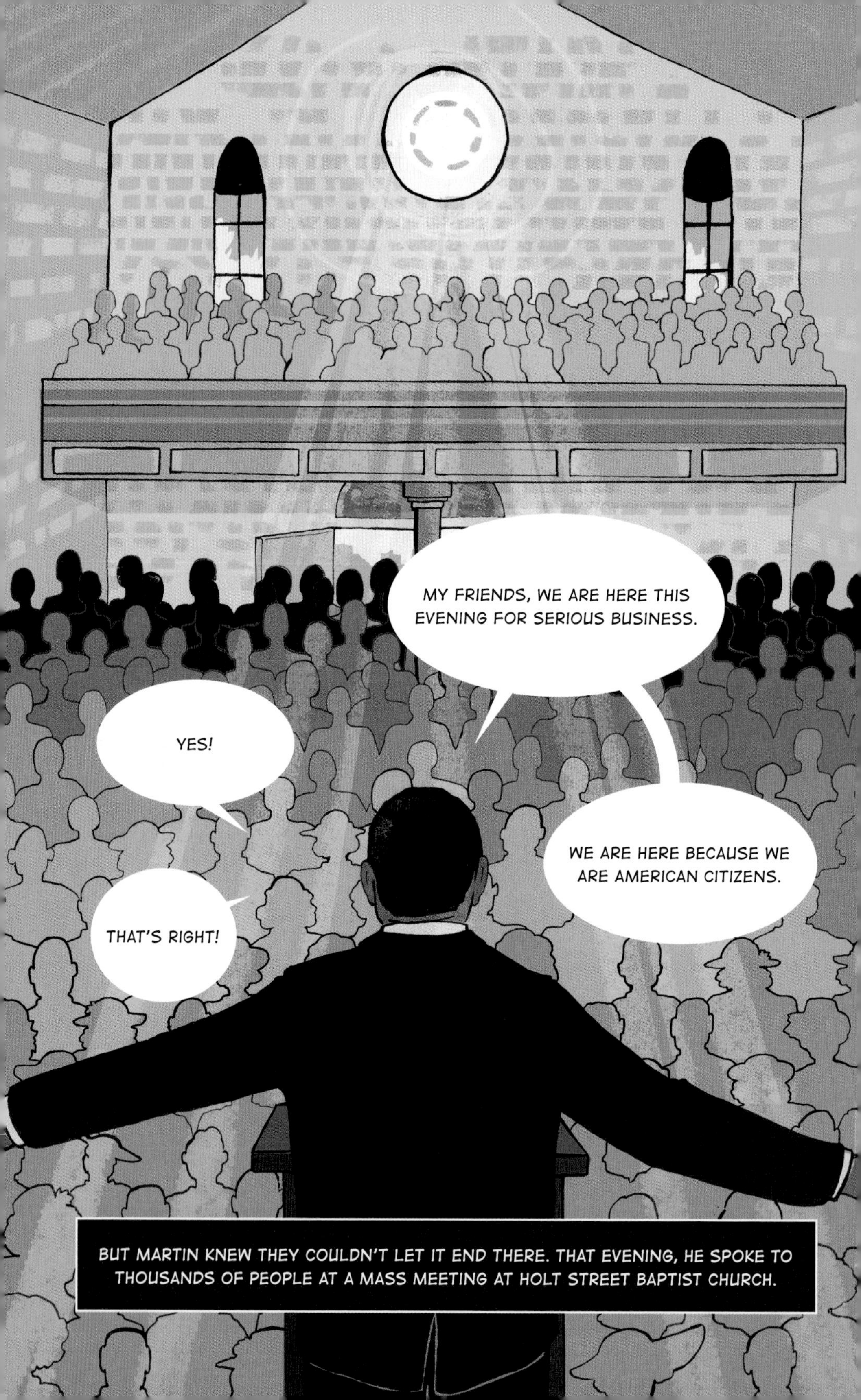
MY FRIENDS, WE ARE HERE THIS EVENING FOR SERIOUS BUSINESS.
YES!
WE ARE HERE BECAUSE WE ARE AMERICAN CITIZENS.
THAT'S RIGHT!
BUT MARTIN KNEW THEY COULDN'T LET IT END THERE. THAT EVENING, HE SPOKE TO THOUSANDS OF PEOPLE AT A MASS MEETING AT HOLT STREET BAPTIST CHURCH.

HE ASKED THEM TO KEEP THE BOYCOTT GOING FOR AS LONG AS IT TOOK TO GET THE SEGREGATION LAWS CHANGED.

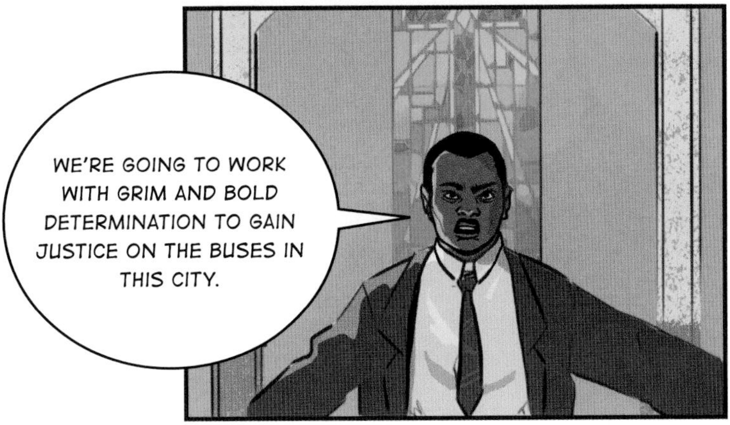
WE'RE GOING TO WORK WITH GRIM AND BOLD DETERMINATION TO GAIN JUSTICE ON THE BUSES IN THIS CITY.

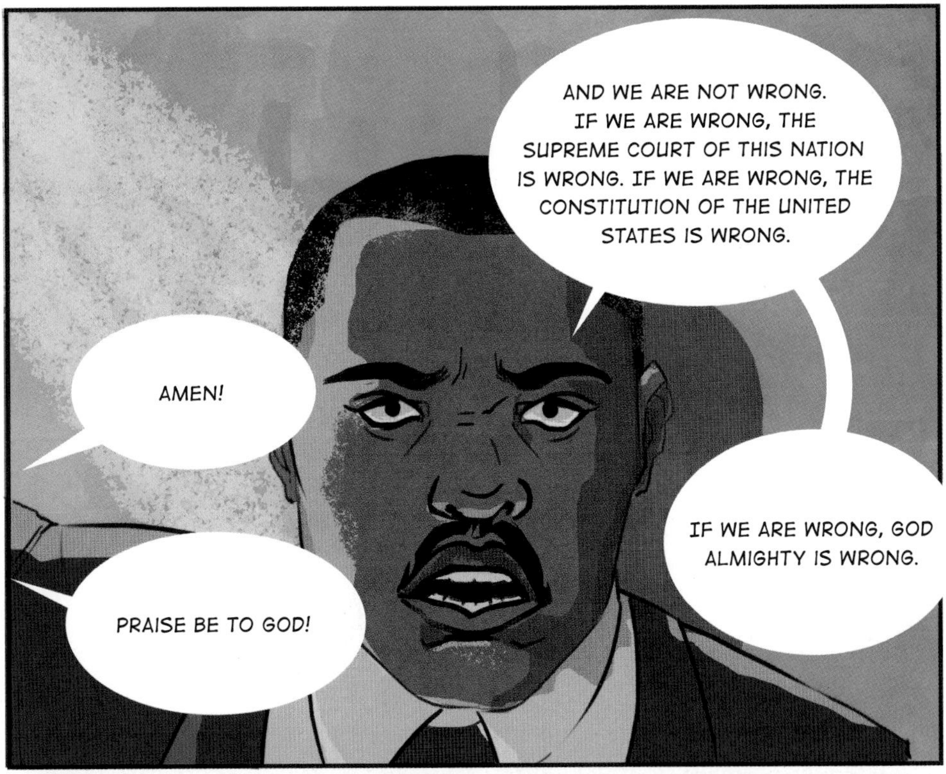
AND WE ARE NOT WRONG. IF WE ARE WRONG, THE SUPREME COURT OF THIS NATION IS WRONG. IF WE ARE WRONG, THE CONSTITUTION OF THE UNITED STATES IS WRONG.
AMEN!
IF WE ARE WRONG, GOD ALMIGHTY IS WRONG.
PRAISE BE TO GOD!

THE BOYCOTT WOULD LAST THIRTEEN LONG MONTHS. MARTIN WAS ENCOURAGED BY THE DETERMINATION OF HIS COMMUNITY.

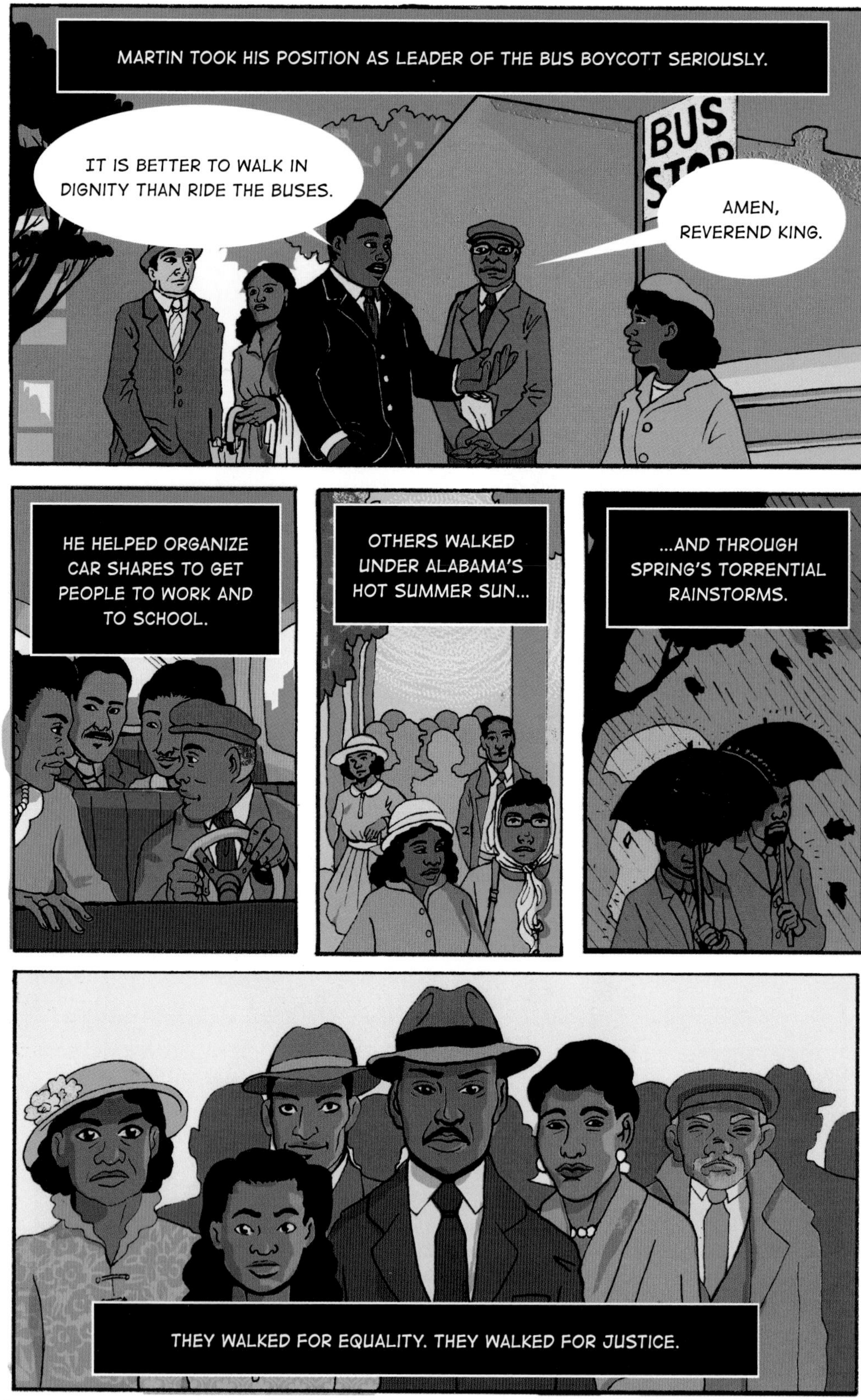
MARTIN TOOK HIS POSITION AS LEADER OF THE BUS BOYCOTT SERIOUSLY.
BUS
IT IS BETTER TO WALK IN DIGNITY THAN RIDE THE BUSES.
AMEN, REVEREND KING.
HE HELPED ORGANIZE CAR SHARES TO GET PEOPLE TO WORK AND TO SCHOOL.
OTHERS WALKED UNDER ALABAMA'S HOT SUMMER SUN...
...AND THROUGH SPRING'S TORRENTIAL RAINSTORMS.
THEY WALKED FOR EQUALITY. THEY WALKED FOR JUSTICE.

1956.

MARTIN'S INVOLVEMENT IN THE BOYCOTT ANGERED MANY PEOPLE IN THE WHITE COMMUNITY.

MONTGOMERY'S CITY OFFICIALS WEREN'T HAPPY EITHER.

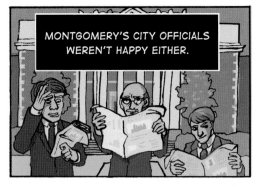

THE CITY TRIED TO PRESSURE MARTIN INTO CALLING OFF THE BOYCOTT. BUT THEY DID IT IN UNDERHANDED WAYS. THEY PRINTED LIES ABOUT HIM IN THE NEWSPAPER. THEY SENT HIM THREATENING LETTERS...

...AND EVEN ARRESTED HIM.

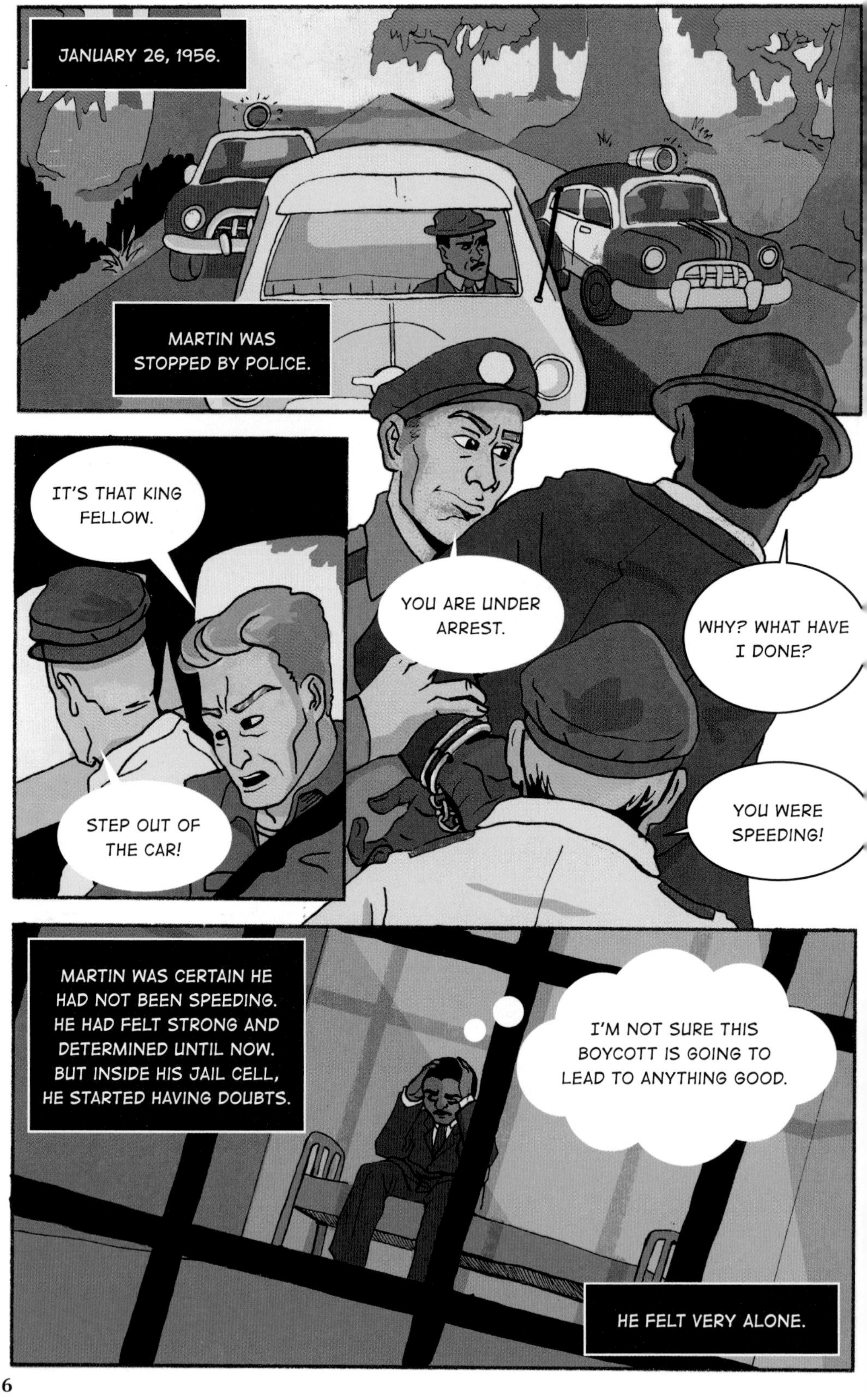
JANUARY 26, 1956.
MARTIN WAS STOPPED BY POLICE.
IT'S THAT KING FELLOW.
STEP OUT OF THE CAR!
YOU ARE UNDER ARREST.
WHY? WHAT HAVE I DONE?
YOU WERE SPEEDING!
MARTIN WAS CERTAIN HE HAD NOT BEEN SPEEDING. HE HAD FELT STRONG AND DETERMINED UNTIL NOW. BUT INSIDE HIS JAIL CELL, HE STARTED HAVING DOUBTS.
I'M NOT SURE THIS BOYCOTT IS GOING TO LEAD TO ANYTHING GOOD.
HE FELT VERY ALONE.

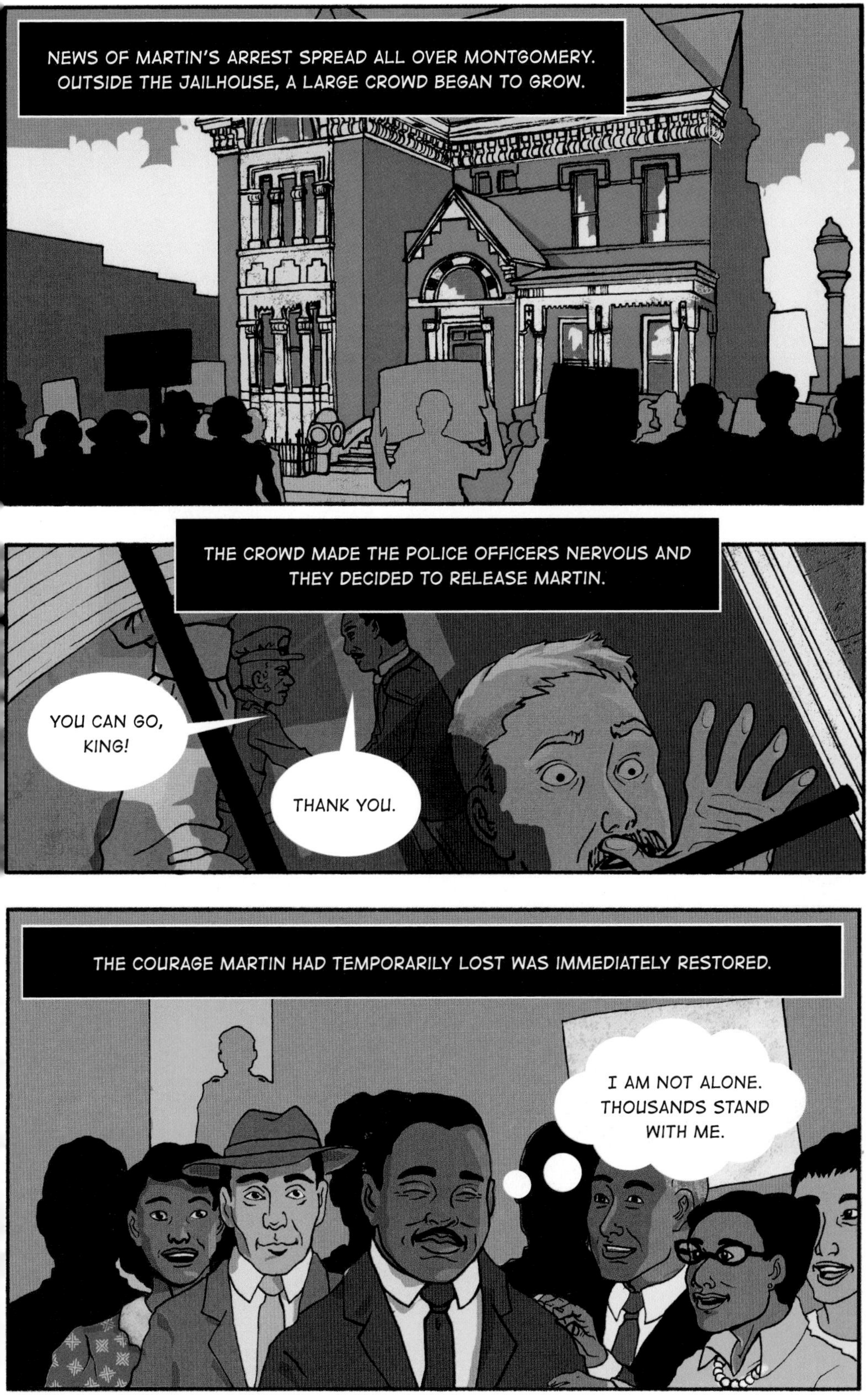
NEWS OF MARTIN'S ARREST SPREAD ALL OVER MONTGOMERY. OUTSIDE THE JAILHOUSE, A LARGE CROWD BEGAN TO GROW.
THE CROWD MADE THE POLICE OFFICERS NERVOUS AND THEY DECIDED TO RELEASE MARTIN.
YOU CAN GO, KING!
THANK YOU.
THE COURAGE MARTIN HAD TEMPORARILY LOST WAS IMMEDIATELY RESTORED.
I AM NOT ALONE. THOUSANDS STAND WITH ME.

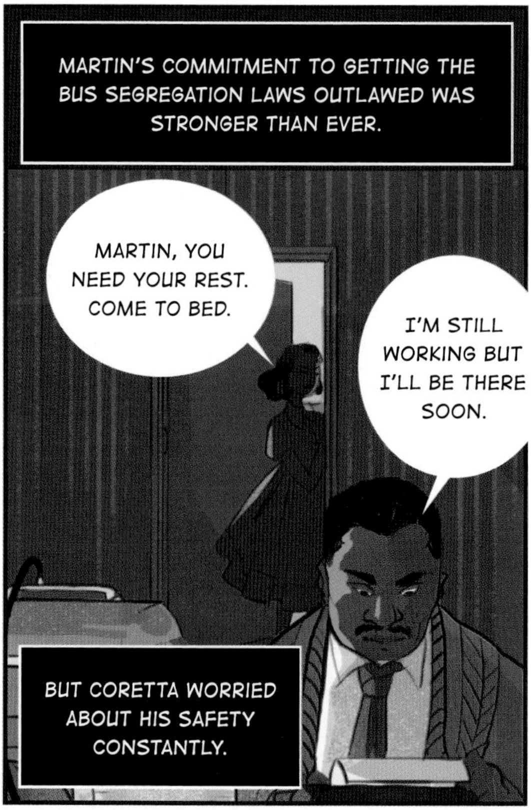
MARTIN'S COMMITMENT TO GETTING THE BUS SEGREGATION LAWS OUTLAWED WAS STRONGER THAN EVER.
MARTIN, YOU NEED YOUR REST. COME TO BED.
I'M STILL WORKING BUT I'LL BE THERE SOON.
BUT CORETTA WORRIED ABOUT HIS SAFETY CONSTANTLY.

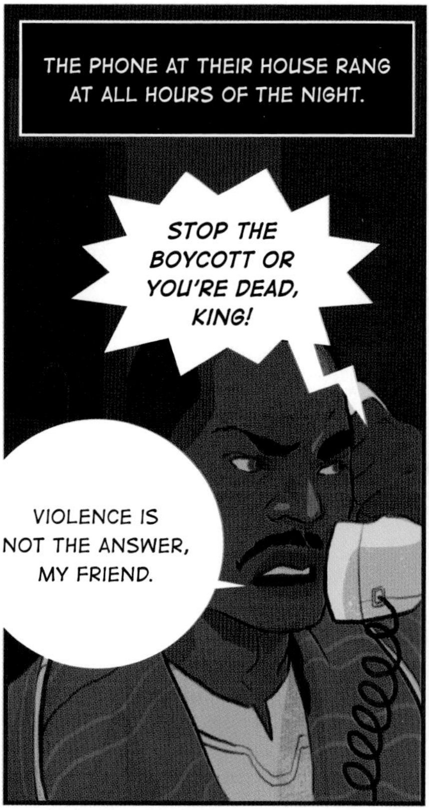
THE PHONE AT THEIR HOUSE RANG AT ALL HOURS OF THE NIGHT.
STOP THE BOYCOTT OR YOU'RE DEAD, KING!
VIOLENCE IS NOT THE ANSWER, MY FRIEND.

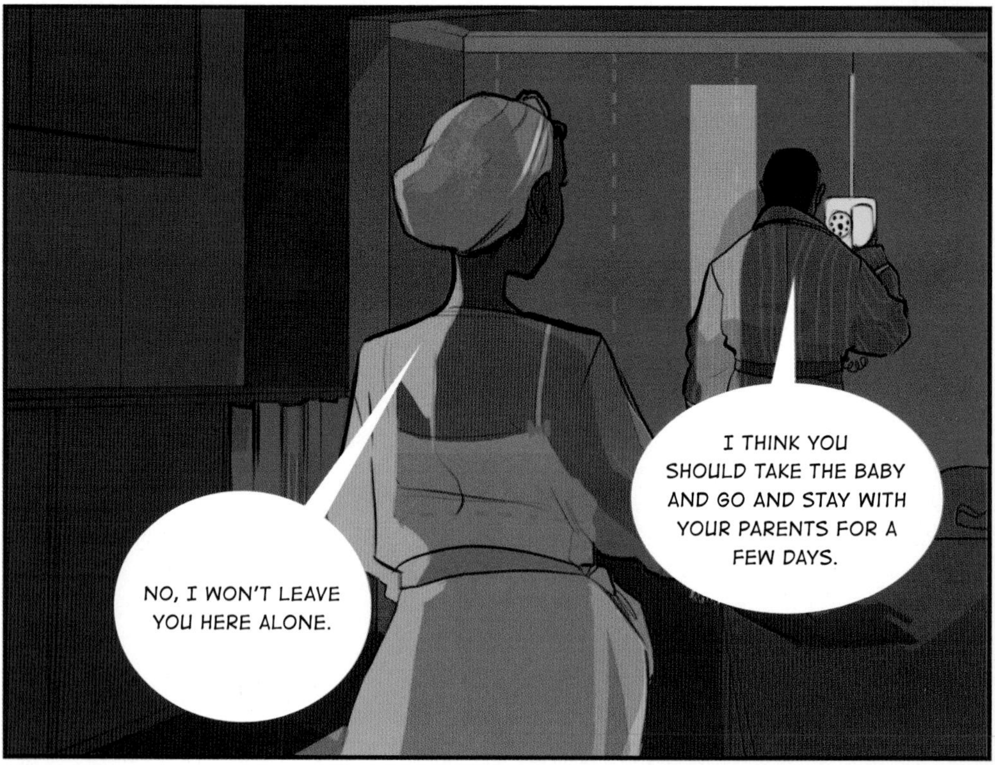
I THINK YOU SHOULD TAKE THE BABY AND GO AND STAY WITH YOUR PARENTS FOR A FEW DAYS.
NO, I WON'T LEAVE YOU HERE ALONE.

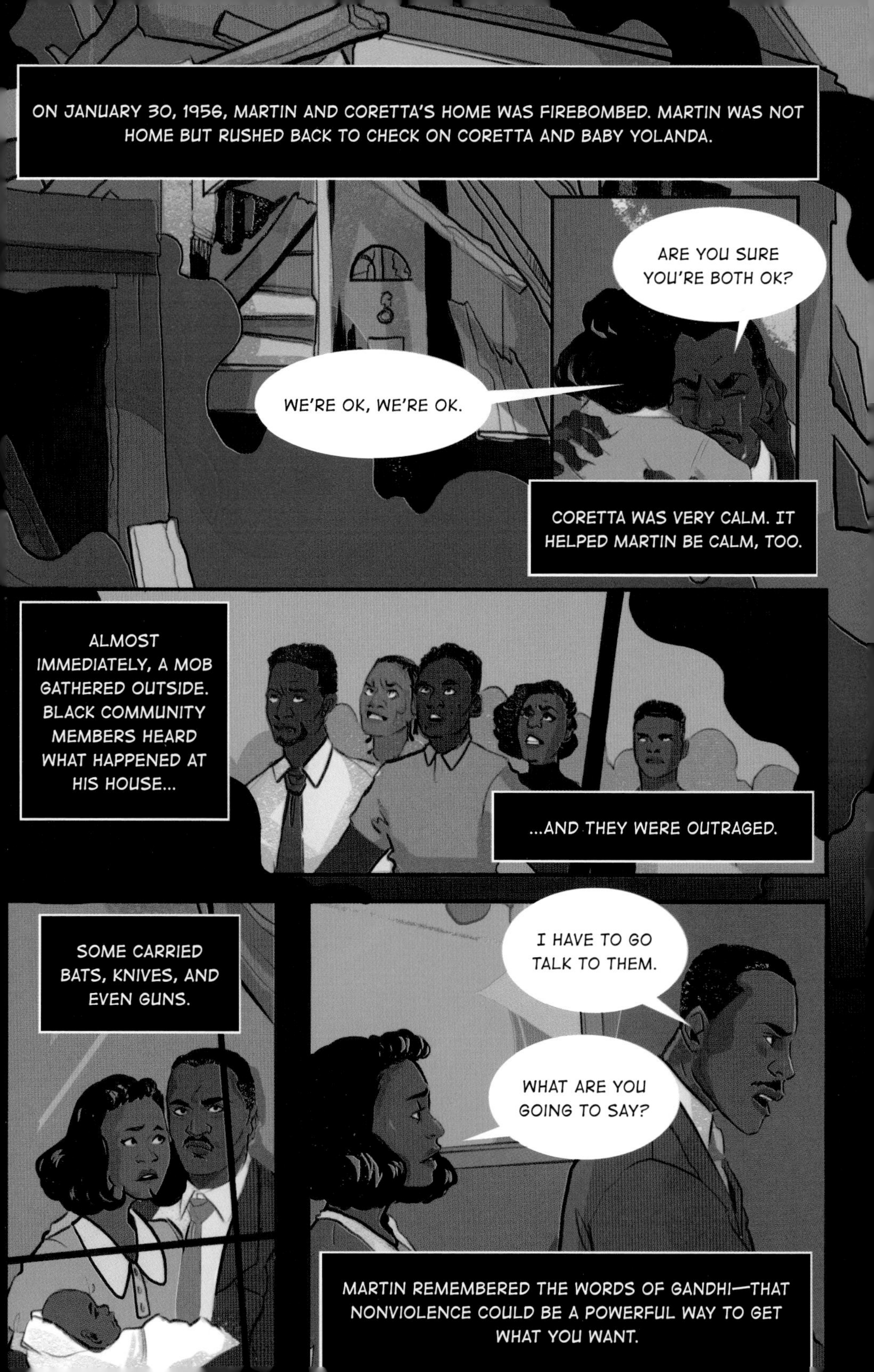
ON JANUARY 30, 1956, MARTIN AND CORETTA'S HOME WAS FIREBOMBED. MARTIN WAS NOT HOME BUT RUSHED BACK TO CHECK ON CORETTA AND BABY YOLANDA.
ARE YOU SURE YOU'RE BOTH OK?
WE'RE OK, WE'RE OK.
CORETTA WAS VERY CALM. IT HELPED MARTIN BE CALM, TOO.
ALMOST IMMEDIATELY, A MOB GATHERED OUTSIDE. BLACK COMMUNITY MEMBERS HEARD WHAT HAPPENED AT HIS HOUSE...
...AND THEY WERE OUTRAGED.
SOME CARRIED BATS, KNIVES, AND EVEN GUNS.
I HAVE TO GO TALK TO THEM.
WHAT ARE YOU GOING TO SAY?
MARTIN REMEMBERED THE WORDS OF GANDHI—THAT NONVIOLENCE COULD BE A POWERFUL WAY TO GET WHAT YOU WANT.

WE'LL KILL 'EM FOR YOU!
JUST SAY THE WORD, REVEREND KING!
I AM OK. MY FAMILY IS OK.
NOW, I ASK YOU ALL TO BE CALM, AS MY FAMILY AND I ARE CALM.

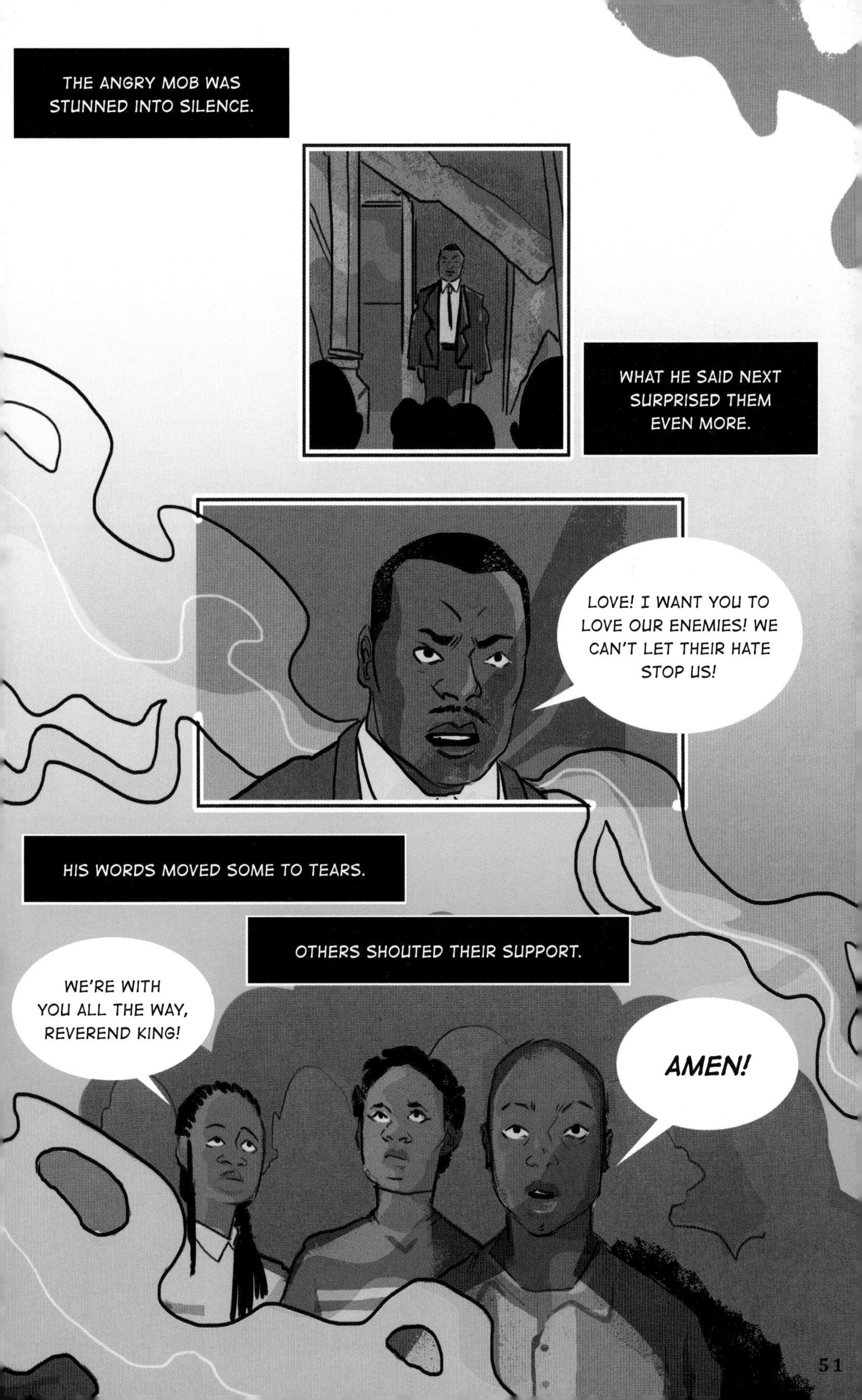
THE ANGRY MOB WAS STUNNED INTO SILENCE.
WHAT HE SAID NEXT SURPRISED THEM EVEN MORE.
LOVE! I WANT YOU TO LOVE OUR ENEMIES! WE CAN'T LET THEIR HATE STOP US!
HIS WORDS MOVED SOME TO TEARS.
OTHERS SHOUTED THEIR SUPPORT.
WE'RE WITH YOU ALL THE WAY, REVEREND KING!
AMEN!

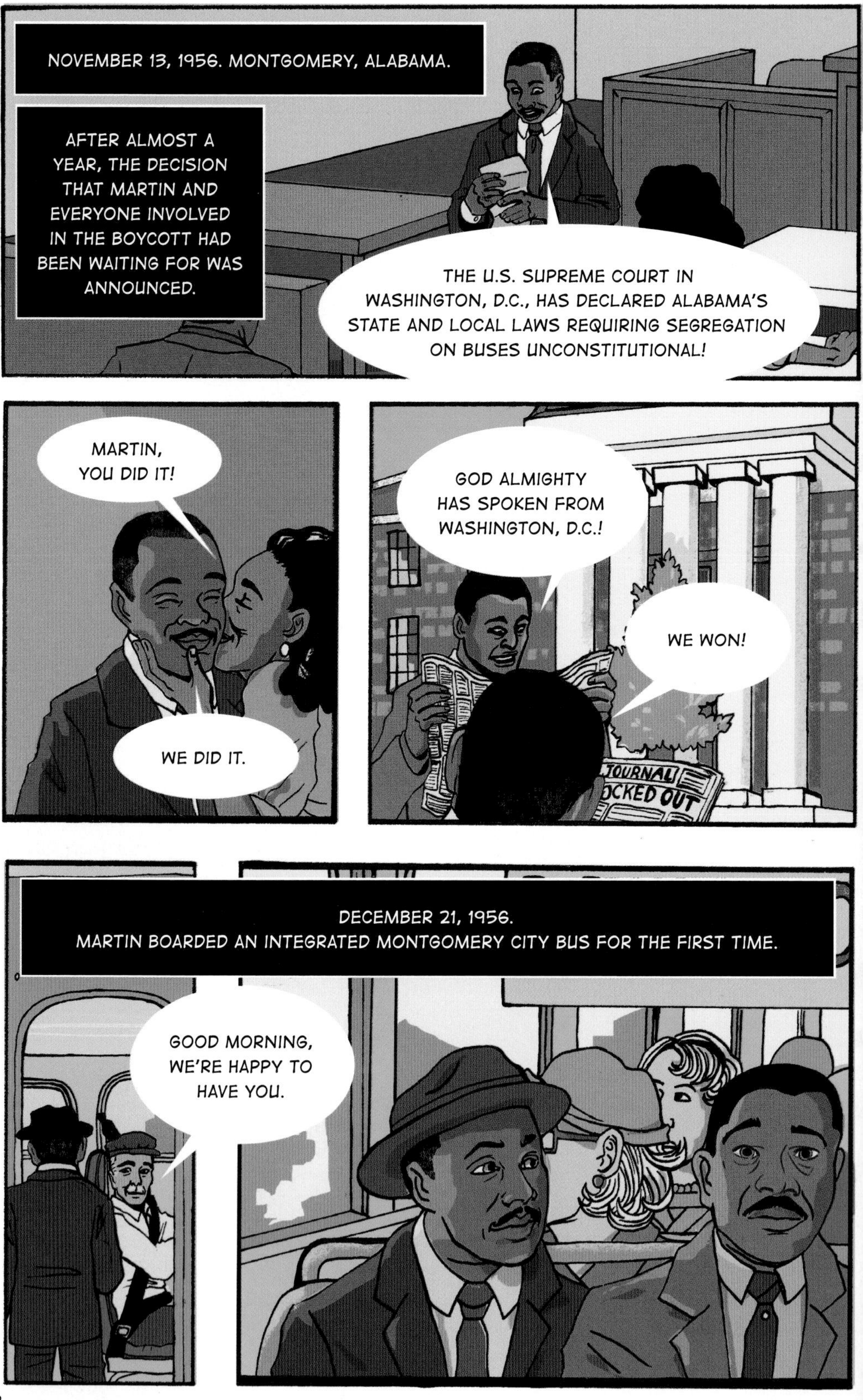
NOVEMBER 13, 1956. MONTGOMERY, ALABAMA.
AFTER ALMOST A YEAR, THE DECISION THAT MARTIN AND EVERYONE INVOLVED IN THE BOYCOTT HAD BEEN WAITING FOR WAS ANNOUNCED.
THE U.S. SUPREME COURT IN WASHINGTON, D.C., HAS DECLARED ALABAMA'S STATE AND LOCAL LAWS REQUIRING SEGREGATION ON BUSES UNCONSTITUTIONAL!
MARTIN, YOU DID IT!
WE DID IT.
GOD ALMIGHTY HAS SPOKEN FROM WASHINGTON, D.C.!
WE WON!
JOURNAL
DECEMBER 21, 1956.
MARTIN BOARDED AN INTEGRATED MONTGOMERY CITY BUS FOR THE FIRST TIME.
GOOD MORNING, WE'RE HAPPY TO HAVE YOU.

ROSA PARKS'S SMALL ACT OF DEFIANCE ON A MONTGOMERY CITY BUS NEARLY THIRTEEN MONTHS EARLIER HAD A BIG IMPACT. IT LED TO CHANGING THE LAW...
PEOPLE SAID I DIDN'T STAND UP BECAUSE I WAS TIRED. THE ONLY TIRED I WAS, WAS TIRED OF GIVING IN.

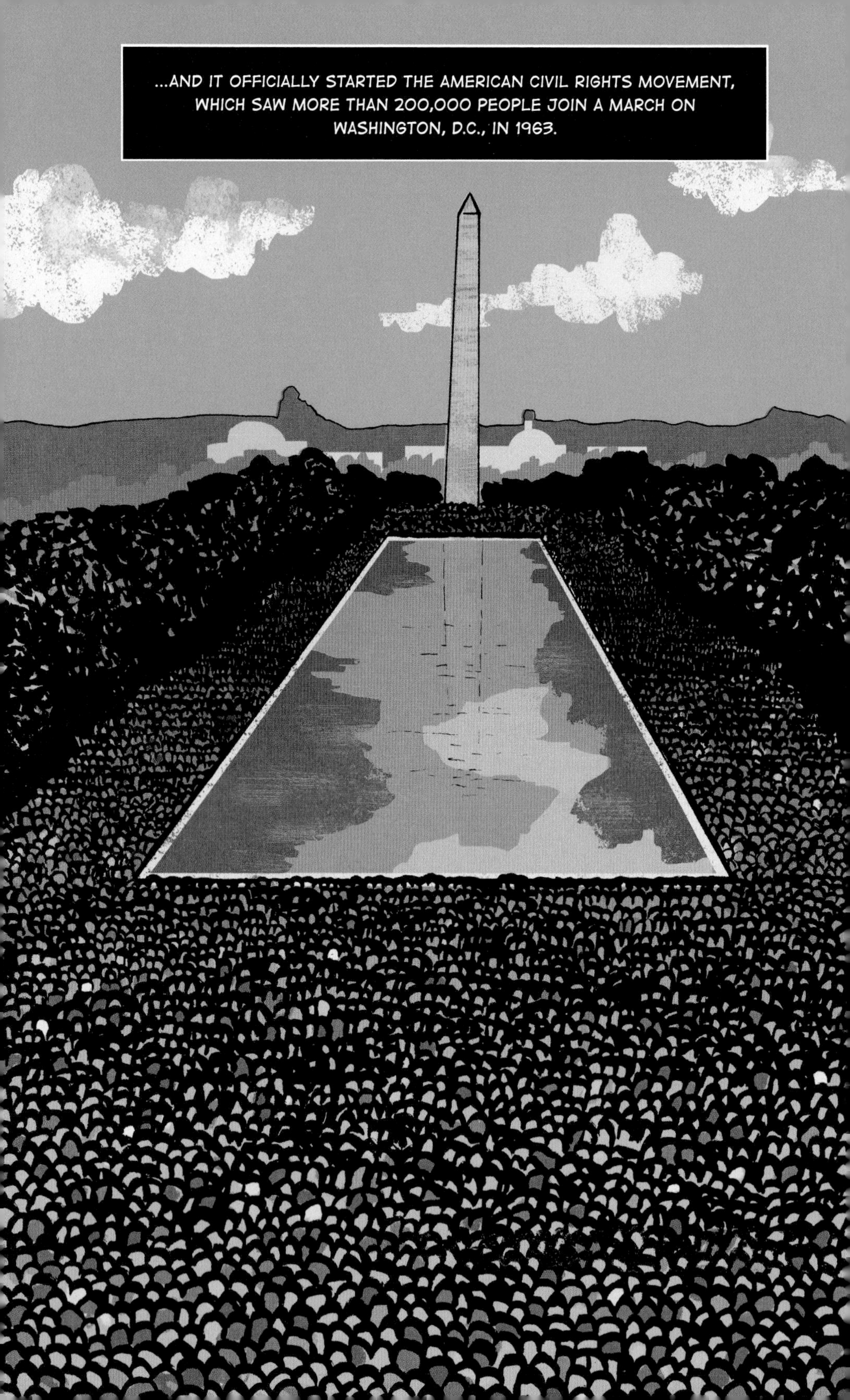
...AND IT OFFICIALLY STARTED THE AMERICAN CIVIL RIGHTS MOVEMENT, WHICH SAW MORE THAN 200,000 PEOPLE JOIN A MARCH ON WASHINGTON, D.C., IN 1963.

CHAPTER 5

CAMPAIGNING FOR CIVIL RIGHTS

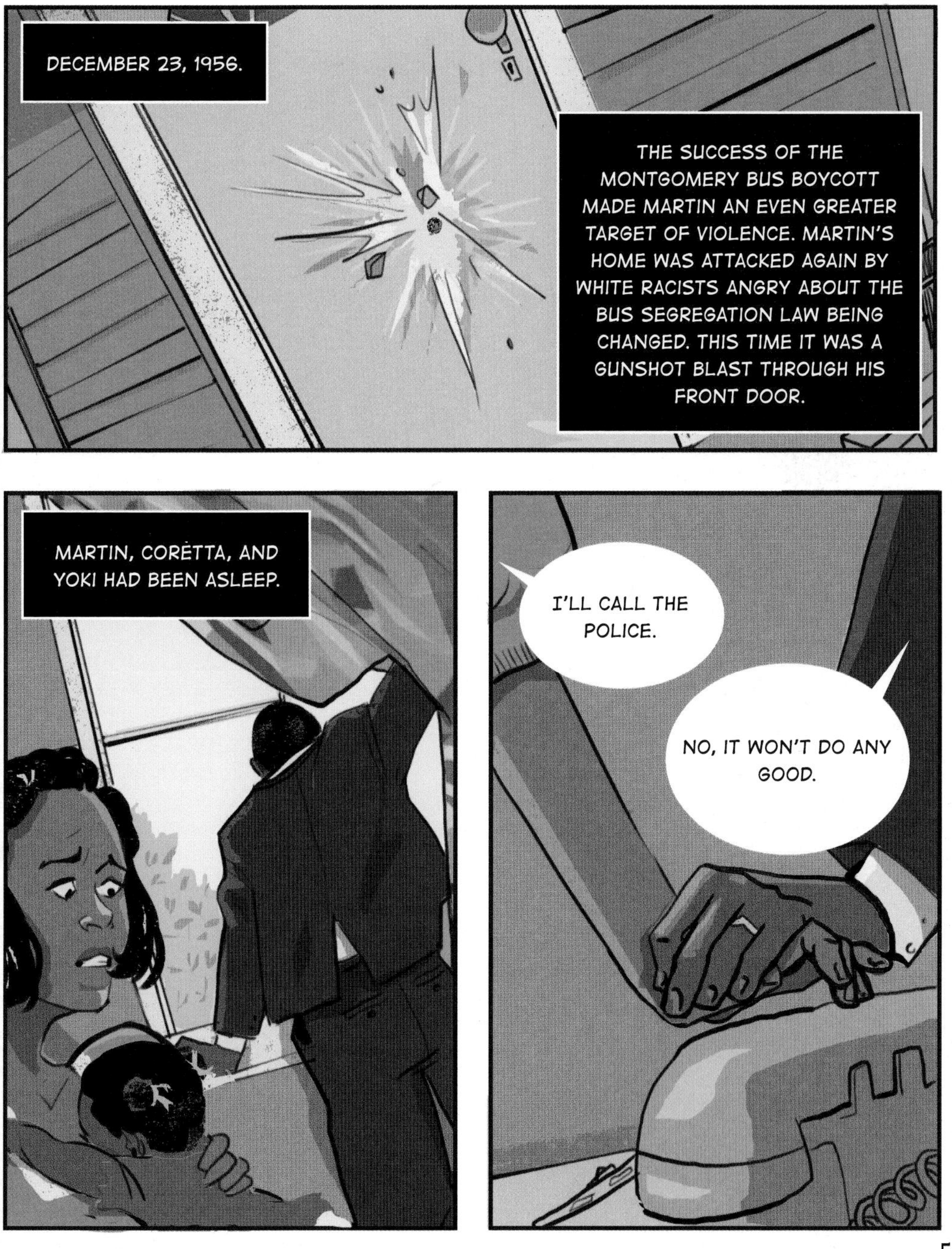
DECEMBER 23, 1956.
THE SUCCESS OF THE MONTGOMERY BUS BOYCOTT MADE MARTIN AN EVEN GREATER TARGET OF VIOLENCE. MARTIN'S HOME WAS ATTACKED AGAIN BY WHITE RACISTS ANGRY ABOUT THE BUS SEGREGATION LAW BEING CHANGED. THIS TIME IT WAS A GUNSHOT BLAST THROUGH HIS FRONT DOOR.
MARTIN, CORETTA, AND YOKI HAD BEEN ASLEEP.
I'LL CALL THE POLICE.
NO, IT WON'T DO ANY GOOD.

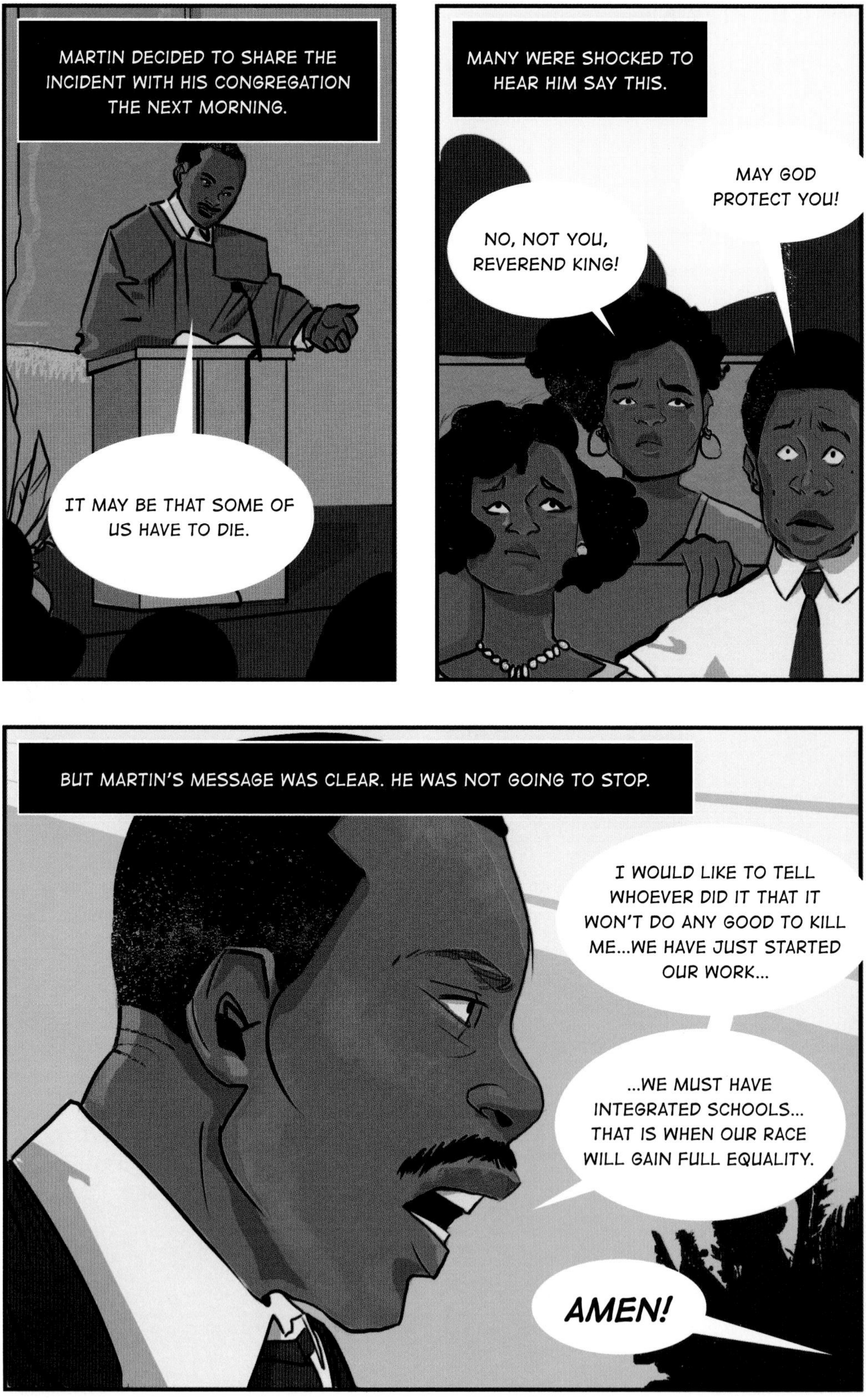
MARTIN DECIDED TO SHARE THE INCIDENT WITH HIS CONGREGATION THE NEXT MORNING.
IT MAY BE THAT SOME OF US HAVE TO DIE.
MANY WERE SHOCKED TO HEAR HIM SAY THIS.
NO, NOT YOU, REVEREND KING!
MAY GOD PROTECT YOU!
BUT MARTIN'S MESSAGE WAS CLEAR. HE WAS NOT GOING TO STOP.
I WOULD LIKE TO TELL WHOEVER DID IT THAT IT WON'T DO ANY GOOD TO KILL ME...WE HAVE JUST STARTED OUR WORK...
...WE MUST HAVE INTEGRATED SCHOOLS... THAT IS WHEN OUR RACE WILL GAIN FULL EQUALITY.
AMEN!

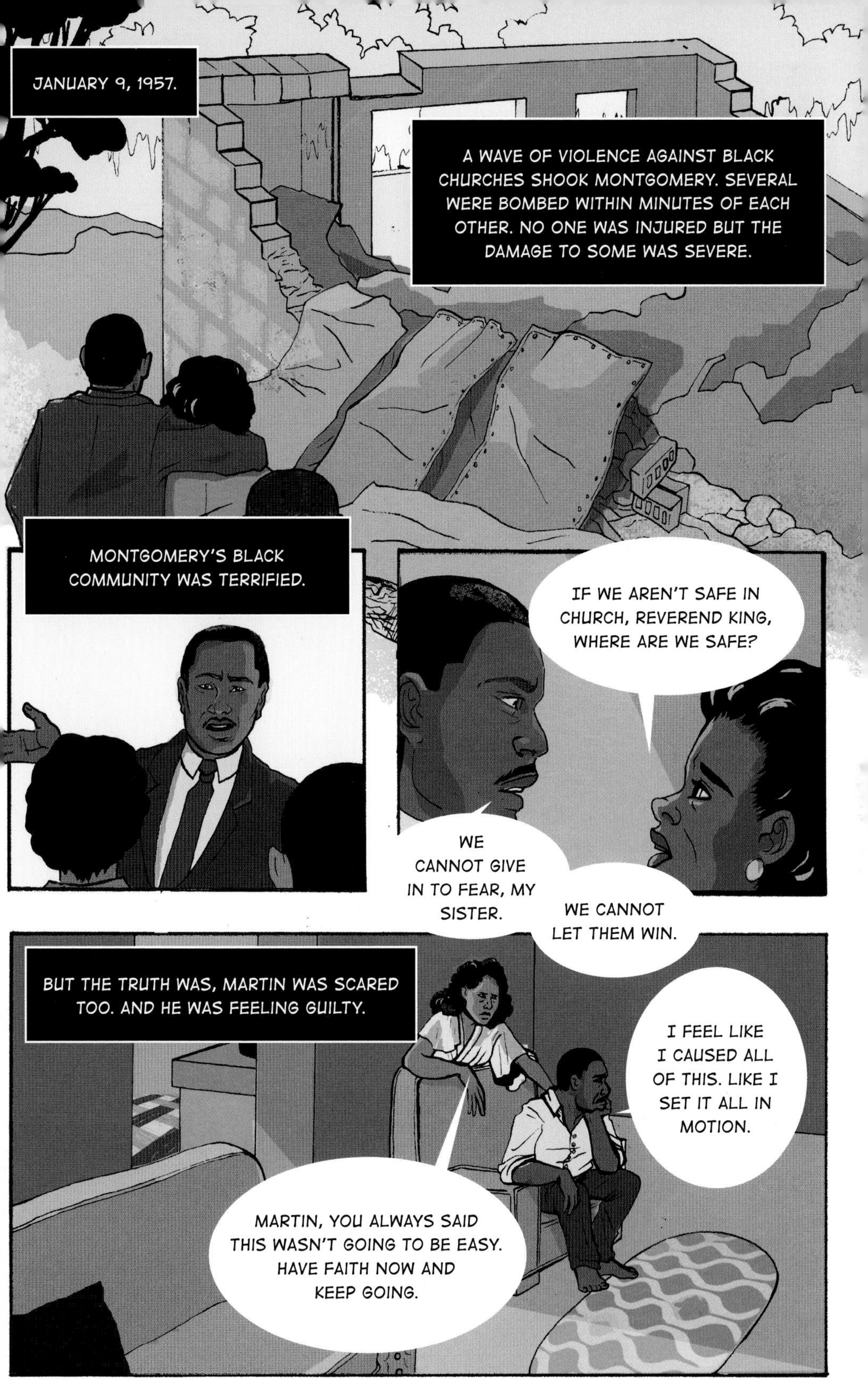

JANUARY 9, 1957.
A WAVE OF VIOLENCE AGAINST BLACK CHURCHES SHOOK MONTGOMERY. SEVERAL WERE BOMBED WITHIN MINUTES OF EACH OTHER. NO ONE WAS INJURED BUT THE DAMAGE TO SOME WAS SEVERE.
MONTGOMERY'S BLACK COMMUNITY WAS TERRIFIED.
IF WE AREN'T SAFE IN CHURCH, REVEREND KING, WHERE ARE WE SAFE?
WE CANNOT GIVE IN TO FEAR, MY SISTER.
WE CANNOT LET THEM WIN.
BUT THE TRUTH WAS, MARTIN WAS SCARED TOO. AND HE WAS FEELING GUILTY.
I FEEL LIKE I CAUSED ALL OF THIS. LIKE I SET IT ALL IN MOTION.
MARTIN, YOU ALWAYS SAID THIS WASN'T GOING TO BE EASY. HAVE FAITH NOW AND KEEP GOING.

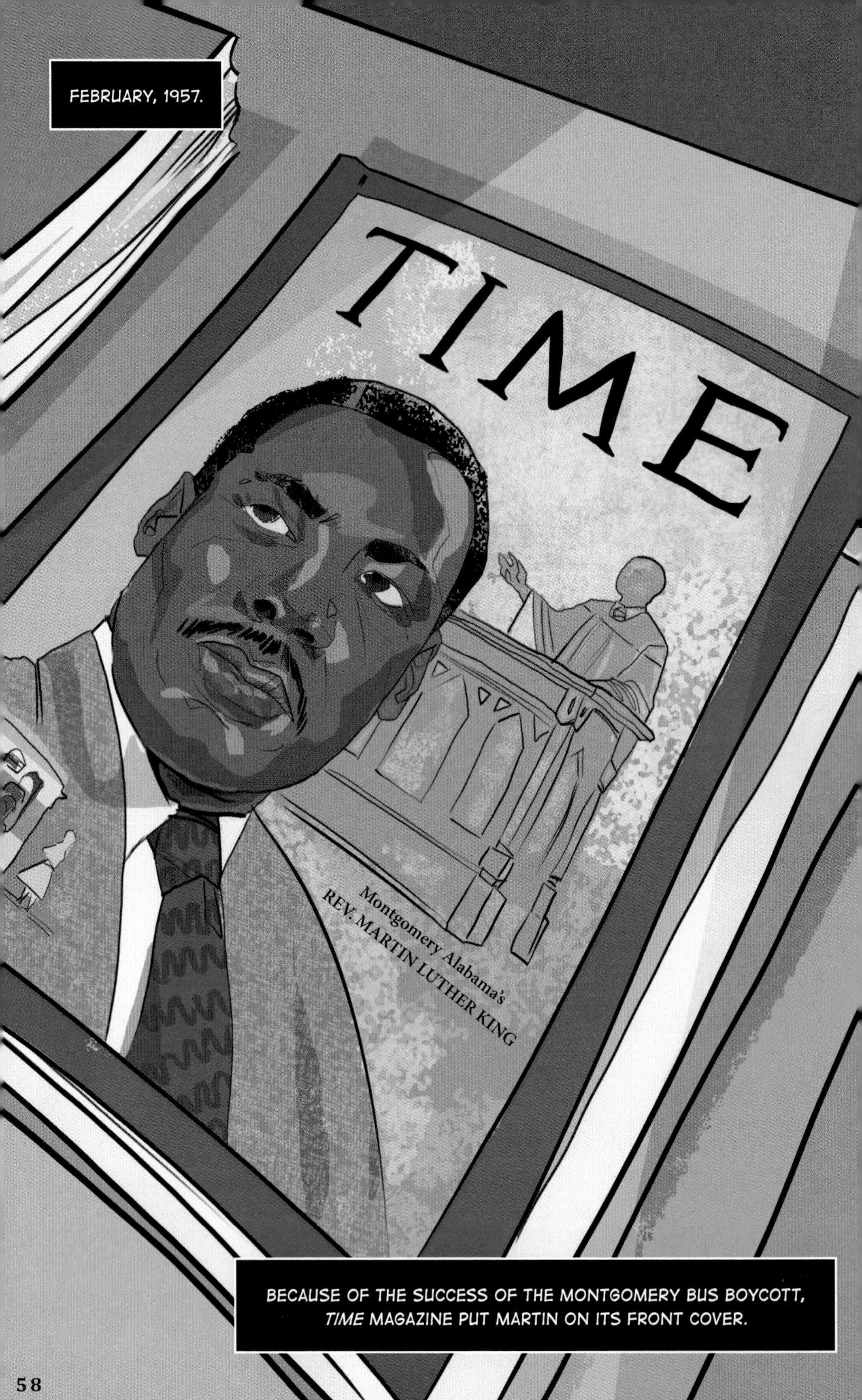
FEBRUARY, 1957.
TIME
Montgomery Alabama's
REV. MARTIN LUTHER KING
BECAUSE OF THE SUCCESS OF THE MONTGOMERY BUS BOYCOTT, *TIME* MAGAZINE PUT MARTIN ON ITS FRONT COVER.

AT TWENTY-SEVEN YEARS OLD, MARTIN HAD BECOME THE LEADER OF THE CIVIL RIGHTS MOVEMENT.

I ALWAYS WANTED TO BE INVOLVED, BUT THIS IS NOT A ROLE I ASKED FOR.

PEOPLE STARTED TO TREAT HIM LIKE A CELEBRITY EVERYWHERE HE WENT.

DR. KING, OVER HERE!

REVEREND KING, SIGN YOUR AUTOGRAPH FOR ME!

SOMETIMES, IT WAS HARD NOT TO LET THE STAR TREATMENT GO TO HIS HEAD.

RIGHT THIS WAY, DR. KING. WE RESERVED A SPECIAL TABLE FOR YOU.

BUT MARTIN KNEW WHILE THINGS WERE BETTER FOR BLACK PEOPLE IN THE SOUTH, THINGS WERE FAR FROM GREAT.

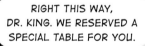

THERE IS STILL MUCH WORK TO BE DONE. I HAVE TO STAY FOCUSED ON THE MISSION.

IN FEBRUARY 1957, MARTIN WAS ASKED TO BE THE LEADER OF THE SOUTHERN CHRISTIAN LEADERSHIP CONFERENCE (SCLC). THE SCLC ADVISED AND SUPPORTED ACTIVISTS WHO WANTED TO LAUNCH THEIR OWN BUS BOYCOTTS AND PROTESTS ACROSS THE SOUTH.

MARTIN'S NEW ROLE HAD HIM BUSIER THAN EVER.

HE TRAVELED ACROSS THE COUNTRY, GIVING LECTURES ON NONVIOLENT PROTESTING.

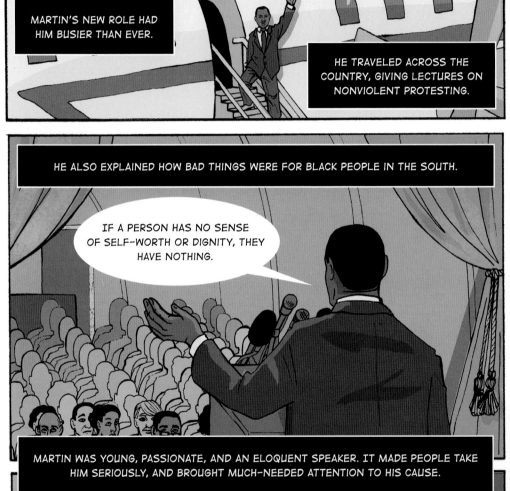

HE ALSO EXPLAINED HOW BAD THINGS WERE FOR BLACK PEOPLE IN THE SOUTH.

IF A PERSON HAS NO SENSE OF SELF-WORTH OR DIGNITY, THEY HAVE NOTHING.

MARTIN WAS YOUNG, PASSIONATE, AND AN ELOQUENT SPEAKER. IT MADE PEOPLE TAKE HIM SERIOUSLY, AND BROUGHT MUCH-NEEDED ATTENTION TO HIS CAUSE.

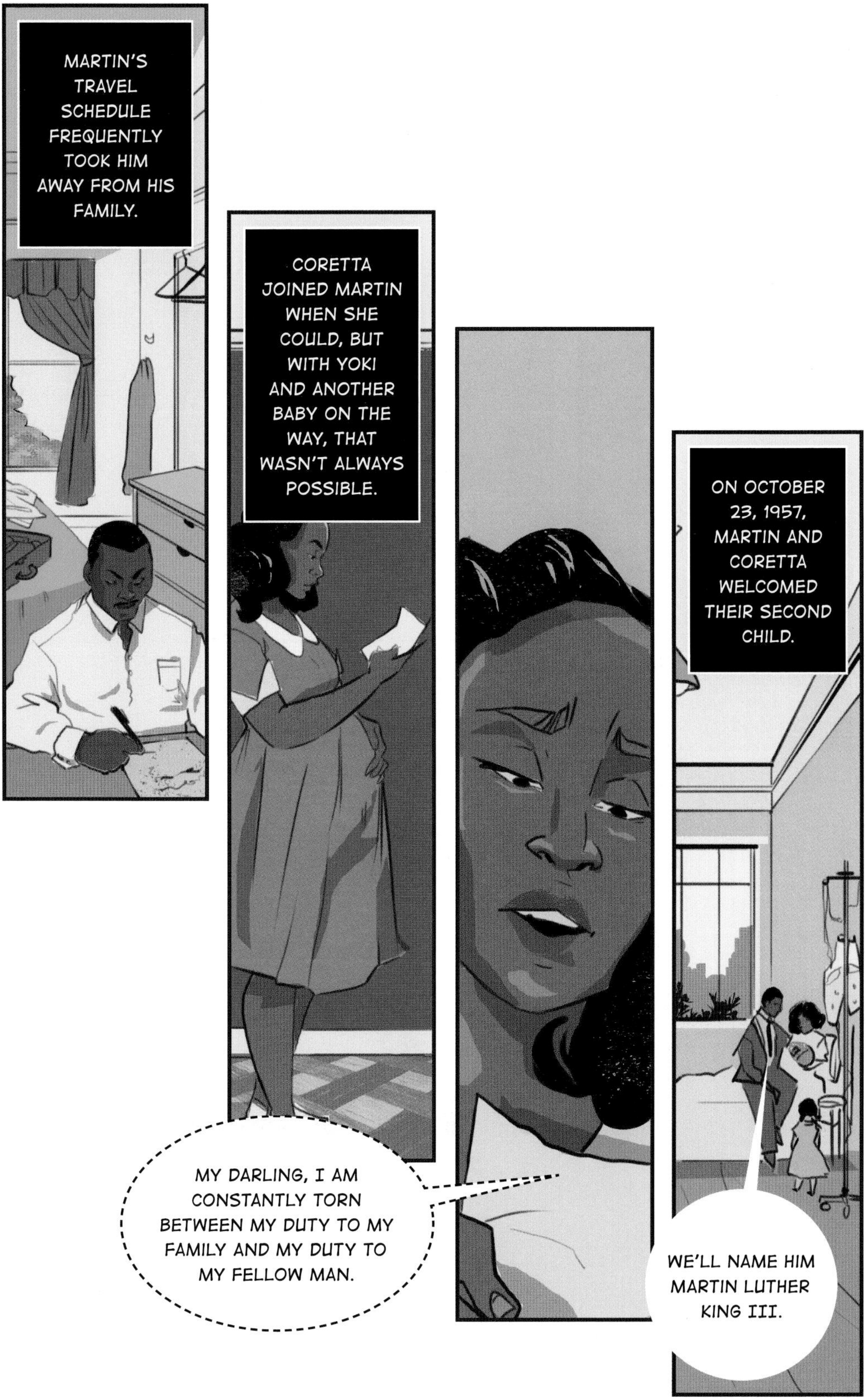
MARTIN'S TRAVEL SCHEDULE FREQUENTLY TOOK HIM AWAY FROM HIS FAMILY.
CORETTA JOINED MARTIN WHEN SHE COULD, BUT WITH YOKI AND ANOTHER BABY ON THE WAY, THAT WASN'T ALWAYS POSSIBLE.
MY DARLING, I AM CONSTANTLY TORN BETWEEN MY DUTY TO MY FAMILY AND MY DUTY TO MY FELLOW MAN.
ON OCTOBER 23, 1957, MARTIN AND CORETTA WELCOMED THEIR SECOND CHILD.
WE'LL NAME HIM MARTIN LUTHER KING III.

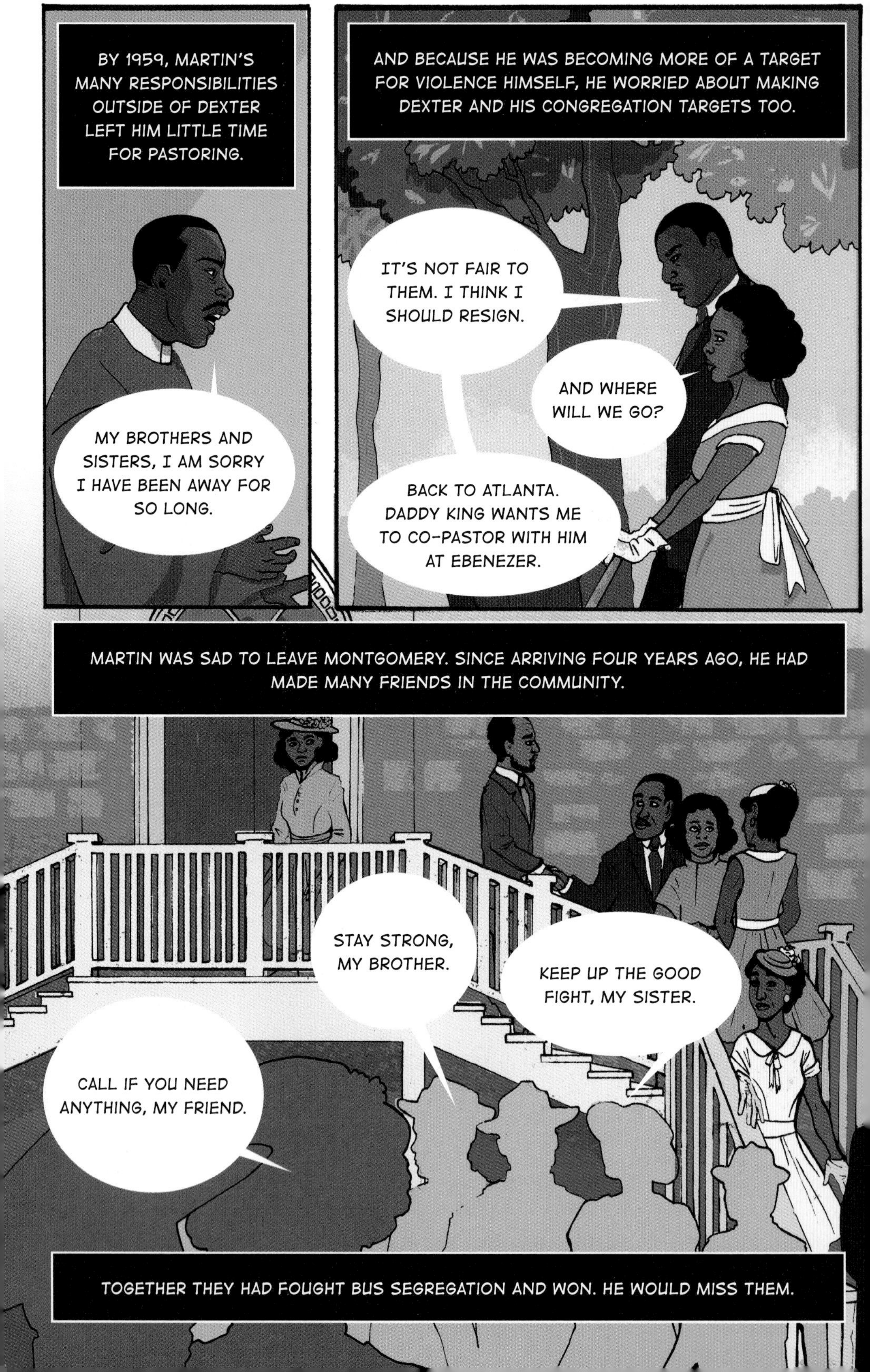
BY 1959, MARTIN'S MANY RESPONSIBILITIES OUTSIDE OF DEXTER LEFT HIM LITTLE TIME FOR PASTORING.
MY BROTHERS AND SISTERS, I AM SORRY I HAVE BEEN AWAY FOR SO LONG.
AND BECAUSE HE WAS BECOMING MORE OF A TARGET FOR VIOLENCE HIMSELF, HE WORRIED ABOUT MAKING DEXTER AND HIS CONGREGATION TARGETS TOO.
IT'S NOT FAIR TO THEM. I THINK I SHOULD RESIGN.
AND WHERE WILL WE GO?
BACK TO ATLANTA. DADDY KING WANTS ME TO CO-PASTOR WITH HIM AT EBENEZER.
MARTIN WAS SAD TO LEAVE MONTGOMERY. SINCE ARRIVING FOUR YEARS AGO, HE HAD MADE MANY FRIENDS IN THE COMMUNITY.
STAY STRONG, MY BROTHER.
KEEP UP THE GOOD FIGHT, MY SISTER.
CALL IF YOU NEED ANYTHING, MY FRIEND.
TOGETHER THEY HAD FOUGHT BUS SEGREGATION AND WON. HE WOULD MISS THEM.

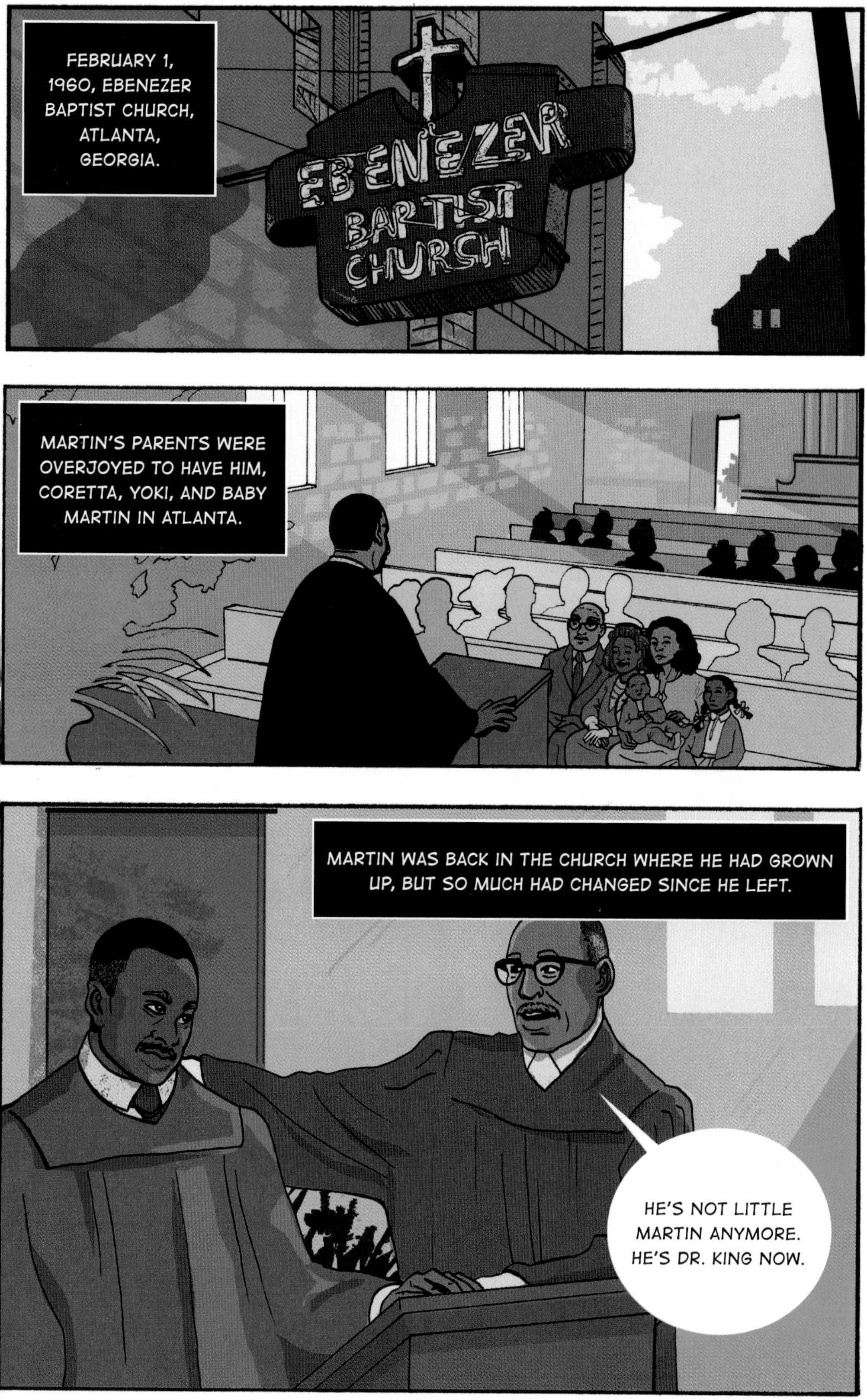
FEBRUARY 1, 1960, EBENEZER BAPTIST CHURCH, ATLANTA, GEORGIA.
EBENEZER BAPTIST CHURCH
MARTIN'S PARENTS WERE OVERJOYED TO HAVE HIM, CORETTA, YOKI, AND BABY MARTIN IN ATLANTA.
MARTIN WAS BACK IN THE CHURCH WHERE HE HAD GROWN UP, BUT SO MUCH HAD CHANGED SINCE HE LEFT.
HE'S NOT LITTLE MARTIN ANYMORE. HE'S DR. KING NOW.

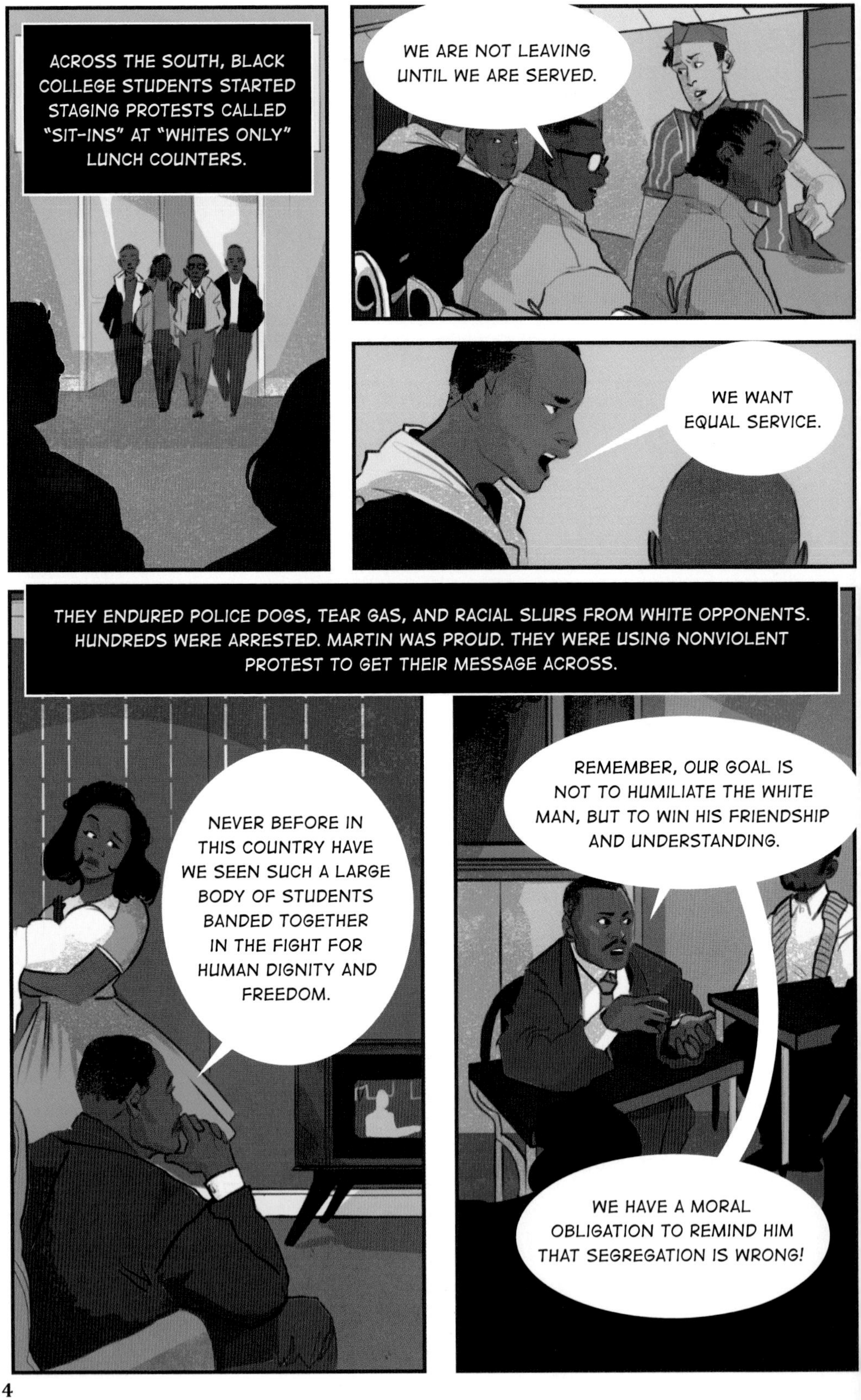
ACROSS THE SOUTH, BLACK COLLEGE STUDENTS STARTED STAGING PROTESTS CALLED "SIT-INS" AT "WHITES ONLY" LUNCH COUNTERS.
WE ARE NOT LEAVING UNTIL WE ARE SERVED.
WE WANT EQUAL SERVICE.
THEY ENDURED POLICE DOGS, TEAR GAS, AND RACIAL SLURS FROM WHITE OPPONENTS. HUNDREDS WERE ARRESTED. MARTIN WAS PROUD. THEY WERE USING NONVIOLENT PROTEST TO GET THEIR MESSAGE ACROSS.
NEVER BEFORE IN THIS COUNTRY HAVE WE SEEN SUCH A LARGE BODY OF STUDENTS BANDED TOGETHER IN THE FIGHT FOR HUMAN DIGNITY AND FREEDOM.
REMEMBER, OUR GOAL IS NOT TO HUMILIATE THE WHITE MAN, BUT TO WIN HIS FRIENDSHIP AND UNDERSTANDING.
WE HAVE A MORAL OBLIGATION TO REMIND HIM THAT SEGREGATION IS WRONG!

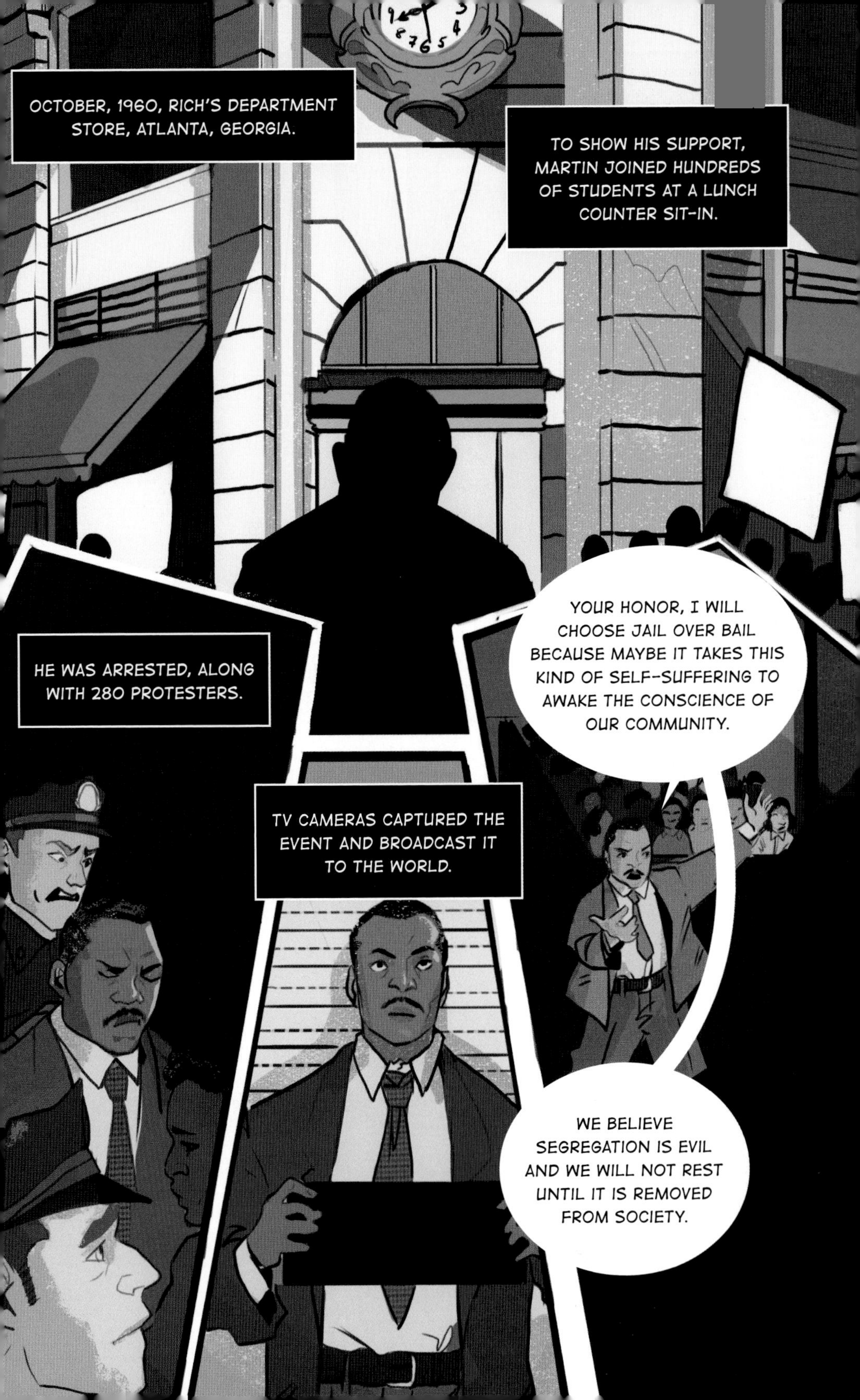
OCTOBER, 1960, RICH'S DEPARTMENT STORE, ATLANTA, GEORGIA.
TO SHOW HIS SUPPORT, MARTIN JOINED HUNDREDS OF STUDENTS AT A LUNCH COUNTER SIT-IN.
HE WAS ARRESTED, ALONG WITH 280 PROTESTERS.
YOUR HONOR, I WILL CHOOSE JAIL OVER BAIL BECAUSE MAYBE IT TAKES THIS KIND OF SELF-SUFFERING TO AWAKE THE CONSCIENCE OF OUR COMMUNITY.
TV CAMERAS CAPTURED THE EVENT AND BROADCAST IT TO THE WORLD.
WE BELIEVE SEGREGATION IS EVIL AND WE WILL NOT REST UNTIL IT IS REMOVED FROM SOCIETY.

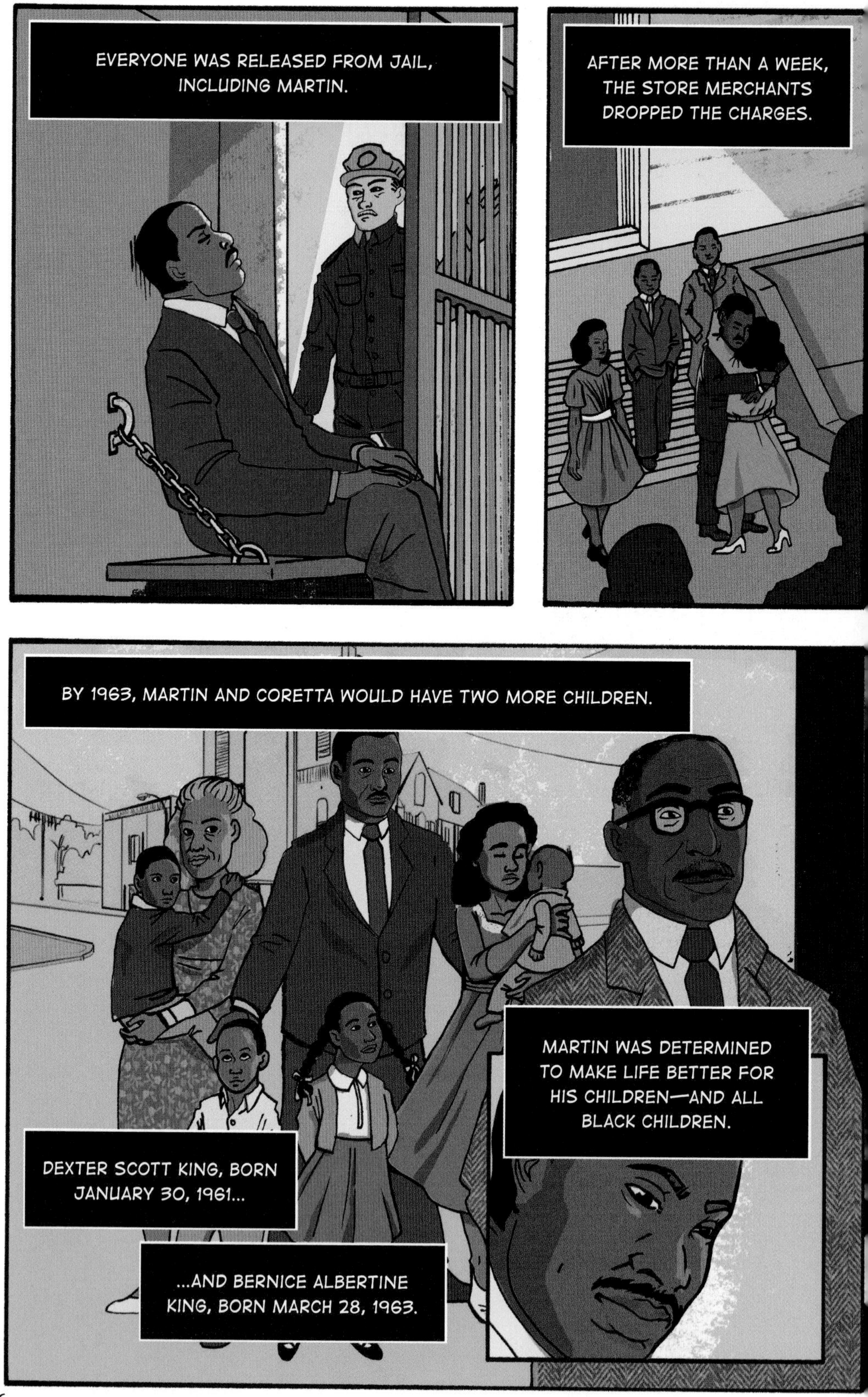
EVERYONE WAS RELEASED FROM JAIL, INCLUDING MARTIN.
AFTER MORE THAN A WEEK, THE STORE MERCHANTS DROPPED THE CHARGES.
BY 1963, MARTIN AND CORETTA WOULD HAVE TWO MORE CHILDREN.
DEXTER SCOTT KING, BORN JANUARY 30, 1961...
...AND BERNICE ALBERTINE KING, BORN MARCH 28, 1963.
MARTIN WAS DETERMINED TO MAKE LIFE BETTER FOR HIS CHILDREN—AND ALL BLACK CHILDREN.

CHAPTER 6

RIDING FOR FREEDOM: THE FREEDOM RIDERS

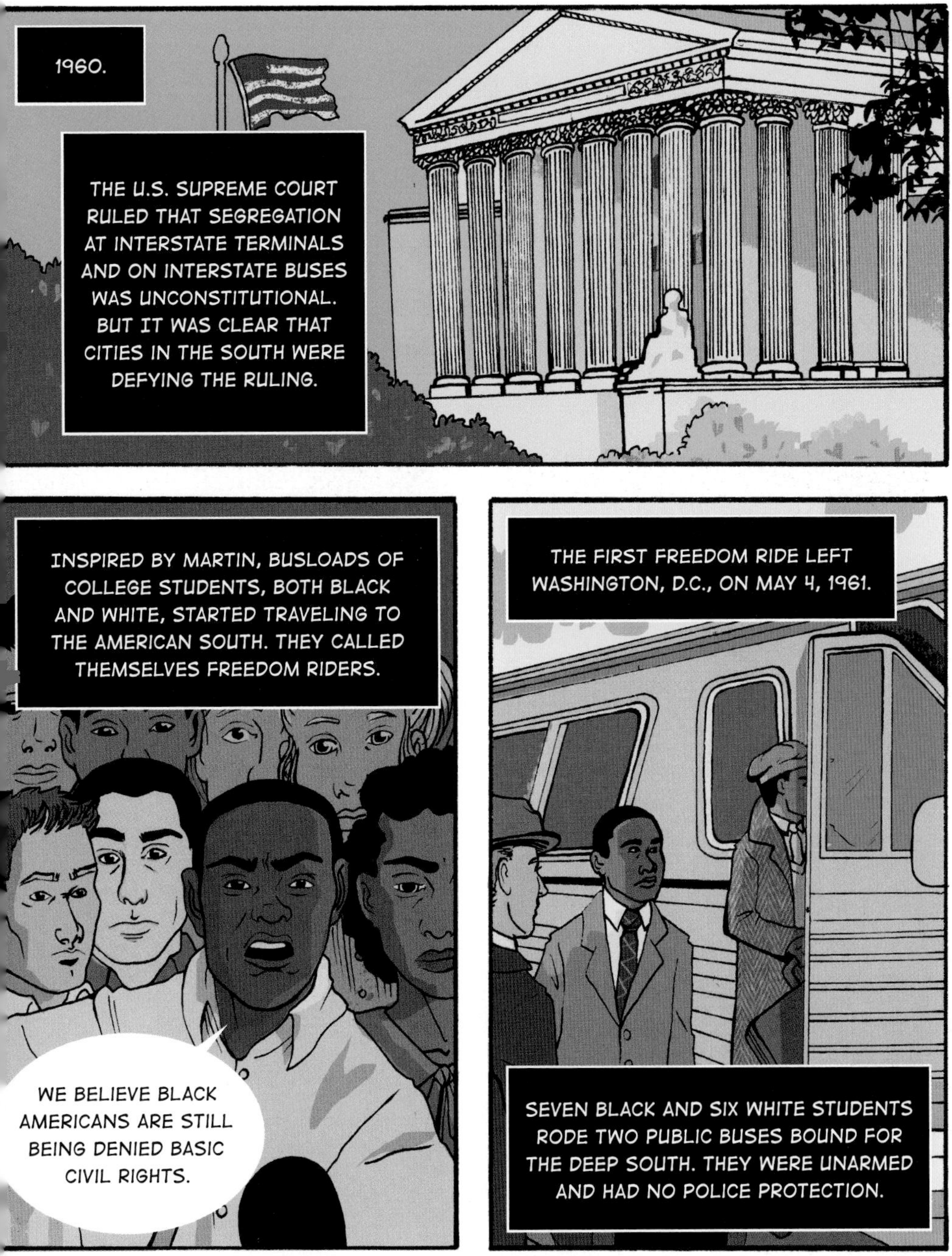

1960.
THE U.S. SUPREME COURT RULED THAT SEGREGATION AT INTERSTATE TERMINALS AND ON INTERSTATE BUSES WAS UNCONSTITUTIONAL. BUT IT WAS CLEAR THAT CITIES IN THE SOUTH WERE DEFYING THE RULING.
INSPIRED BY MARTIN, BUSLOADS OF COLLEGE STUDENTS, BOTH BLACK AND WHITE, STARTED TRAVELING TO THE AMERICAN SOUTH. THEY CALLED THEMSELVES FREEDOM RIDERS.
WE BELIEVE BLACK AMERICANS ARE STILL BEING DENIED BASIC CIVIL RIGHTS.
THE FIRST FREEDOM RIDE LEFT WASHINGTON, D.C., ON MAY 4, 1961.
SEVEN BLACK AND SIX WHITE STUDENTS RODE TWO PUBLIC BUSES BOUND FOR THE DEEP SOUTH. THEY WERE UNARMED AND HAD NO POLICE PROTECTION.

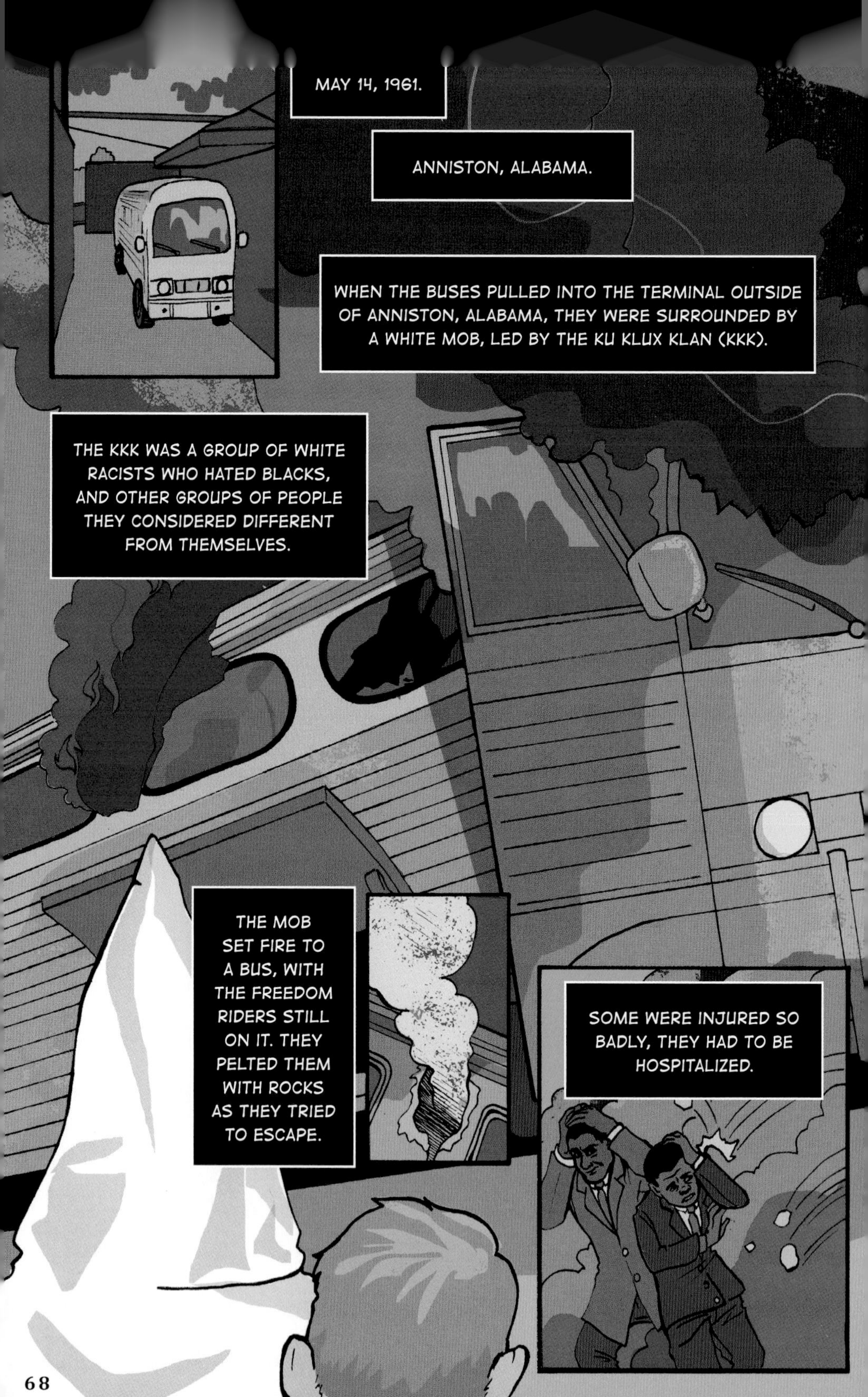
MAY 14, 1961.
ANNISTON, ALABAMA.
WHEN THE BUSES PULLED INTO THE TERMINAL OUTSIDE OF ANNISTON, ALABAMA, THEY WERE SURROUNDED BY A WHITE MOB, LED BY THE KU KLUX KLAN (KKK).
THE KKK WAS A GROUP OF WHITE RACISTS WHO HATED BLACKS, AND OTHER GROUPS OF PEOPLE THEY CONSIDERED DIFFERENT FROM THEMSELVES.
THE MOB SET FIRE TO A BUS, WITH THE FREEDOM RIDERS STILL ON IT. THEY PELTED THEM WITH ROCKS AS THEY TRIED TO ESCAPE.
SOME WERE INJURED SO BADLY, THEY HAD TO BE HOSPITALIZED.

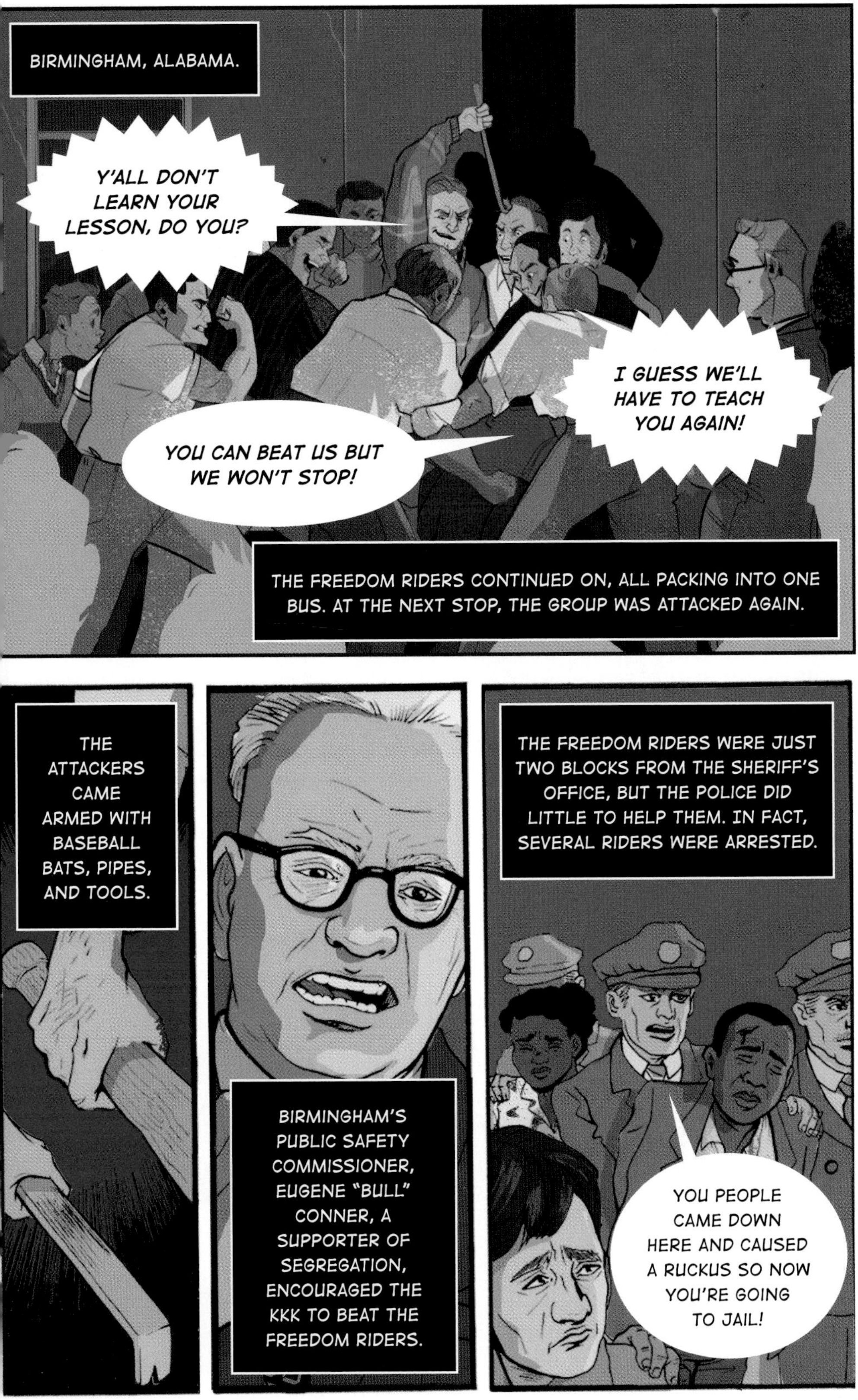
BIRMINGHAM, ALABAMA.
Y'ALL DON'T LEARN YOUR LESSON, DO YOU?
I GUESS WE'LL HAVE TO TEACH YOU AGAIN!
YOU CAN BEAT US BUT WE WON'T STOP!
THE FREEDOM RIDERS CONTINUED ON, ALL PACKING INTO ONE BUS. AT THE NEXT STOP, THE GROUP WAS ATTACKED AGAIN.
THE ATTACKERS CAME ARMED WITH BASEBALL BATS, PIPES, AND TOOLS.
BIRMINGHAM'S PUBLIC SAFETY COMMISSIONER, EUGENE "BULL" CONNER, A SUPPORTER OF SEGREGATION, ENCOURAGED THE KKK TO BEAT THE FREEDOM RIDERS.
THE FREEDOM RIDERS WERE JUST TWO BLOCKS FROM THE SHERIFF'S OFFICE, BUT THE POLICE DID LITTLE TO HELP THEM. IN FACT, SEVERAL RIDERS WERE ARRESTED.
YOU PEOPLE CAME DOWN HERE AND CAUSED A RUCKUS SO NOW YOU'RE GOING TO JAIL!

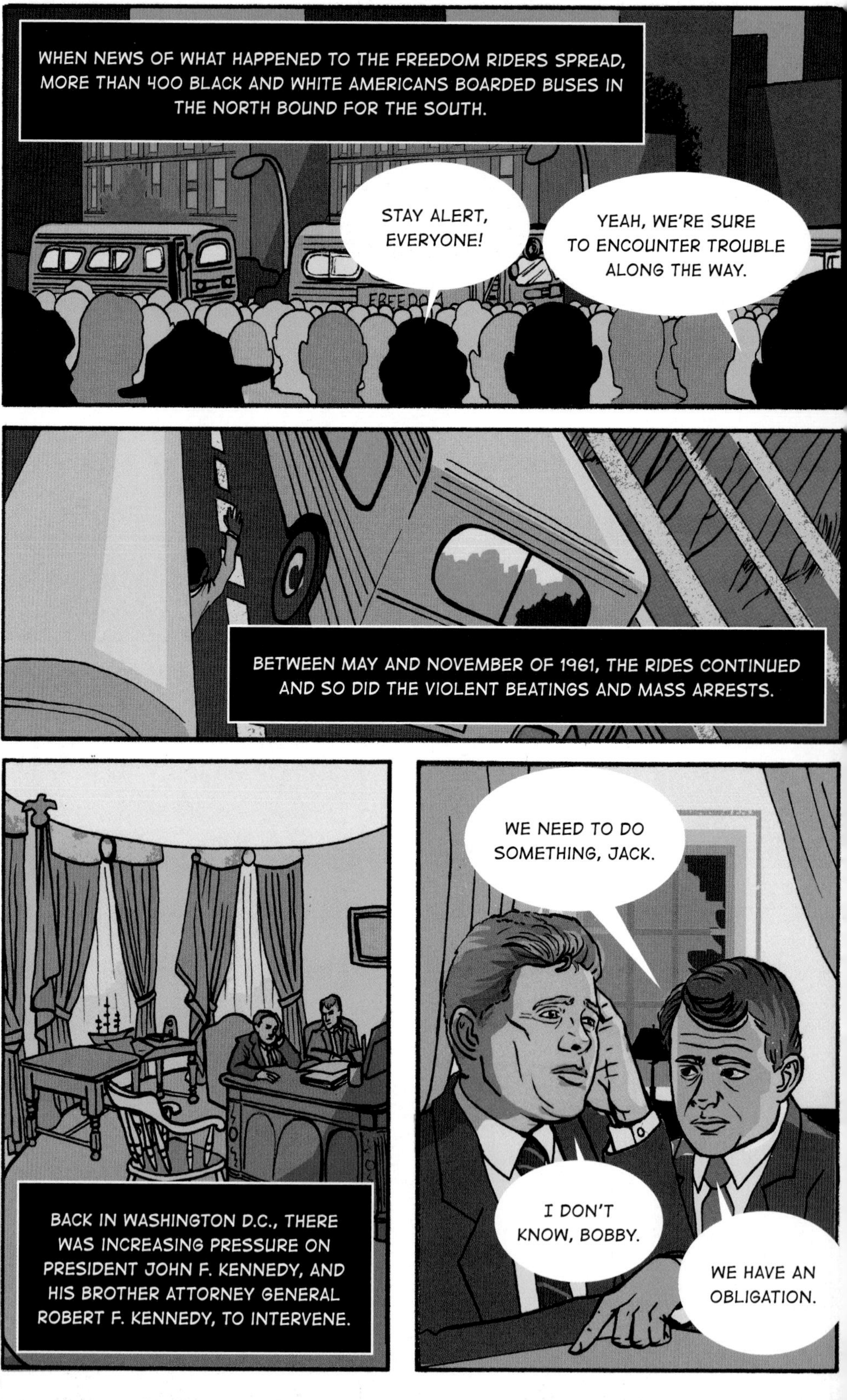
WHEN NEWS OF WHAT HAPPENED TO THE FREEDOM RIDERS SPREAD, MORE THAN 400 BLACK AND WHITE AMERICANS BOARDED BUSES IN THE NORTH BOUND FOR THE SOUTH.
STAY ALERT, EVERYONE!
YEAH, WE'RE SURE TO ENCOUNTER TROUBLE ALONG THE WAY.
BETWEEN MAY AND NOVEMBER OF 1961, THE RIDES CONTINUED AND SO DID THE VIOLENT BEATINGS AND MASS ARRESTS.
BACK IN WASHINGTON D.C., THERE WAS INCREASING PRESSURE ON PRESIDENT JOHN F. KENNEDY, AND HIS BROTHER ATTORNEY GENERAL ROBERT F. KENNEDY, TO INTERVENE.
WE NEED TO DO SOMETHING, JACK.
I DON'T KNOW, BOBBY.
WE HAVE AN OBLIGATION.

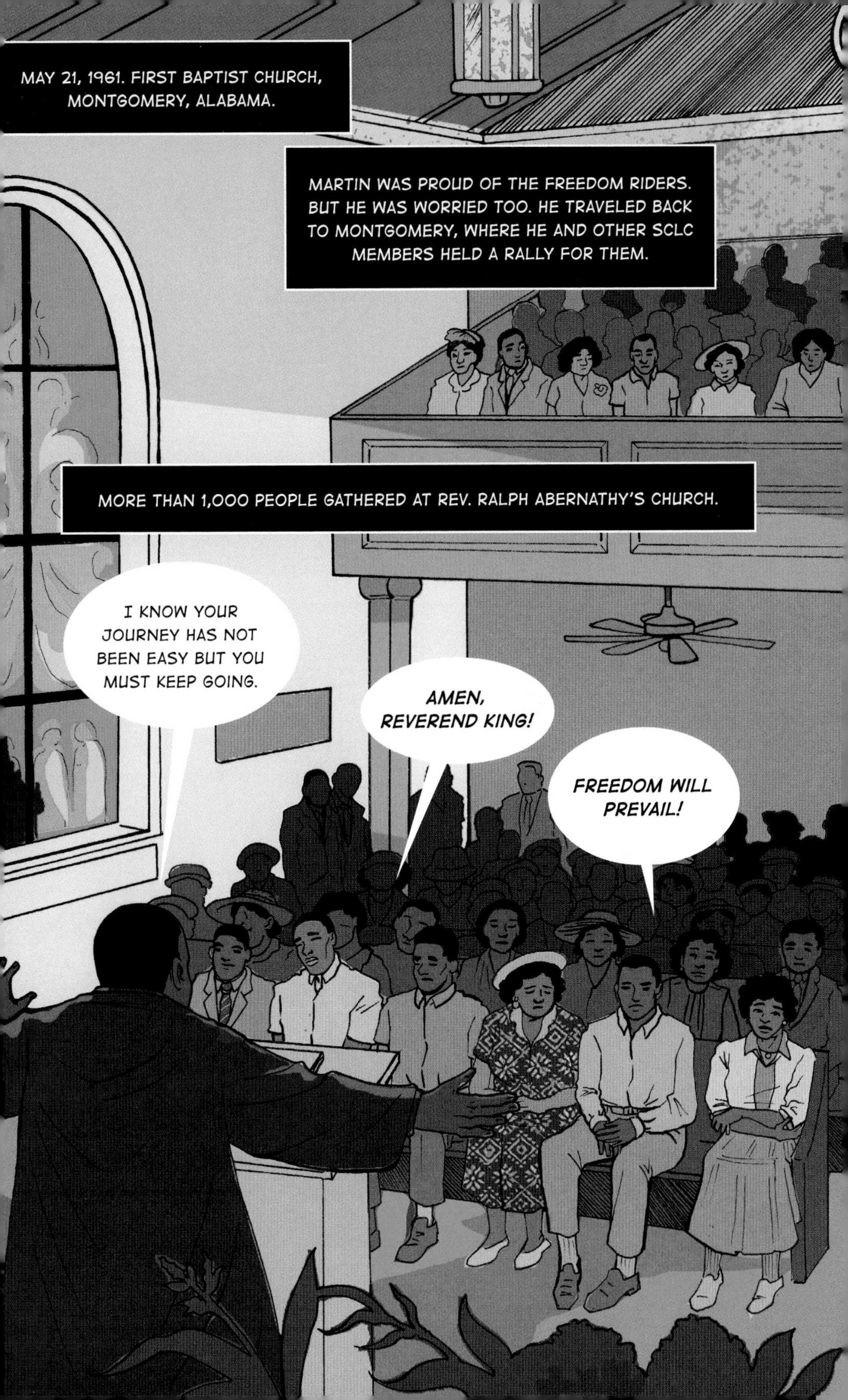
MAY 21, 1961. FIRST BAPTIST CHURCH, MONTGOMERY, ALABAMA.
MARTIN WAS PROUD OF THE FREEDOM RIDERS. BUT HE WAS WORRIED TOO. HE TRAVELED BACK TO MONTGOMERY, WHERE HE AND OTHER SCLC MEMBERS HELD A RALLY FOR THEM.
MORE THAN 1,000 PEOPLE GATHERED AT REV. RALPH ABERNATHY'S CHURCH.
I KNOW YOUR JOURNEY HAS NOT BEEN EASY BUT YOU MUST KEEP GOING.
AMEN, REVEREND KING!
FREEDOM WILL PREVAIL!

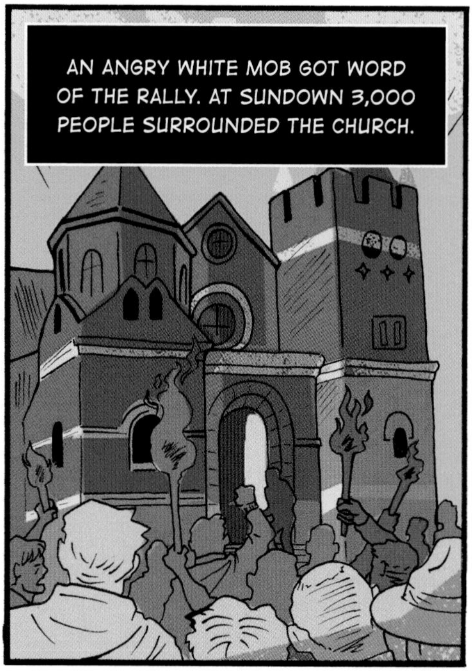
AN ANGRY WHITE MOB GOT WORD OF THE RALLY. AT SUNDOWN 3,000 PEOPLE SURROUNDED THE CHURCH.

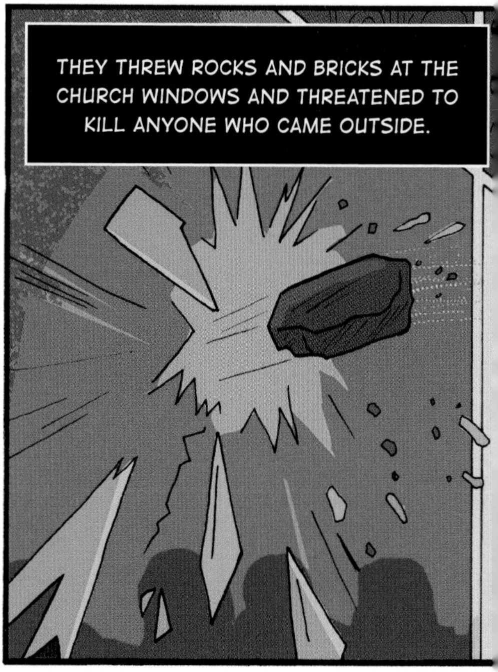
THEY THREW ROCKS AND BRICKS AT THE CHURCH WINDOWS AND THREATENED TO KILL ANYONE WHO CAME OUTSIDE.

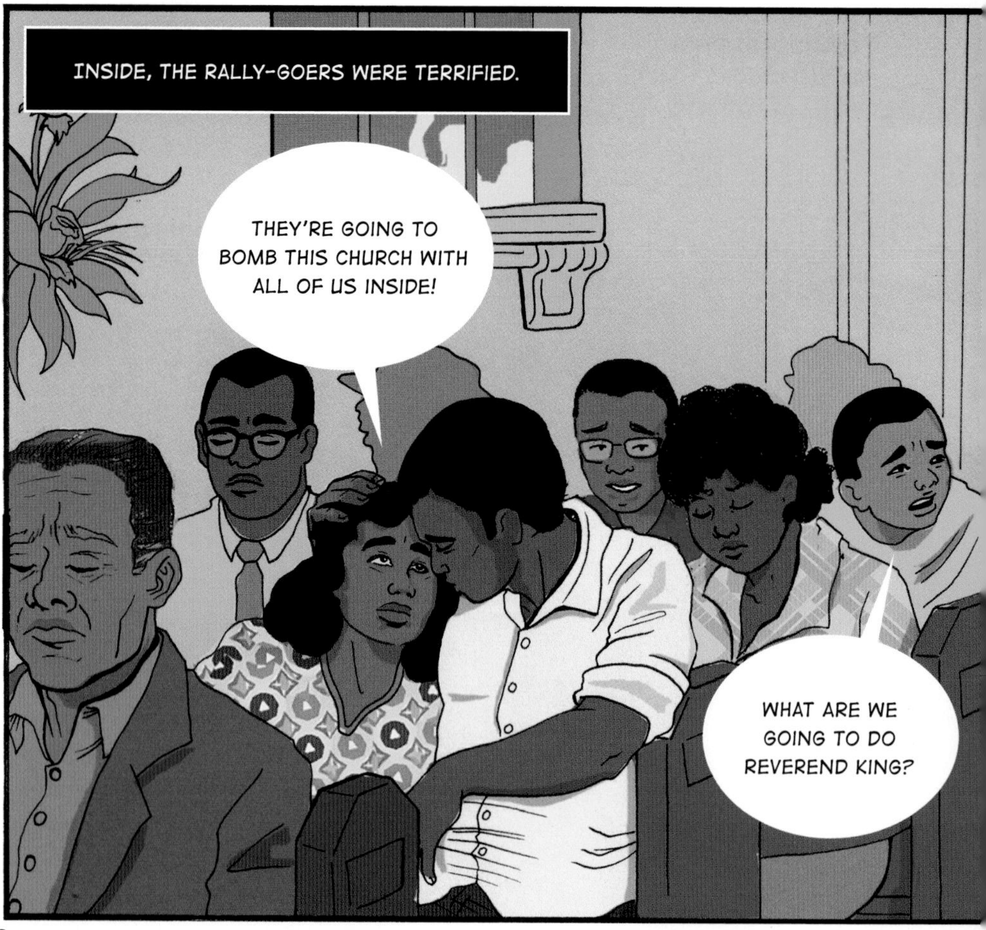
INSIDE, THE RALLY-GOERS WERE TERRIFIED.
THEY'RE GOING TO BOMB THIS CHURCH WITH ALL OF US INSIDE!
WHAT ARE WE GOING TO DO REVEREND KING?

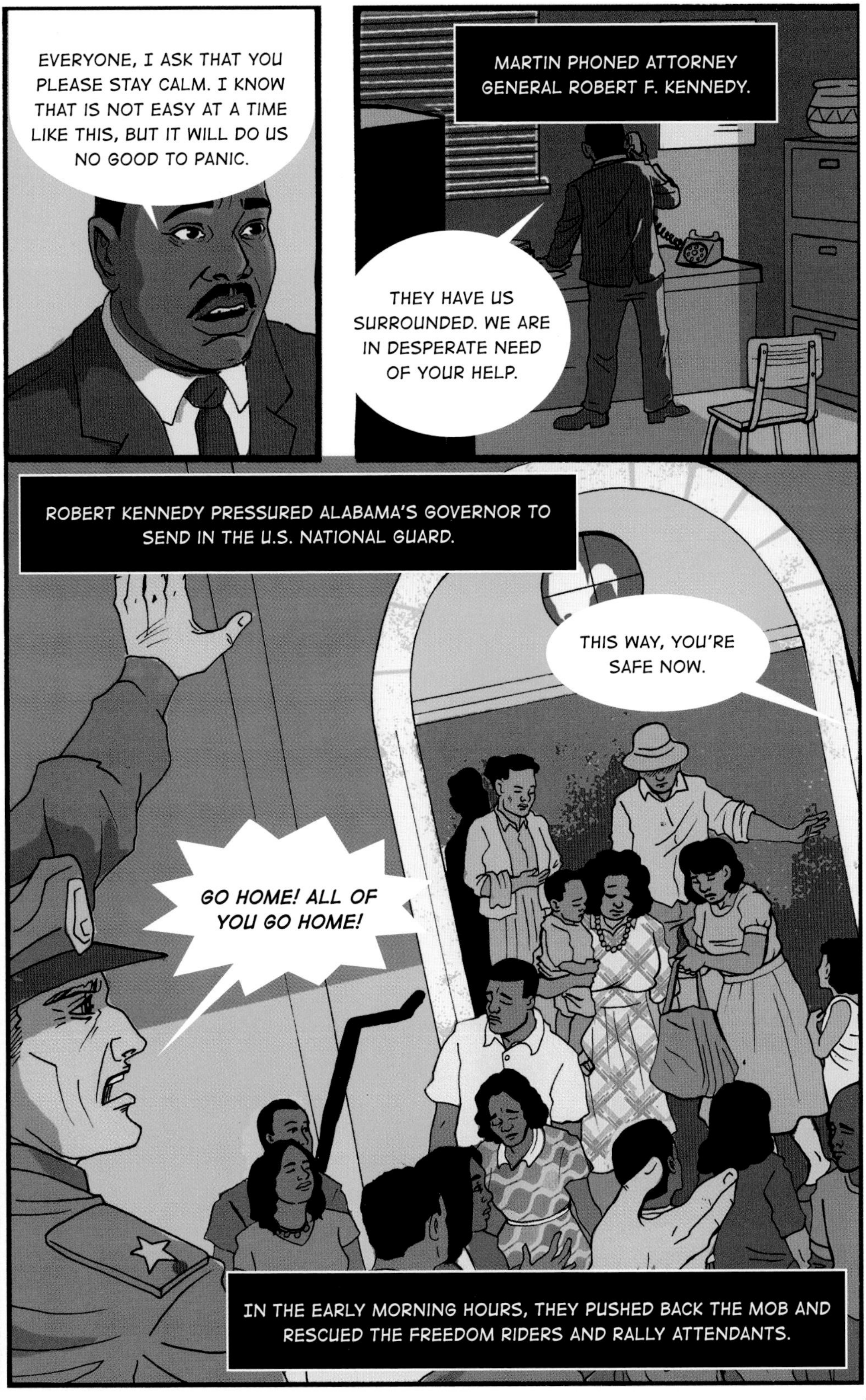
EVERYONE, I ASK THAT YOU PLEASE STAY CALM. I KNOW THAT IS NOT EASY AT A TIME LIKE THIS, BUT IT WILL DO US NO GOOD TO PANIC.
MARTIN PHONED ATTORNEY GENERAL ROBERT F. KENNEDY.
THEY HAVE US SURROUNDED. WE ARE IN DESPERATE NEED OF YOUR HELP.
ROBERT KENNEDY PRESSURED ALABAMA'S GOVERNOR TO SEND IN THE U.S. NATIONAL GUARD.
THIS WAY, YOU'RE SAFE NOW.
GO HOME! ALL OF YOU GO HOME!
IN THE EARLY MORNING HOURS, THEY PUSHED BACK THE MOB AND RESCUED THE FREEDOM RIDERS AND RALLY ATTENDANTS.

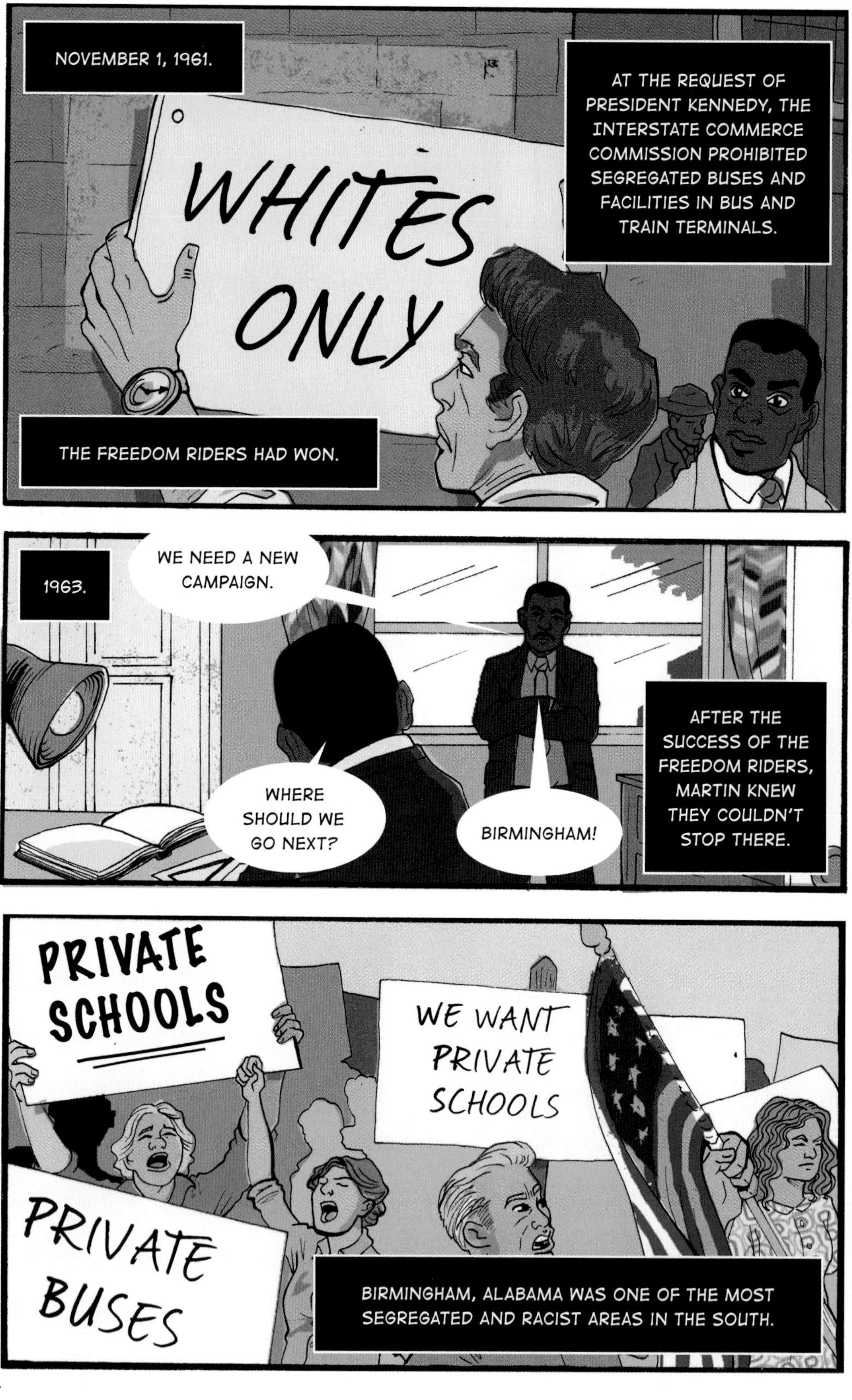
NOVEMBER 1, 1961.
AT THE REQUEST OF PRESIDENT KENNEDY, THE INTERSTATE COMMERCE COMMISSION PROHIBITED SEGREGATED BUSES AND FACILITIES IN BUS AND TRAIN TERMINALS.
WHITES ONLY
THE FREEDOM RIDERS HAD WON.
1963.
WE NEED A NEW CAMPAIGN.
AFTER THE SUCCESS OF THE FREEDOM RIDERS, MARTIN KNEW THEY COULDN'T STOP THERE.
WHERE SHOULD WE GO NEXT?
BIRMINGHAM!
PRIVATE SCHOOLS
WE WANT PRIVATE SCHOOLS
PRIVATE BUSES
BIRMINGHAM, ALABAMA WAS ONE OF THE MOST SEGREGATED AND RACIST AREAS IN THE SOUTH.

GEORGE WALLACE, THE GOVERNOR FOR ALABAMA, WAS FAMOUS FOR DECLARING...

"SEGREGATION TODAY, SEGREGATION TOMORROW, SEGREGATION FOREVER!"

MARTIN THOUGHT IF THEY COULD SUCCEED IN RULING OUT SEGREGATION THERE, THEY COULD SUCCEED ANYWHERE.

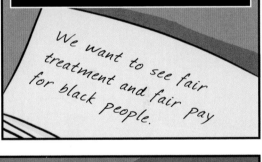

RALPH WROTE A LIST OF DEMANDS THEY WANTED THE CITY OF BIRMINGHAM TO MEET AND MAILED IT TO GOVERNOR WALLACE.

We want to see fair treatment and fair pay for black people.

BUT GOVERNOR WALLACE RESPONDED "NEVER."

IT'S TIME WE TAKE ACTION.

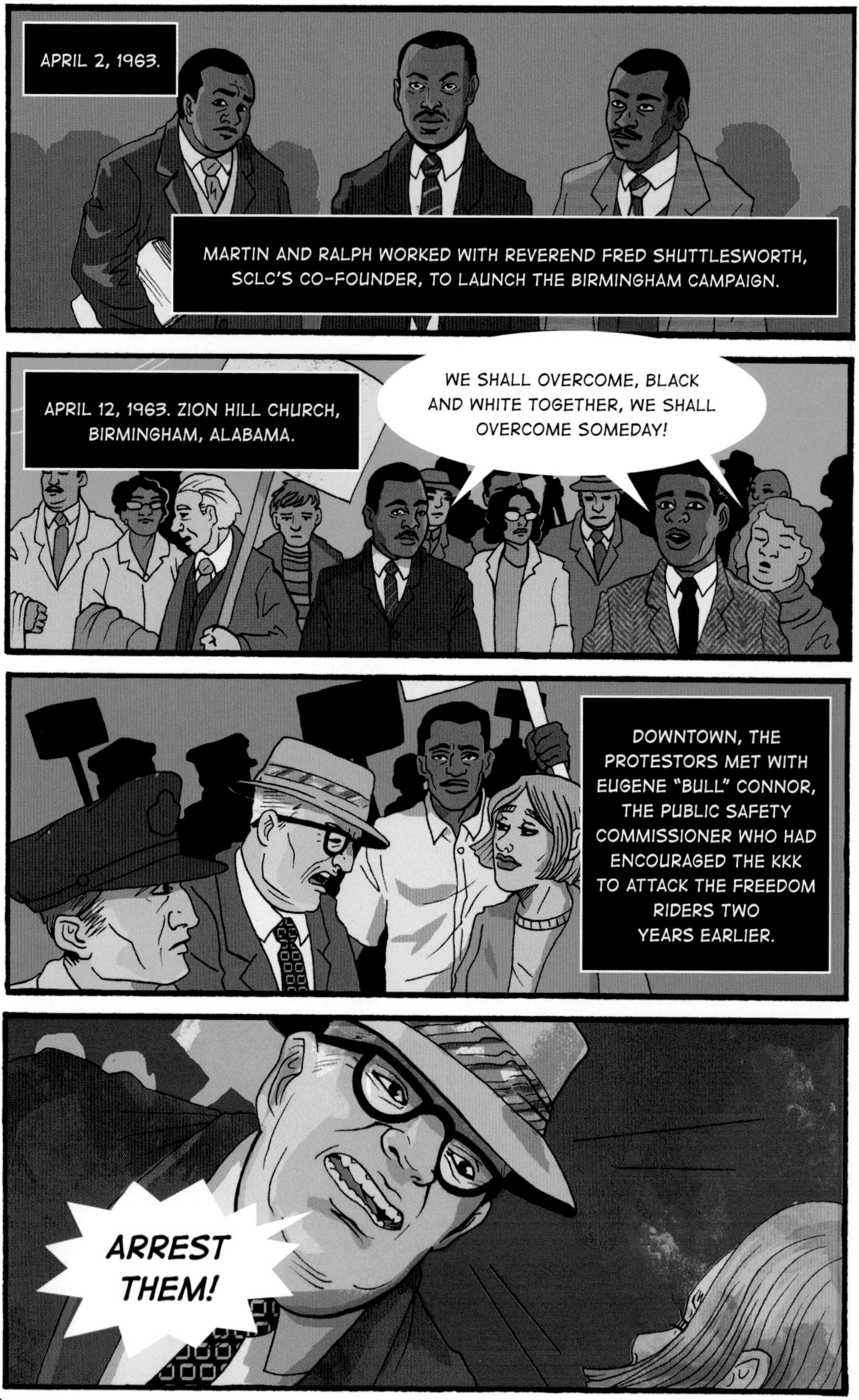
APRIL 2, 1963.
MARTIN AND RALPH WORKED WITH REVEREND FRED SHUTTLESWORTH, SCLC'S CO-FOUNDER, TO LAUNCH THE BIRMINGHAM CAMPAIGN.
APRIL 12, 1963. ZION HILL CHURCH, BIRMINGHAM, ALABAMA.
WE SHALL OVERCOME, BLACK AND WHITE TOGETHER, WE SHALL OVERCOME SOMEDAY!
DOWNTOWN, THE PROTESTORS MET WITH EUGENE "BULL" CONNOR, THE PUBLIC SAFETY COMMISSIONER WHO HAD ENCOURAGED THE KKK TO ATTACK THE FREEDOM RIDERS TWO YEARS EARLIER.
ARREST THEM!

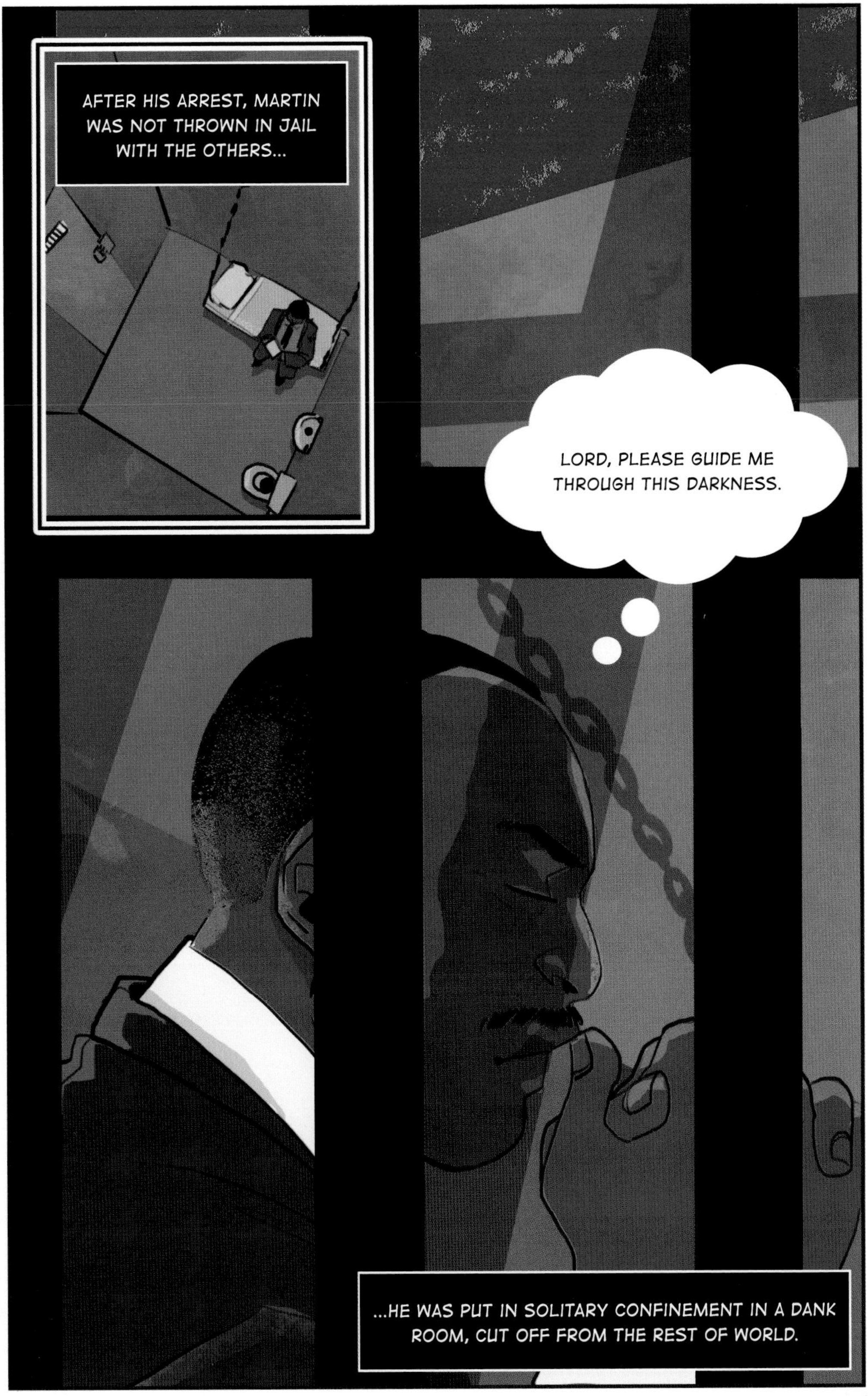
AFTER HIS ARREST, MARTIN WAS NOT THROWN IN JAIL WITH THE OTHERS...
LORD, PLEASE GUIDE ME THROUGH THIS DARKNESS.
...HE WAS PUT IN SOLITARY CONFINEMENT IN A DANK ROOM, CUT OFF FROM THE REST OF WORLD.

BACK IN ATLANTA, CORETTA GOT WORD OF MARTIN'S ARREST.

MARTIN ALWAYS CALLED AFTER AN ARREST, BUT 24 HOURS WENT BY AND SHE DIDN'T HEAR FROM HIM. CORETTA WAS WORRIED.

I WOULD LIKE TO SPEAK TO PRESIDENT KENNEDY. I AM CONCERNED FOR MY HUSBAND'S LIFE.

WITHIN HOURS, PRESIDENT KENNEDY PERSONALLY CALLED BIRMINGHAM CITY OFFICIALS.

YOU MUST NOT MISTREAT REVEREND KING. LET HIM CALL HIS WIFE.

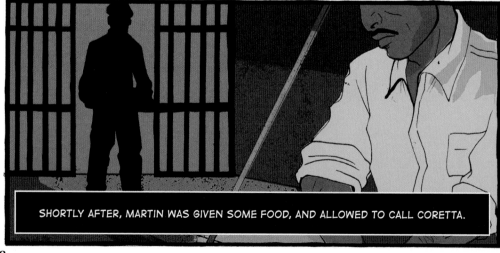

SHORTLY AFTER, MARTIN WAS GIVEN SOME FOOD, AND ALLOWED TO CALL CORETTA.

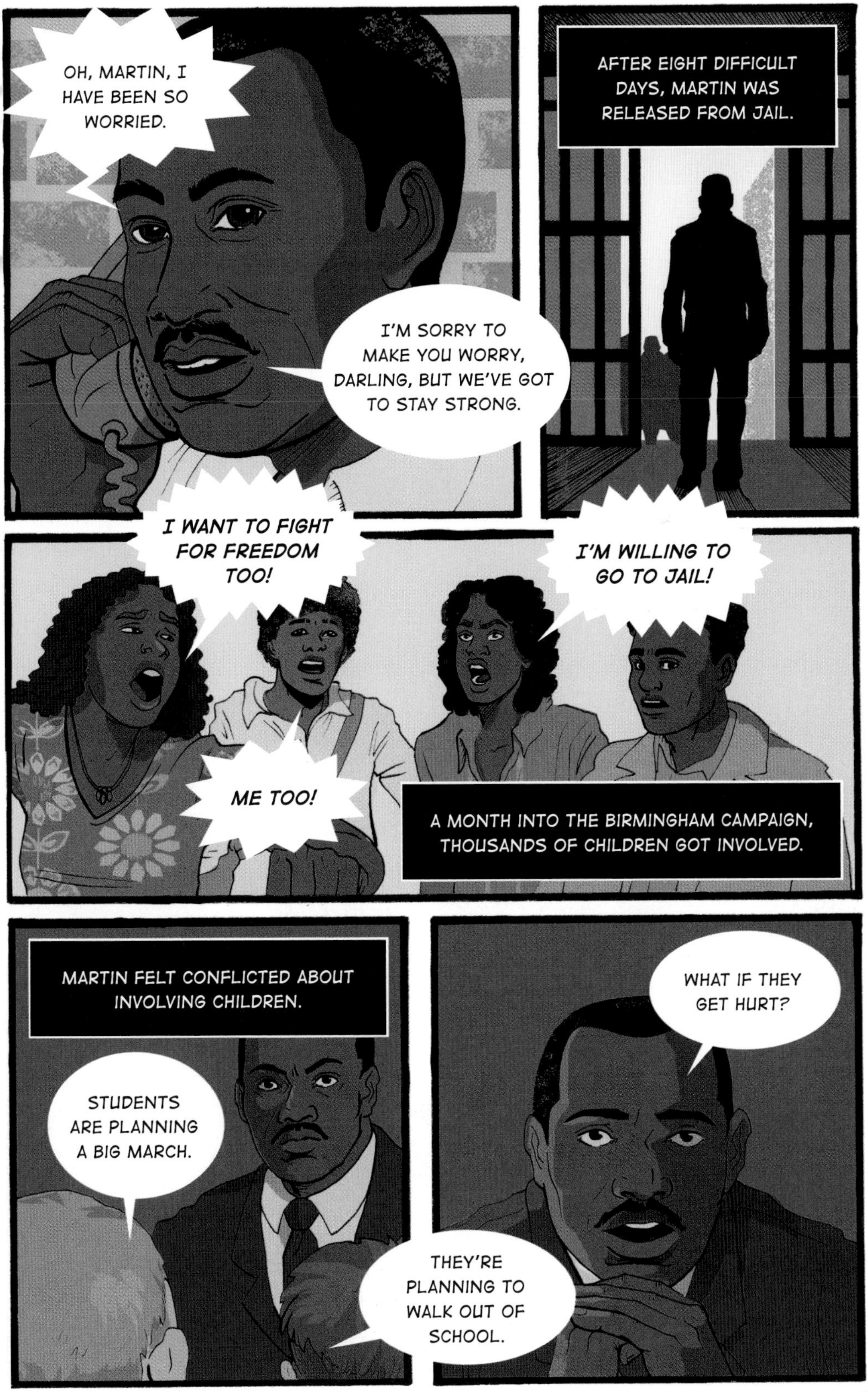
OH, MARTIN, I HAVE BEEN SO WORRIED.
I'M SORRY TO MAKE YOU WORRY, DARLING, BUT WE'VE GOT TO STAY STRONG.
AFTER EIGHT DIFFICULT DAYS, MARTIN WAS RELEASED FROM JAIL.
I WANT TO FIGHT FOR FREEDOM TOO!
I'M WILLING TO GO TO JAIL!
ME TOO!
A MONTH INTO THE BIRMINGHAM CAMPAIGN, THOUSANDS OF CHILDREN GOT INVOLVED.
MARTIN FELT CONFLICTED ABOUT INVOLVING CHILDREN.
STUDENTS ARE PLANNING A BIG MARCH.
THEY'RE PLANNING TO WALK OUT OF SCHOOL.
WHAT IF THEY GET HURT?

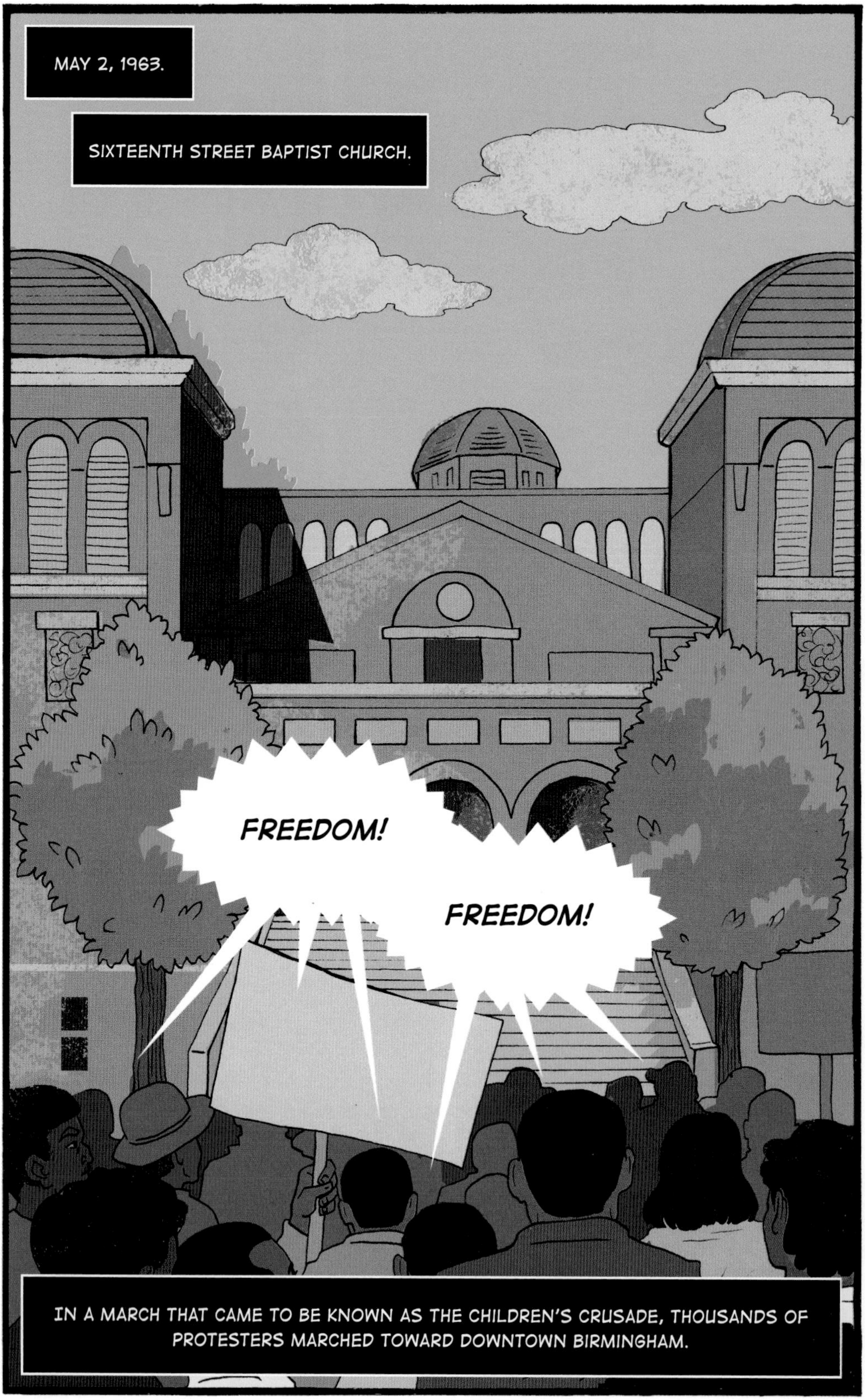
MAY 2, 1963.
SIXTEENTH STREET BAPTIST CHURCH.
FREEDOM!
FREEDOM!
IN A MARCH THAT CAME TO BE KNOWN AS THE CHILDREN'S CRUSADE, THOUSANDS OF PROTESTERS MARCHED TOWARD DOWNTOWN BIRMINGHAM.

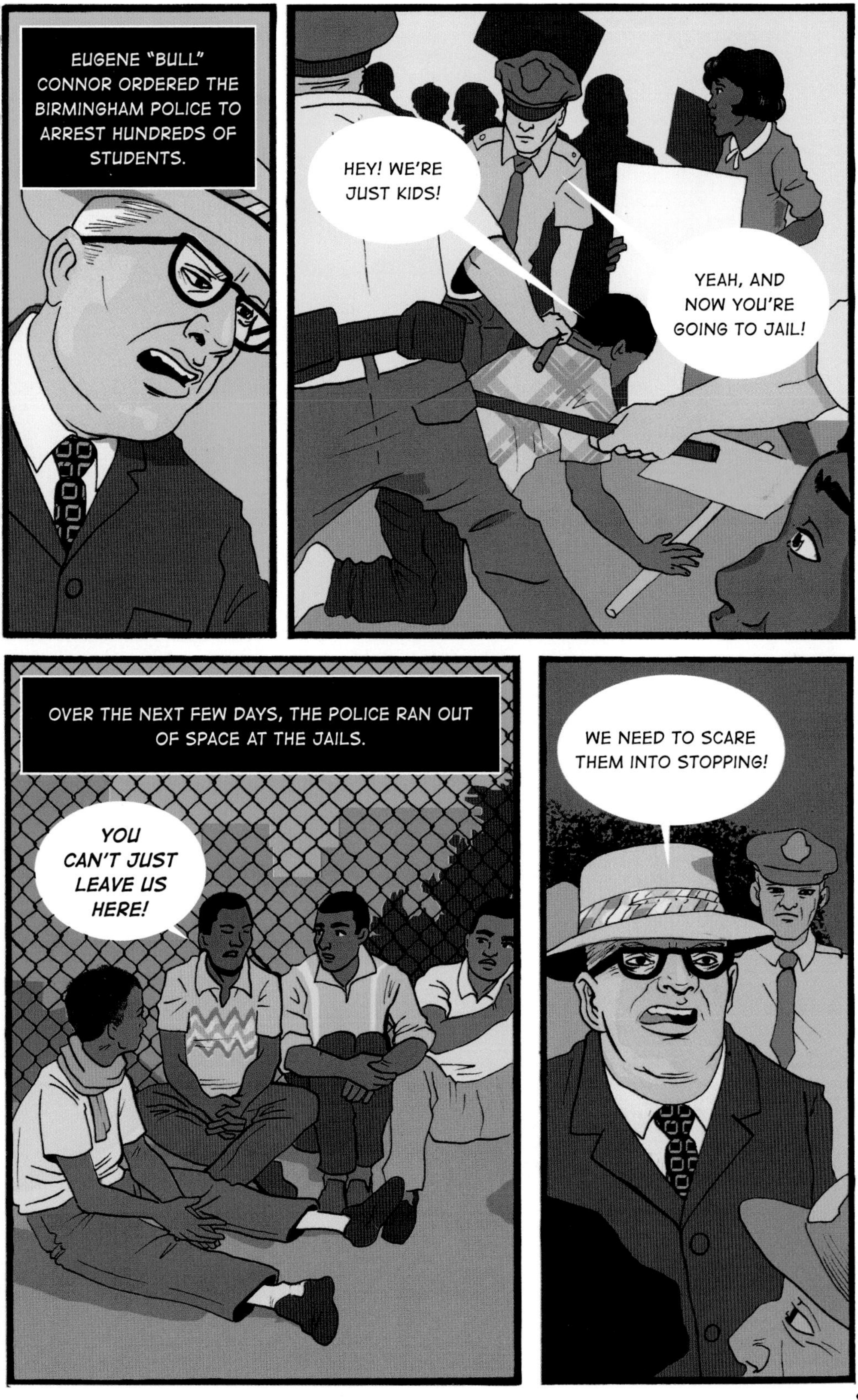
EUGENE "BULL" CONNOR ORDERED THE BIRMINGHAM POLICE TO ARREST HUNDREDS OF STUDENTS.
HEY! WE'RE JUST KIDS!
YEAH, AND NOW YOU'RE GOING TO JAIL!
OVER THE NEXT FEW DAYS, THE POLICE RAN OUT OF SPACE AT THE JAILS.
YOU CAN'T JUST LEAVE US HERE!
WE NEED TO SCARE THEM INTO STOPPING!

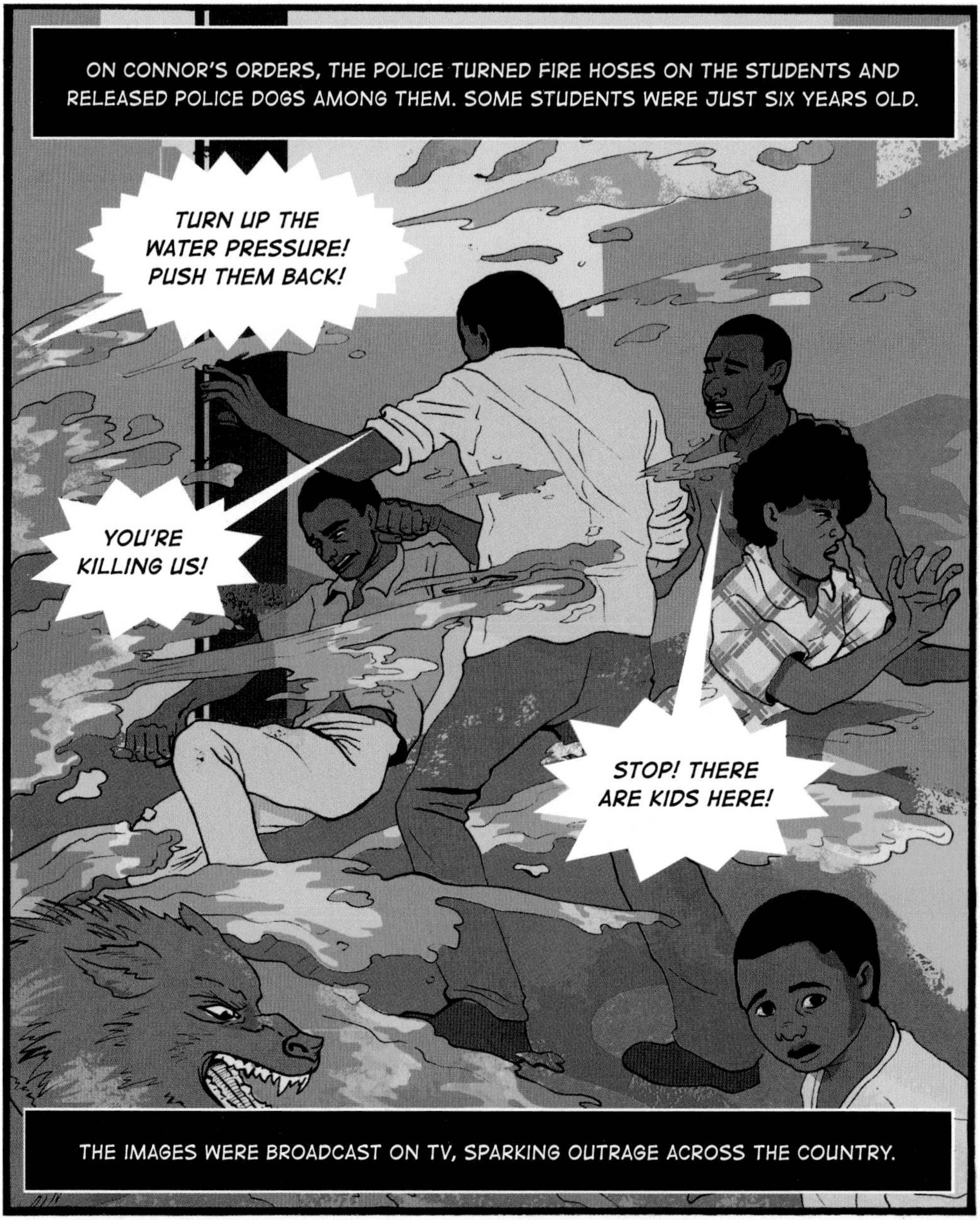
ON CONNOR'S ORDERS, THE POLICE TURNED FIRE HOSES ON THE STUDENTS AND RELEASED POLICE DOGS AMONG THEM. SOME STUDENTS WERE JUST SIX YEARS OLD.
TURN UP THE WATER PRESSURE! PUSH THEM BACK!
YOU'RE KILLING US!
STOP! THERE ARE KIDS HERE!
THE IMAGES WERE BROADCAST ON TV, SPARKING OUTRAGE ACROSS THE COUNTRY.

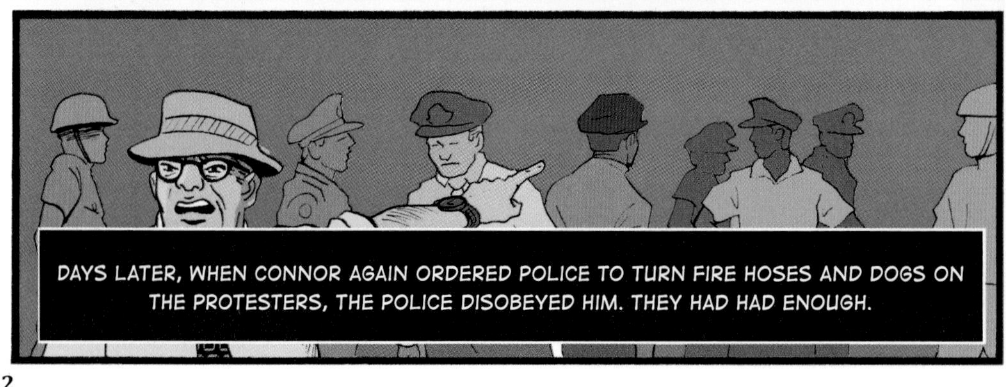
DAYS LATER, WHEN CONNOR AGAIN ORDERED POLICE TO TURN FIRE HOSES AND DOGS ON THE PROTESTERS, THE POLICE DISOBEYED HIM. THEY HAD HAD ENOUGH.

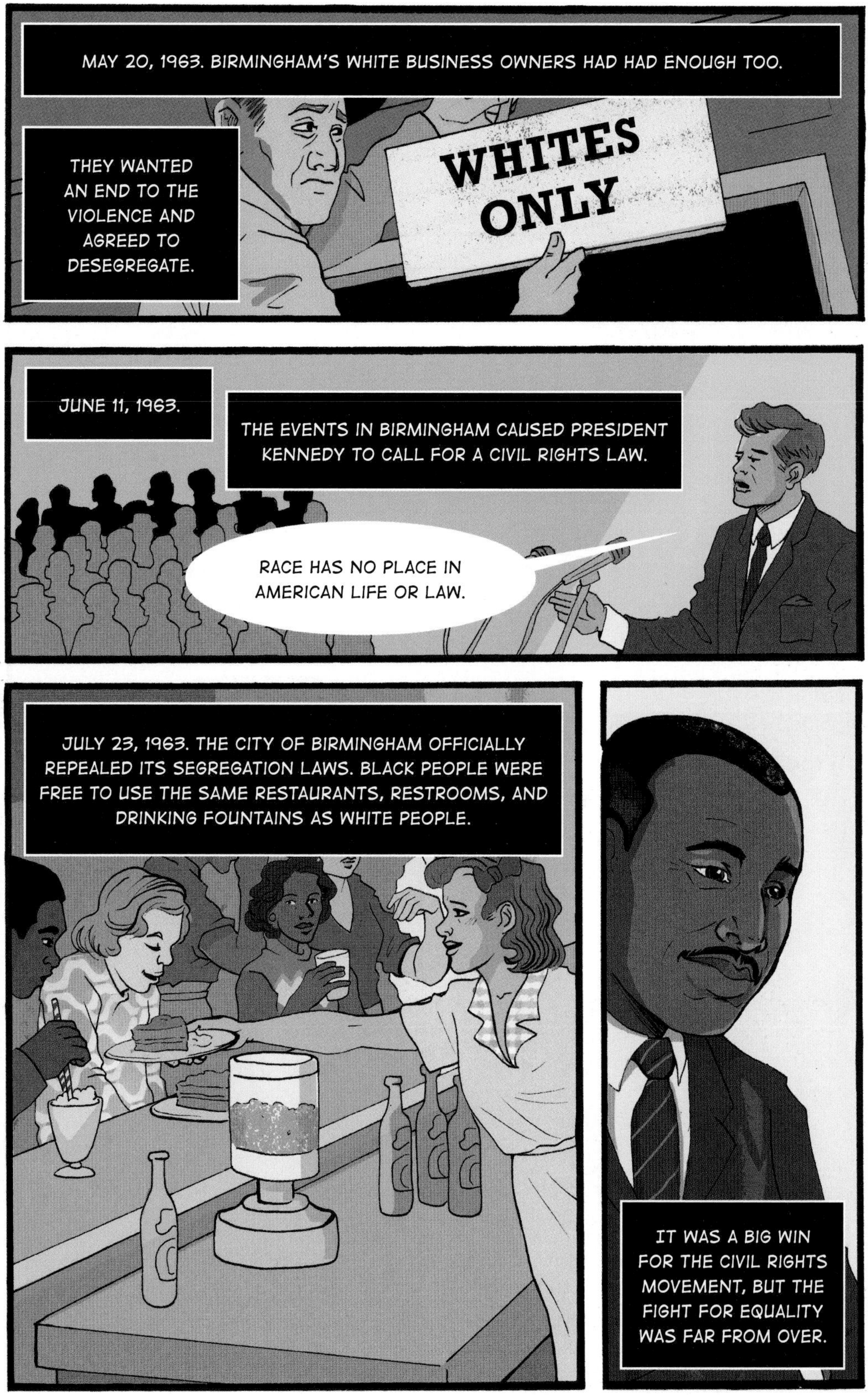
MAY 20, 1963. BIRMINGHAM'S WHITE BUSINESS OWNERS HAD HAD ENOUGH TOO.
THEY WANTED AN END TO THE VIOLENCE AND AGREED TO DESEGREGATE.
WHITES ONLY
JUNE 11, 1963.
THE EVENTS IN BIRMINGHAM CAUSED PRESIDENT KENNEDY TO CALL FOR A CIVIL RIGHTS LAW.
RACE HAS NO PLACE IN AMERICAN LIFE OR LAW.
JULY 23, 1963. THE CITY OF BIRMINGHAM OFFICIALLY REPEALED ITS SEGREGATION LAWS. BLACK PEOPLE WERE FREE TO USE THE SAME RESTAURANTS, RESTROOMS, AND DRINKING FOUNTAINS AS WHITE PEOPLE.
IT WAS A BIG WIN FOR THE CIVIL RIGHTS MOVEMENT, BUT THE FIGHT FOR EQUALITY WAS FAR FROM OVER.

CHAPTER 7

"I HAVE A DREAM"

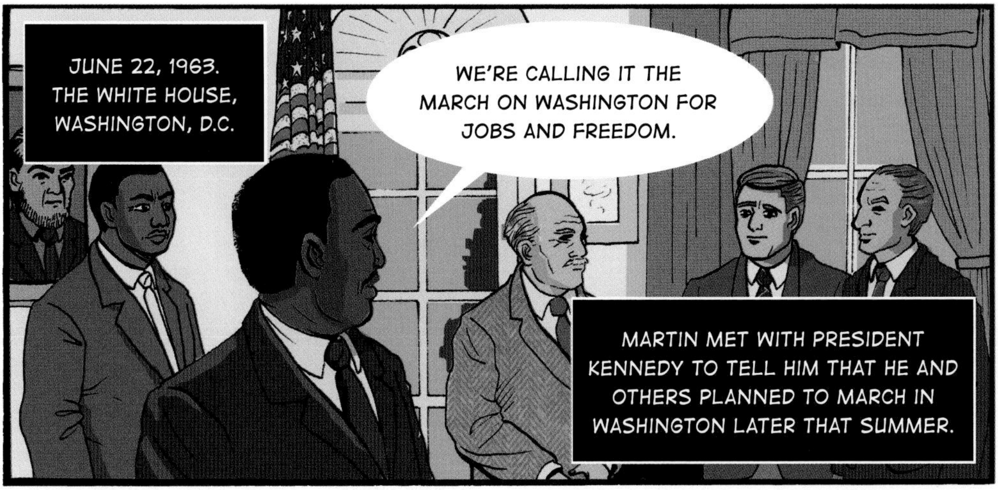
JUNE 22, 1963. THE WHITE HOUSE, WASHINGTON, D.C.
WE'RE CALLING IT THE MARCH ON WASHINGTON FOR JOBS AND FREEDOM.
MARTIN MET WITH PRESIDENT KENNEDY TO TELL HIM THAT HE AND OTHERS PLANNED TO MARCH IN WASHINGTON LATER THAT SUMMER.

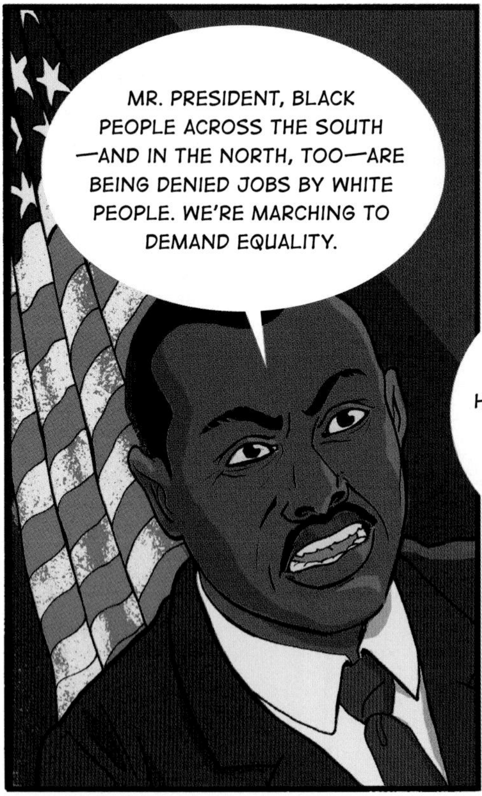
MR. PRESIDENT, BLACK PEOPLE ACROSS THE SOUTH—AND IN THE NORTH, TOO—ARE BEING DENIED JOBS BY WHITE PEOPLE. WE'RE MARCHING TO DEMAND EQUALITY.

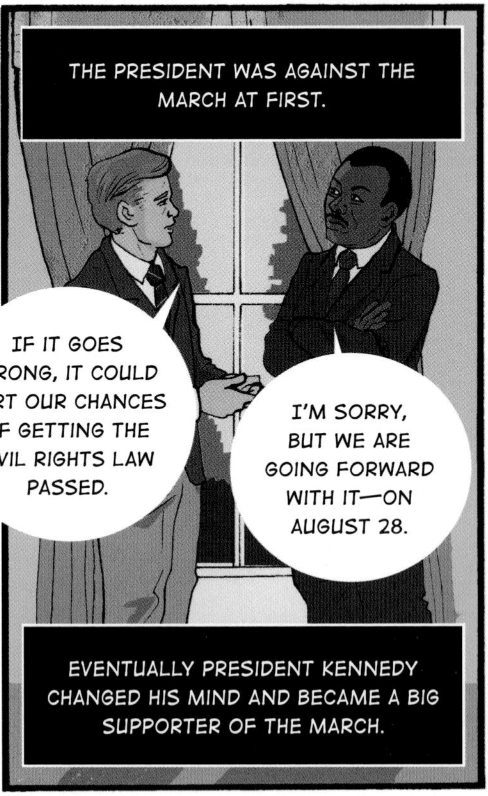
THE PRESIDENT WAS AGAINST THE MARCH AT FIRST.
IF IT GOES WRONG, IT COULD HURT OUR CHANCES OF GETTING THE CIVIL RIGHTS LAW PASSED.
I'M SORRY, BUT WE ARE GOING FORWARD WITH IT—ON AUGUST 28.
EVENTUALLY PRESIDENT KENNEDY CHANGED HIS MIND AND BECAME A BIG SUPPORTER OF THE MARCH.

AUGUST 27, 1963.

WASHINGTON, D.C.

MARTIN WAS DUE TO GIVE THE CLOSING REMARKS AT THE MARCH THE NEXT DAY...

...BUT BECAUSE OF HIS BUSY SCHEDULE, HE DIDN'T HAVE TIME TO WORK ON HIS SPEECH.

I KNOW WHAT I WANT TO SAY. NOW I JUST HAVE TO WRITE IT.

HE STAYED UP ALL NIGHT WRITING AND FINISHED AROUND 5 A.M.

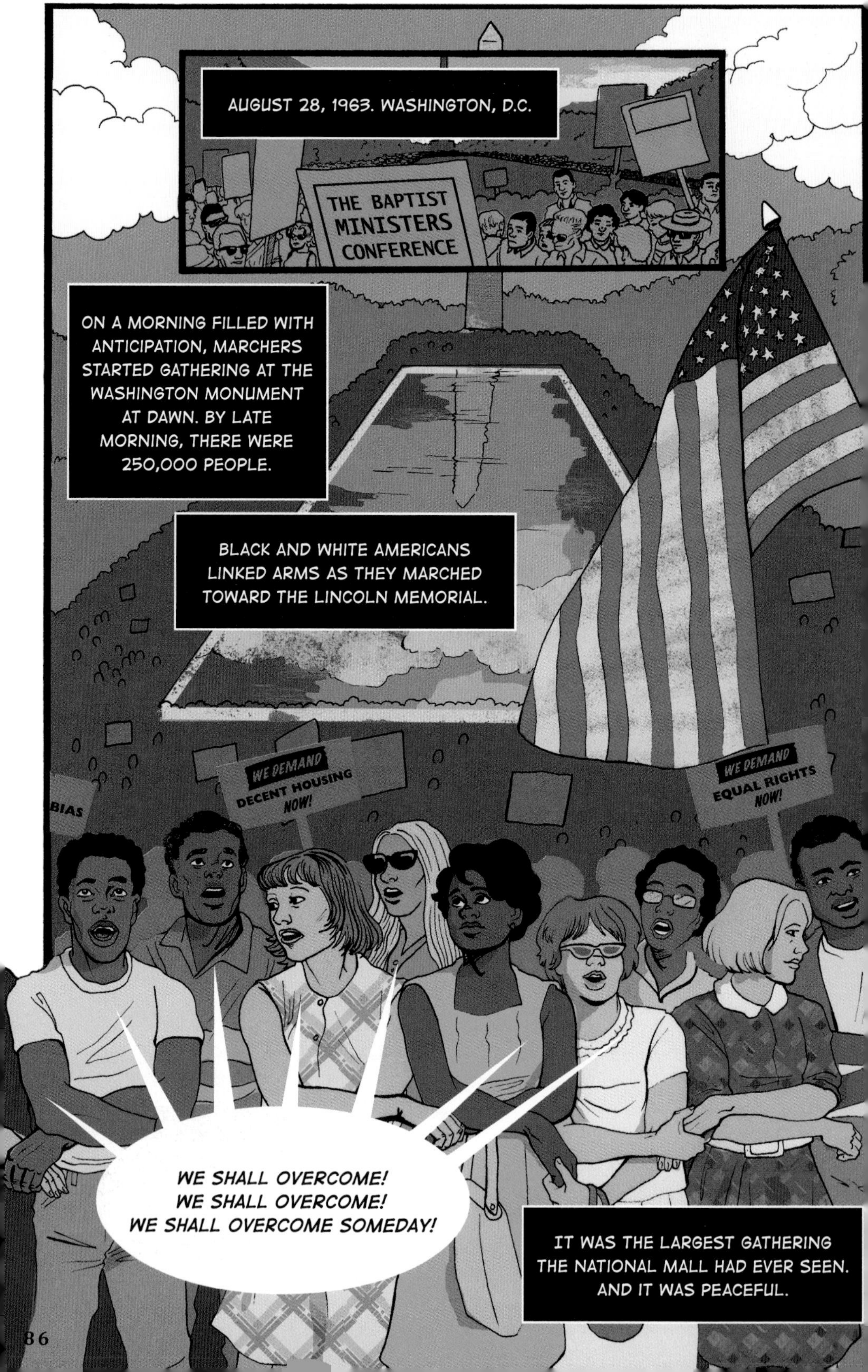
AUGUST 28, 1963. WASHINGTON, D.C.
THE BAPTIST MINISTERS CONFERENCE
ON A MORNING FILLED WITH ANTICIPATION, MARCHERS STARTED GATHERING AT THE WASHINGTON MONUMENT AT DAWN. BY LATE MORNING, THERE WERE 250,000 PEOPLE.
BLACK AND WHITE AMERICANS LINKED ARMS AS THEY MARCHED TOWARD THE LINCOLN MEMORIAL.
BIAS
WE DEMAND DECENT HOUSING NOW!
WE DEMAND EQUAL RIGHTS NOW!
WE SHALL OVERCOME! WE SHALL OVERCOME! WE SHALL OVERCOME SOMEDAY!
IT WAS THE LARGEST GATHERING THE NATIONAL MALL HAD EVER SEEN. AND IT WAS PEACEFUL.

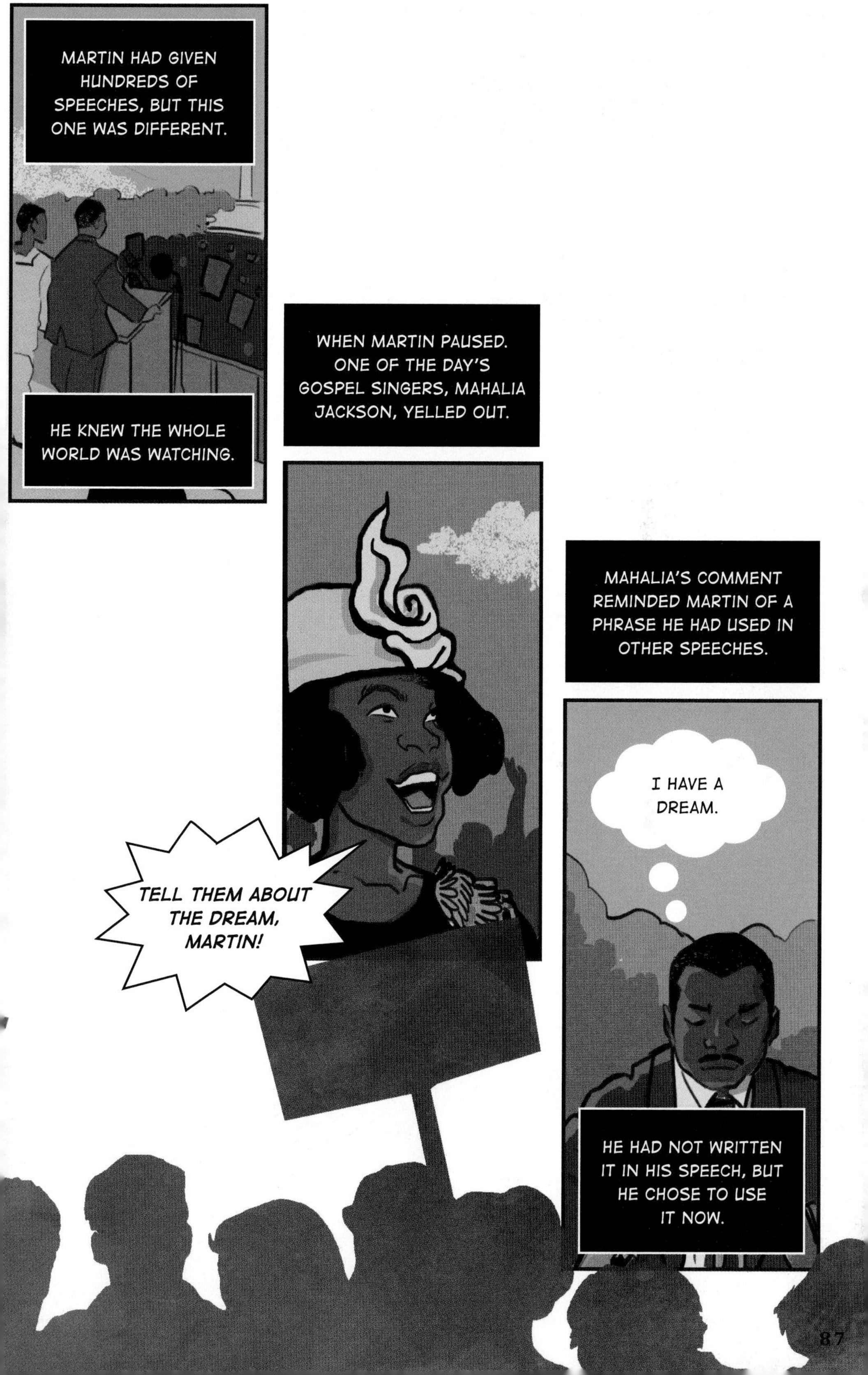
MARTIN HAD GIVEN HUNDREDS OF SPEECHES, BUT THIS ONE WAS DIFFERENT.
HE KNEW THE WHOLE WORLD WAS WATCHING.
WHEN MARTIN PAUSED. ONE OF THE DAY'S GOSPEL SINGERS, MAHALIA JACKSON, YELLED OUT.
TELL THEM ABOUT THE DREAM, MARTIN!
MAHALIA'S COMMENT REMINDED MARTIN OF A PHRASE HE HAD USED IN OTHER SPEECHES.
I HAVE A DREAM.
HE HAD NOT WRITTEN IT IN HIS SPEECH, BUT HE CHOSE TO USE IT NOW.

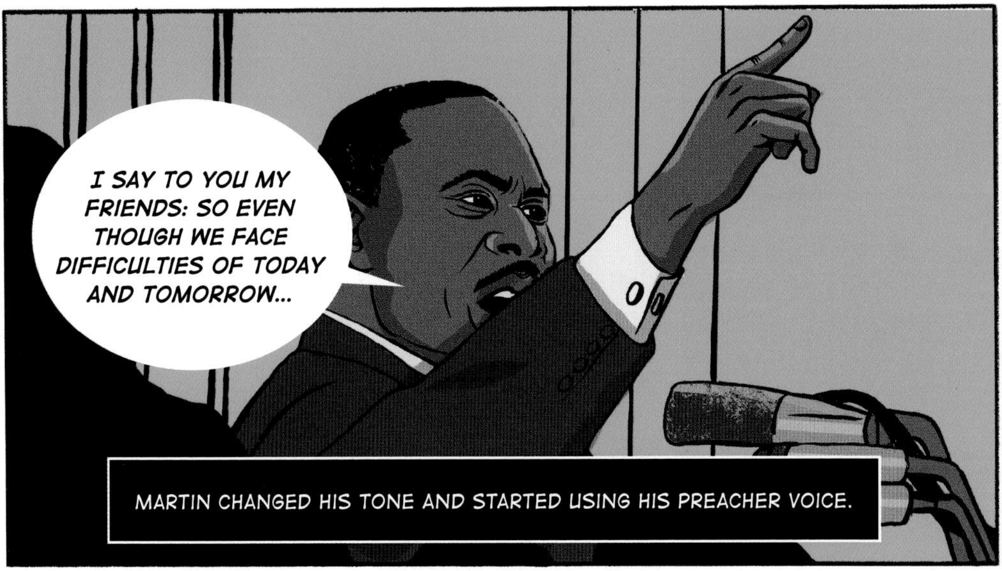
I SAY TO YOU MY FRIENDS: SO EVEN THOUGH WE FACE DIFFICULTIES OF TODAY AND TOMORROW...
MARTIN CHANGED HIS TONE AND STARTED USING HIS PREACHER VOICE.

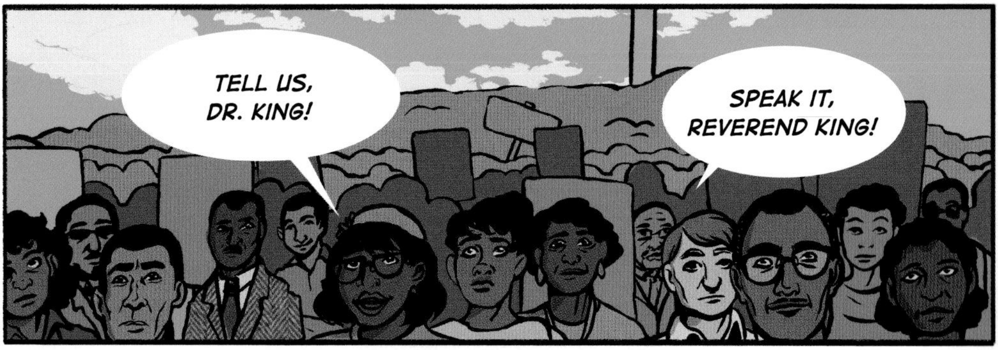
TELL US, DR. KING!
SPEAK IT, REVEREND KING!

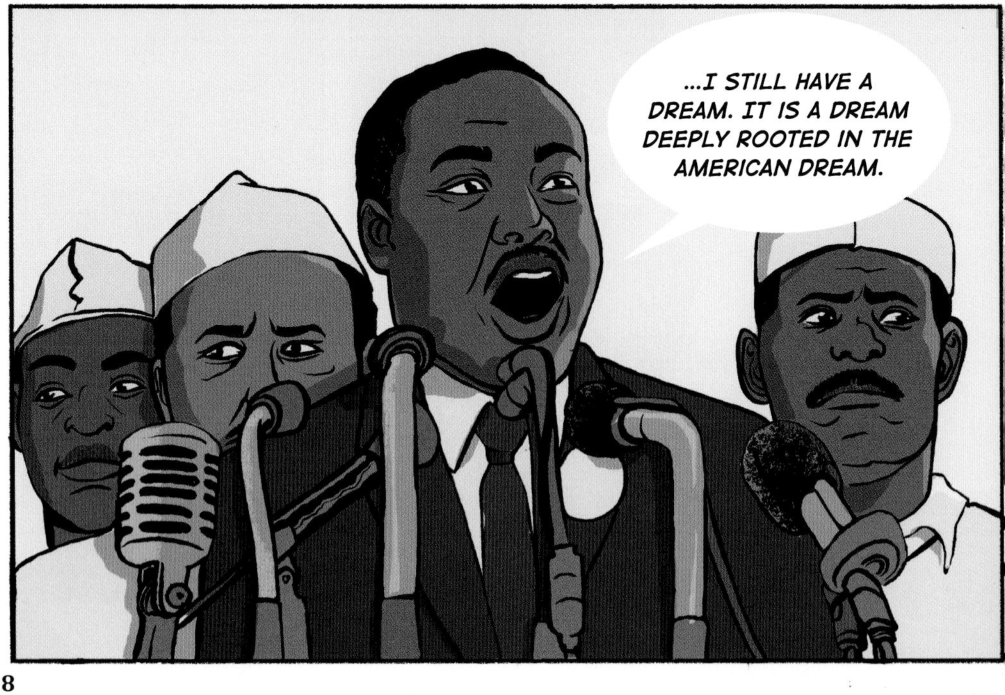
...I STILL HAVE A DREAM. IT IS A DREAM DEEPLY ROOTED IN THE AMERICAN DREAM.

I HAVE A DREAM THAT MY FOUR LITTLE CHILDREN WILL ONE DAY LIVE IN A NATION...

...WHERE THEY WILL BE JUDGED NOT BY THE COLOR OF THEIR SKIN, BUT BY THE CONTENT OF THEIR CHARACTER.
I HAVE A DREAM TODAY.

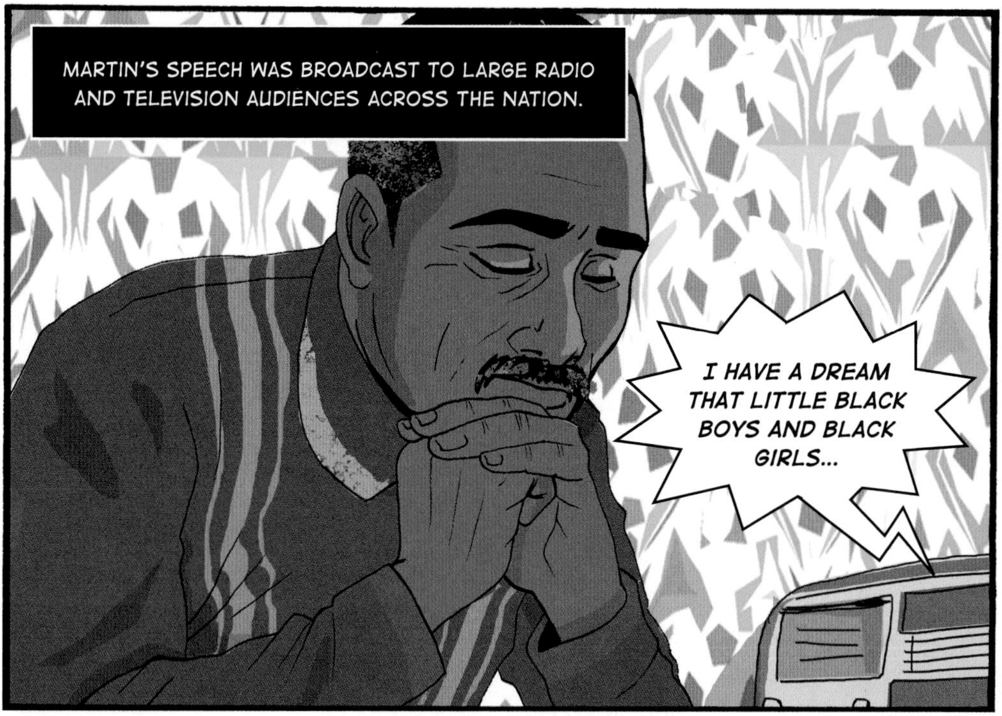
MARTIN'S SPEECH WAS BROADCAST TO LARGE RADIO AND TELEVISION AUDIENCES ACROSS THE NATION.
I HAVE A DREAM THAT LITTLE BLACK BOYS AND BLACK GIRLS...

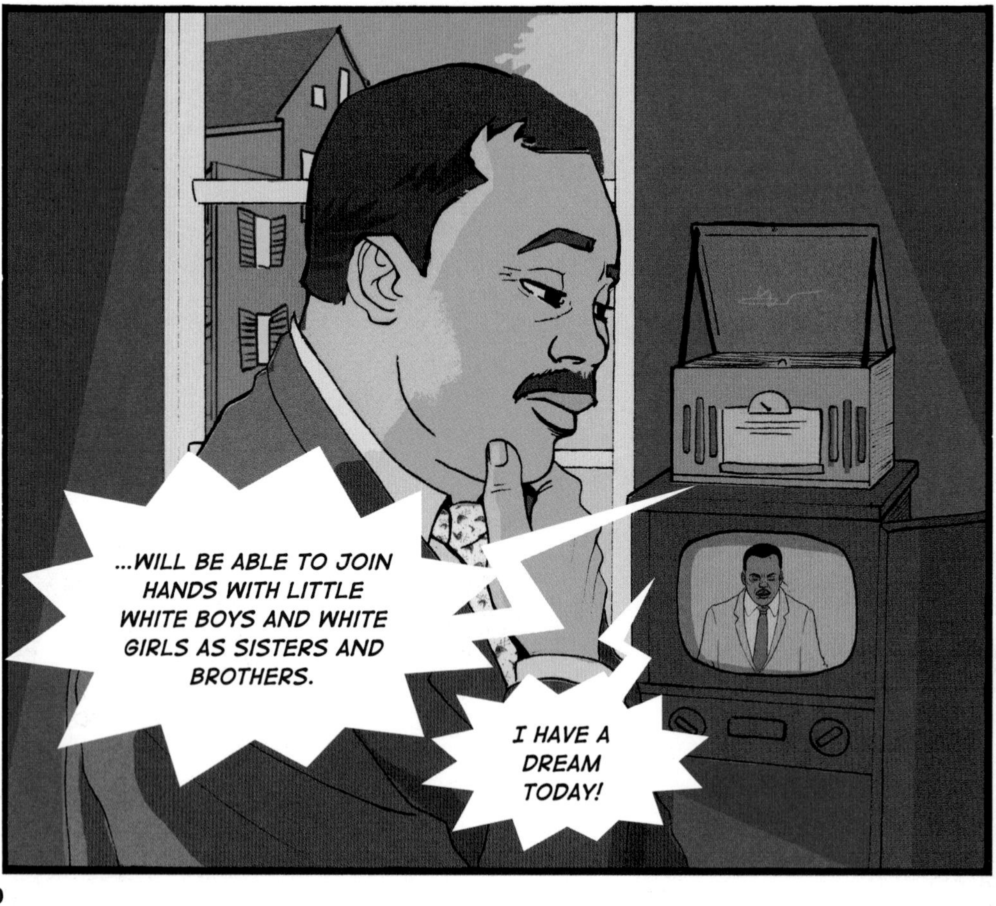
...WILL BE ABLE TO JOIN HANDS WITH LITTLE WHITE BOYS AND WHITE GIRLS AS SISTERS AND BROTHERS.
I HAVE A DREAM TODAY!

SO LET FREEDOM RING FROM THE PRODIGIOUS HILLTOPS OF NEW HAMPSHIRE...
...LET FREEDOM RING FROM EVERY HILL AND MOLEHILL OF MISSISSIPPI...
...AND WHEN THIS HAPPENS, AND WHEN WE ALLOW FREEDOM TO RING...
...(WE) WILL BE ABLE TO JOIN HANDS AND SING... "FREE AT LAST. FREE AT LAST. THANK GOD ALMIGHTY, WE ARE FREE AT LAST."

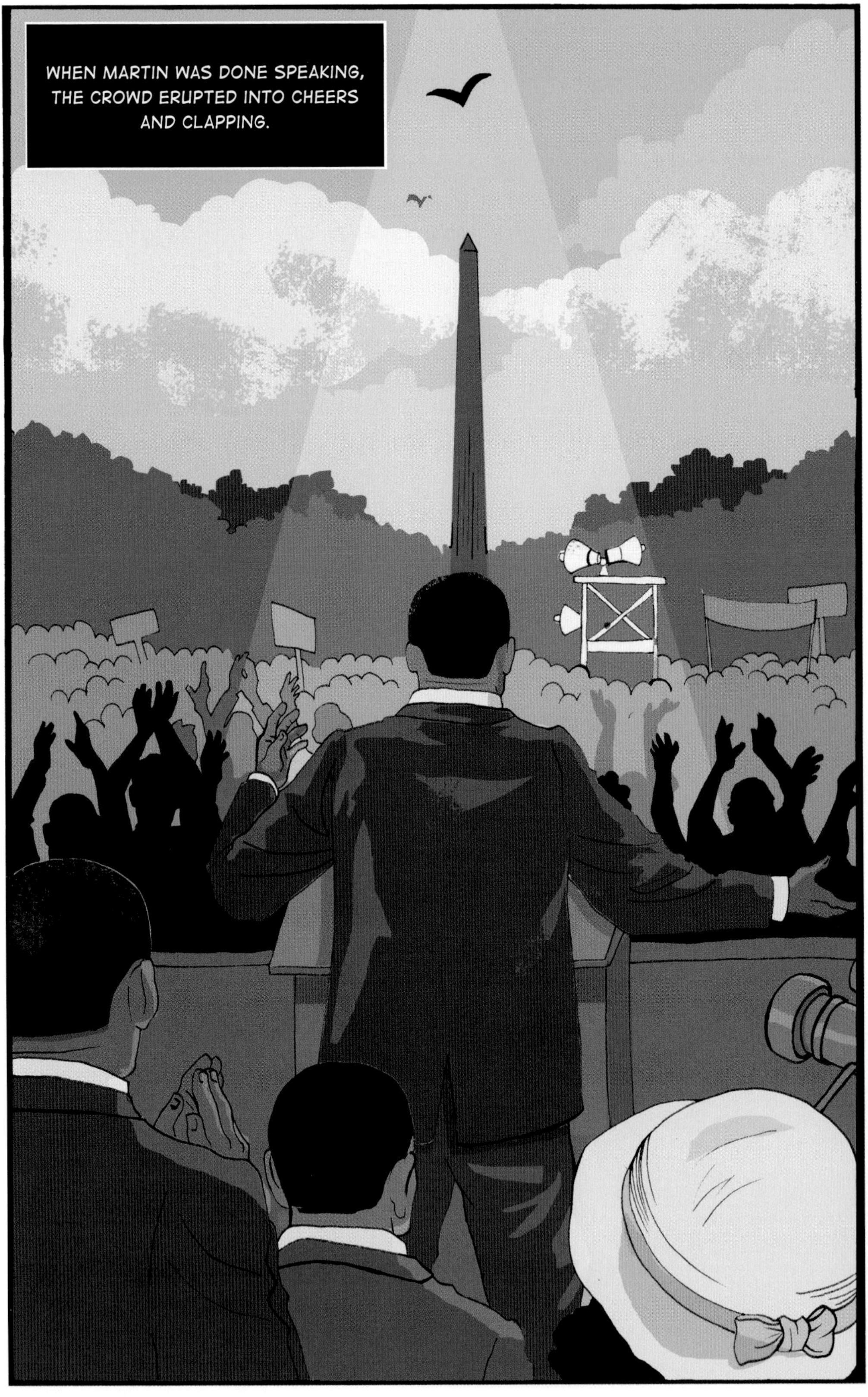
WHEN MARTIN WAS DONE SPEAKING, THE CROWD ERUPTED INTO CHEERS AND CLAPPING.

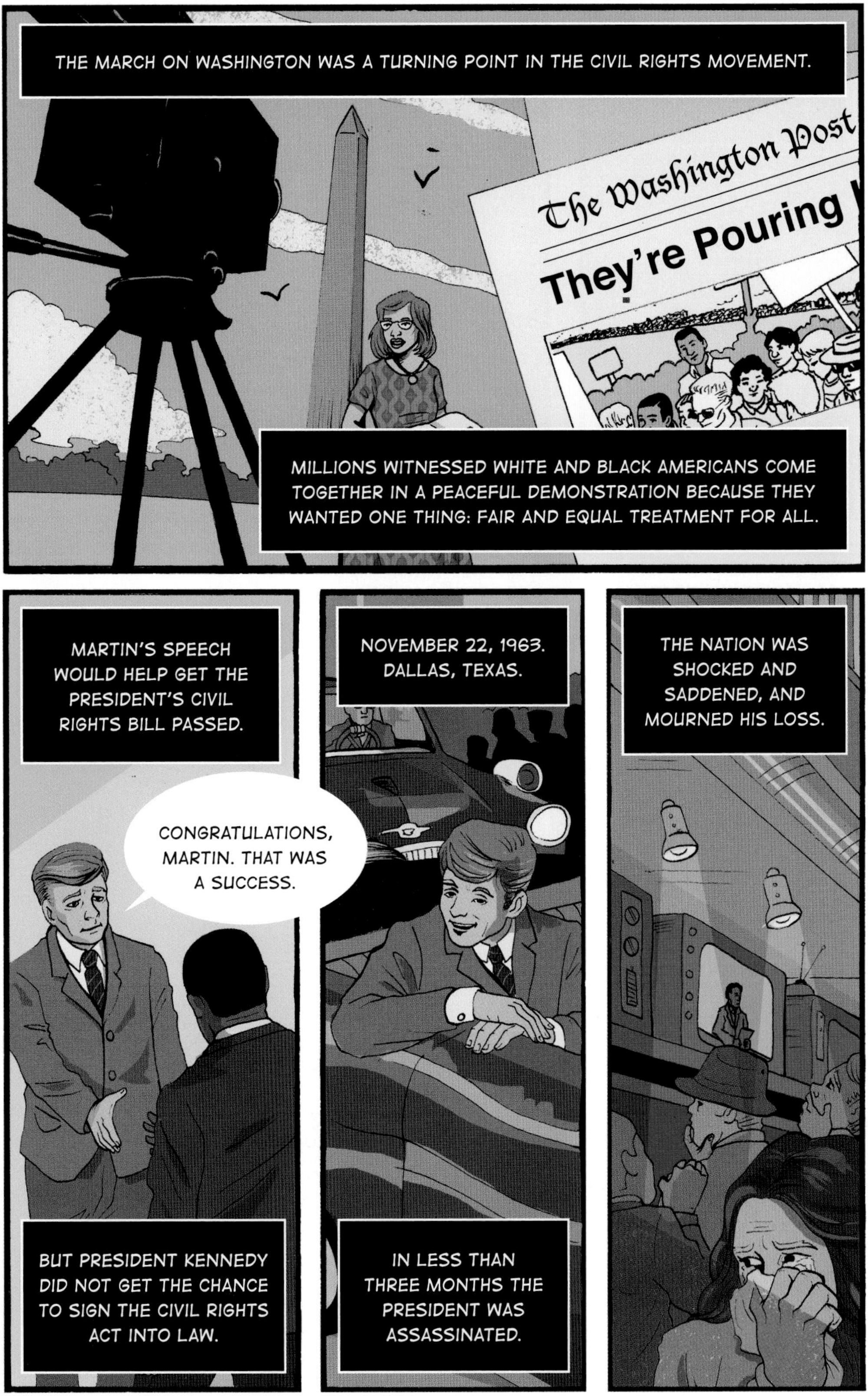
THE MARCH ON WASHINGTON WAS A TURNING POINT IN THE CIVIL RIGHTS MOVEMENT.
The Washington Post
They're Pouring
MILLIONS WITNESSED WHITE AND BLACK AMERICANS COME TOGETHER IN A PEACEFUL DEMONSTRATION BECAUSE THEY WANTED ONE THING: FAIR AND EQUAL TREATMENT FOR ALL.
MARTIN'S SPEECH WOULD HELP GET THE PRESIDENT'S CIVIL RIGHTS BILL PASSED.
CONGRATULATIONS, MARTIN. THAT WAS A SUCCESS.
BUT PRESIDENT KENNEDY DID NOT GET THE CHANCE TO SIGN THE CIVIL RIGHTS ACT INTO LAW.
NOVEMBER 22, 1963. DALLAS, TEXAS.
IN LESS THAN THREE MONTHS THE PRESIDENT WAS ASSASSINATED.
THE NATION WAS SHOCKED AND SADDENED, AND MOURNED HIS LOSS.

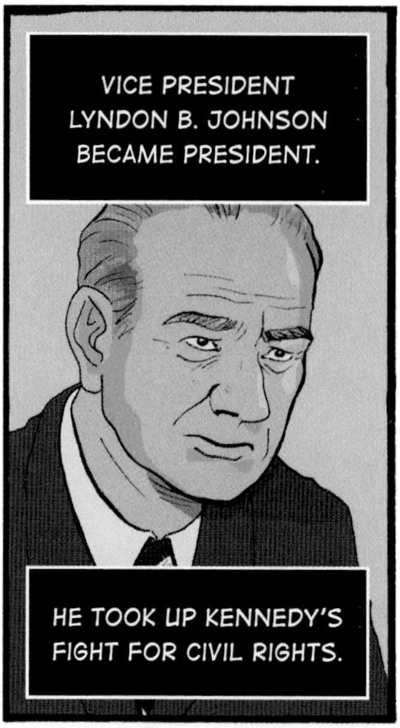
VICE PRESIDENT LYNDON B. JOHNSON BECAME PRESIDENT.
HE TOOK UP KENNEDY'S FIGHT FOR CIVIL RIGHTS.

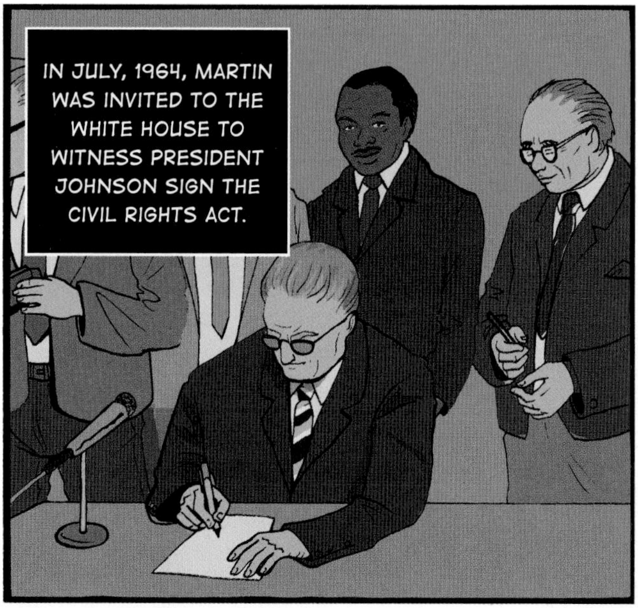
IN JULY, 1964, MARTIN WAS INVITED TO THE WHITE HOUSE TO WITNESS PRESIDENT JOHNSON SIGN THE CIVIL RIGHTS ACT.

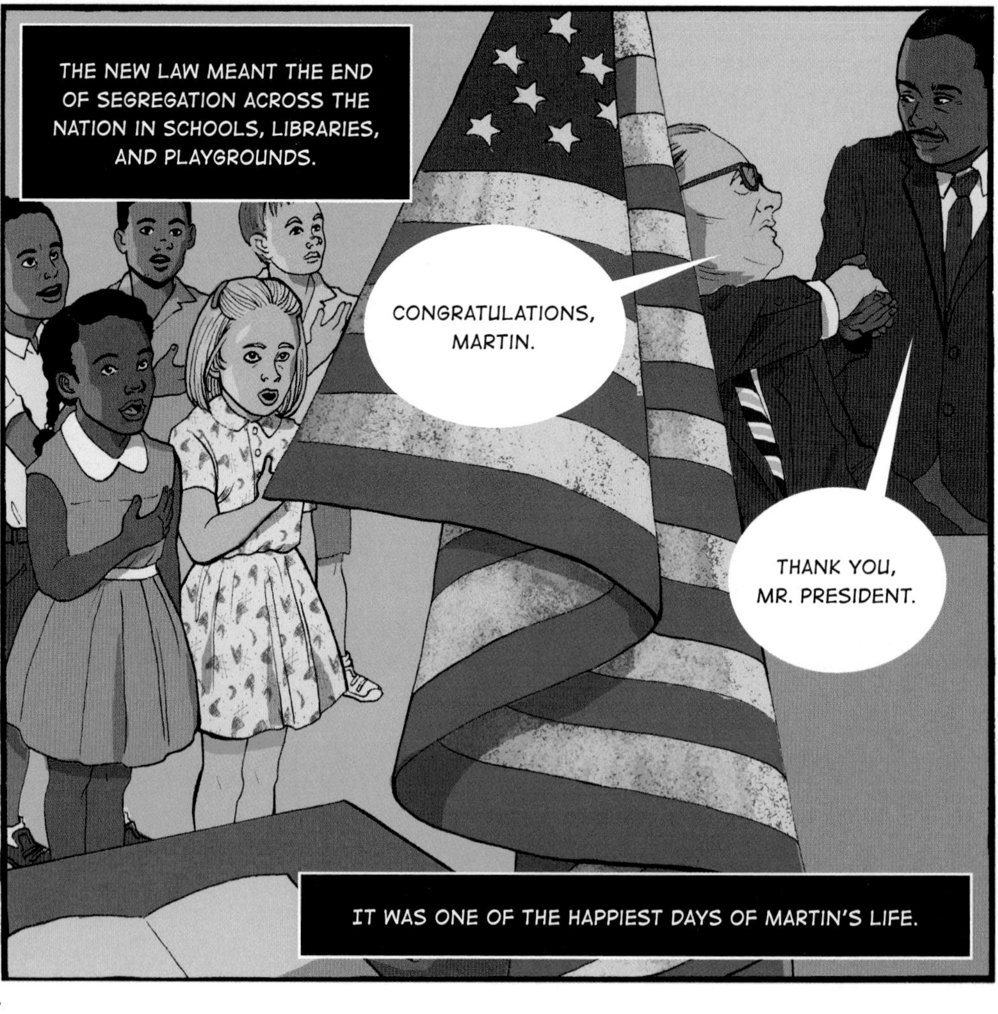
THE NEW LAW MEANT THE END OF SEGREGATION ACROSS THE NATION IN SCHOOLS, LIBRARIES, AND PLAYGROUNDS.
CONGRATULATIONS, MARTIN.
THANK YOU, MR. PRESIDENT.
IT WAS ONE OF THE HAPPIEST DAYS OF MARTIN'S LIFE.

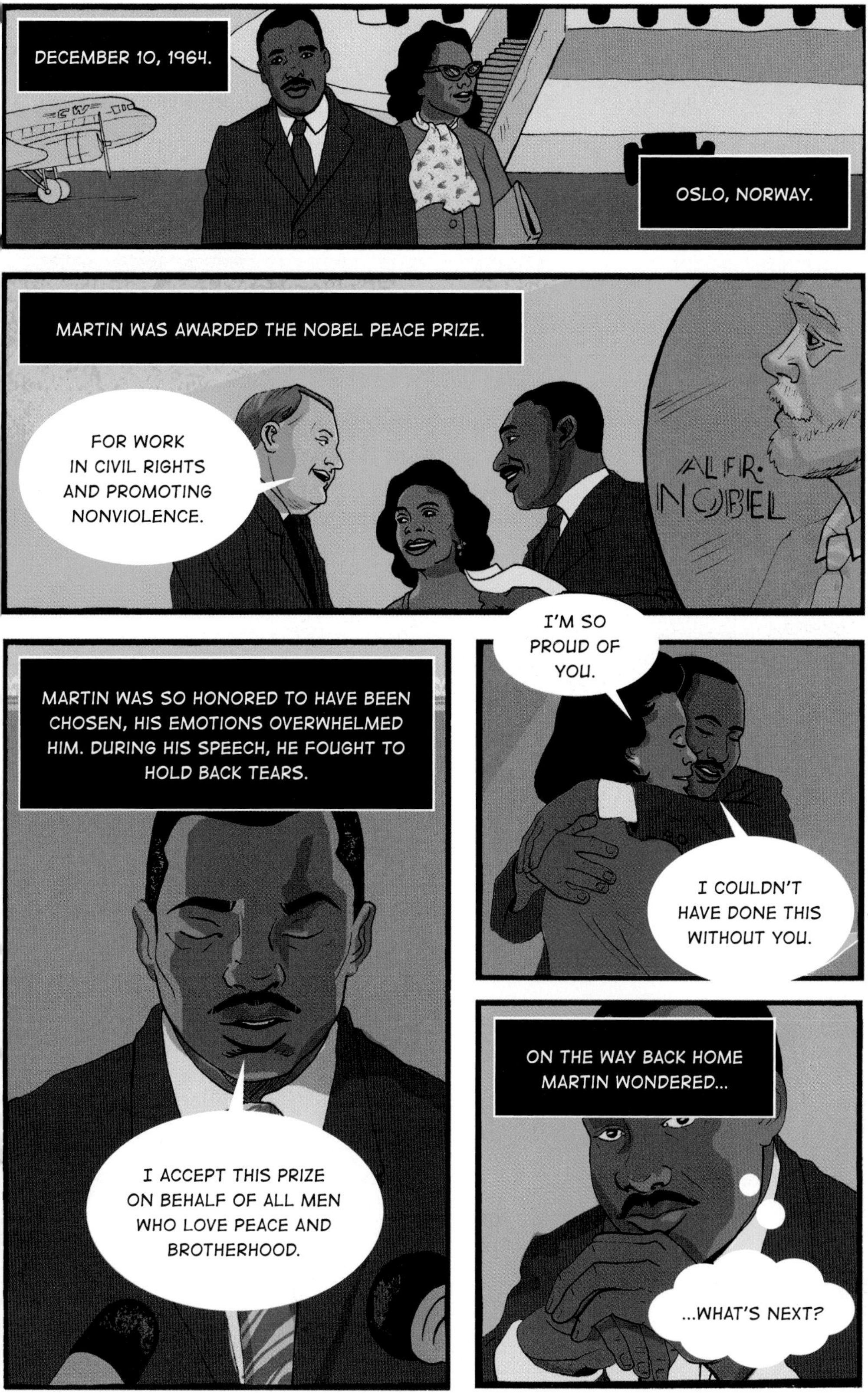
DECEMBER 10, 1964.
OSLO, NORWAY.
MARTIN WAS AWARDED THE NOBEL PEACE PRIZE.
FOR WORK IN CIVIL RIGHTS AND PROMOTING NONVIOLENCE.
ALFR. NOBEL
MARTIN WAS SO HONORED TO HAVE BEEN CHOSEN, HIS EMOTIONS OVERWHELMED HIM. DURING HIS SPEECH, HE FOUGHT TO HOLD BACK TEARS.
I ACCEPT THIS PRIZE ON BEHALF OF ALL MEN WHO LOVE PEACE AND BROTHERHOOD.
I'M SO PROUD OF YOU.
I COULDN'T HAVE DONE THIS WITHOUT YOU.
ON THE WAY BACK HOME MARTIN WONDERED...
...WHAT'S NEXT?

CHAPTER 8

SELMA AND THE FIGHT FOR THE RIGHT TO VOTE

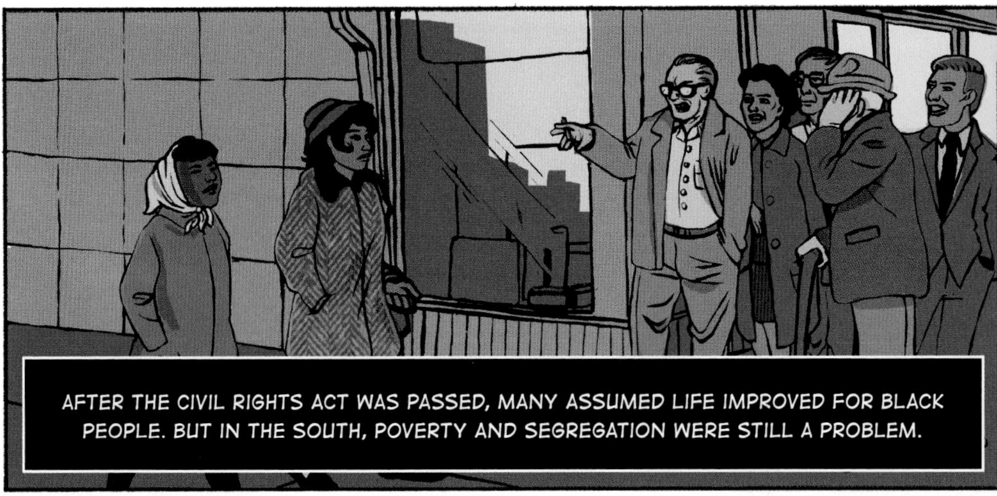
AFTER THE CIVIL RIGHTS ACT WAS PASSED, MANY ASSUMED LIFE IMPROVED FOR BLACK PEOPLE. BUT IN THE SOUTH, POVERTY AND SEGREGATION WERE STILL A PROBLEM.

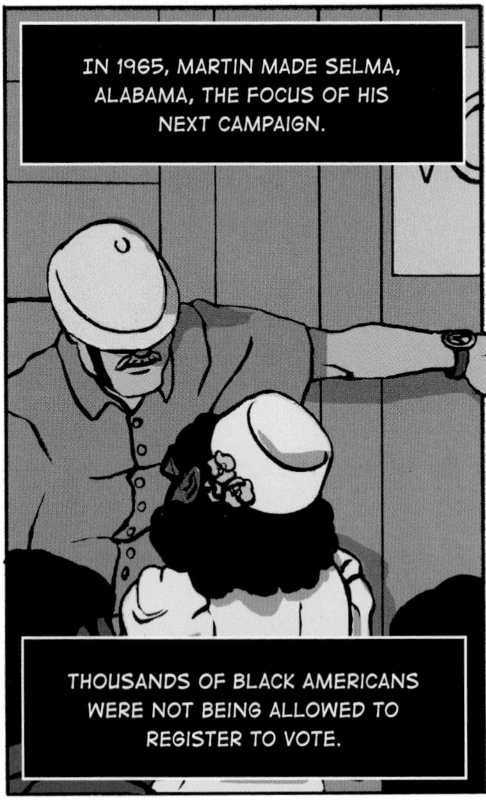
IN 1965, MARTIN MADE SELMA, ALABAMA, THE FOCUS OF HIS NEXT CAMPAIGN.
THOUSANDS OF BLACK AMERICANS WERE NOT BEING ALLOWED TO REGISTER TO VOTE.

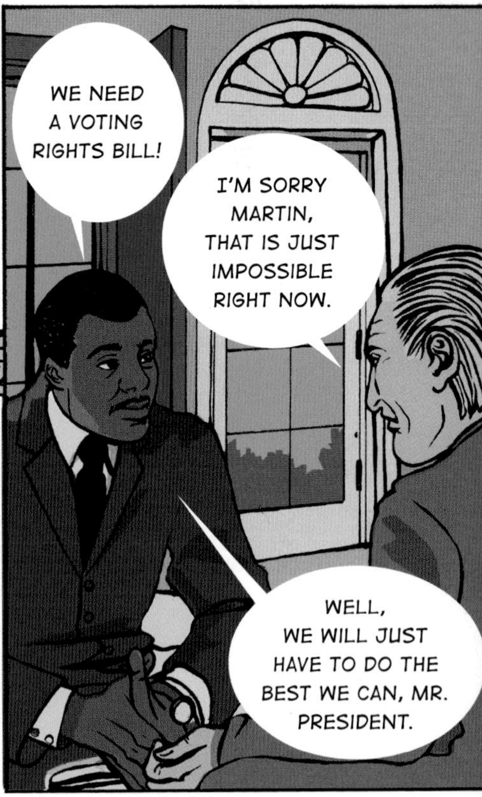
WE NEED A VOTING RIGHTS BILL!
I'M SORRY MARTIN, THAT IS JUST IMPOSSIBLE RIGHT NOW.
WELL, WE WILL JUST HAVE TO DO THE BEST WE CAN, MR. PRESIDENT.

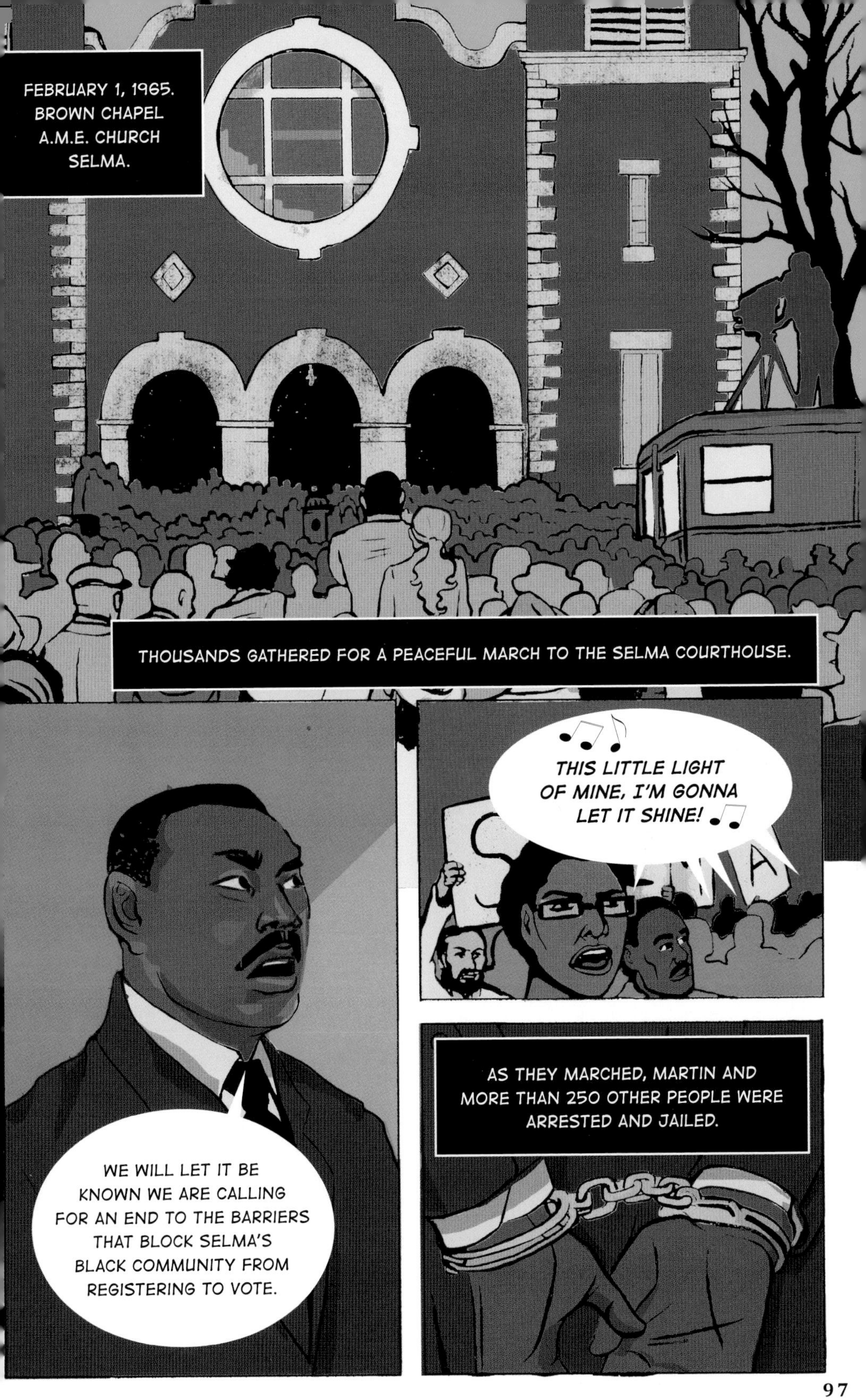
FEBRUARY 1, 1965.
BROWN CHAPEL
A.M.E. CHURCH
SELMA.
THOUSANDS GATHERED FOR A PEACEFUL MARCH TO THE SELMA COURTHOUSE.
WE WILL LET IT BE KNOWN WE ARE CALLING FOR AN END TO THE BARRIERS THAT BLOCK SELMA'S BLACK COMMUNITY FROM REGISTERING TO VOTE.
THIS LITTLE LIGHT OF MINE, I'M GONNA LET IT SHINE!
AS THEY MARCHED, MARTIN AND MORE THAN 250 OTHER PEOPLE WERE ARRESTED AND JAILED.

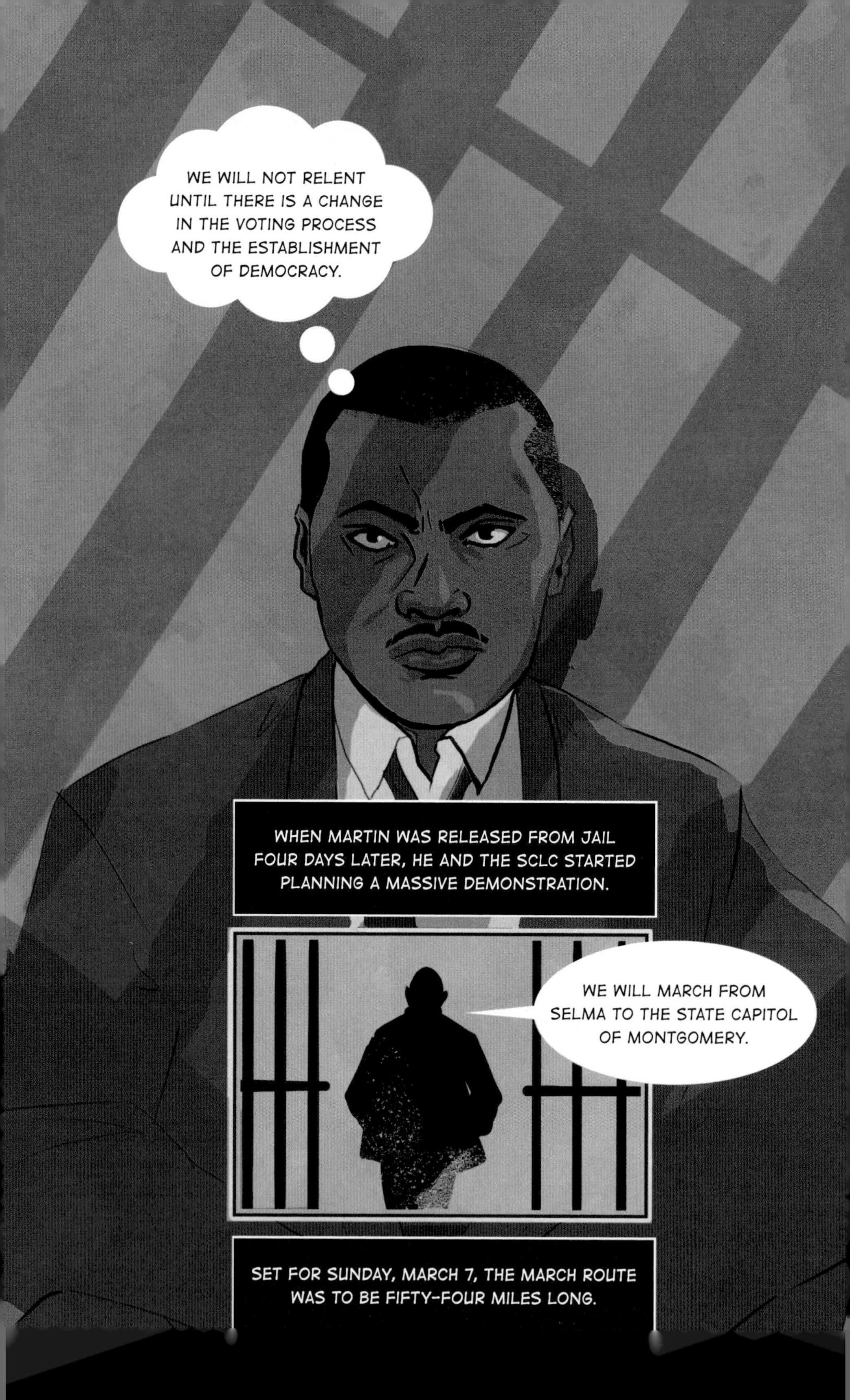
WE WILL NOT RELENT UNTIL THERE IS A CHANGE IN THE VOTING PROCESS AND THE ESTABLISHMENT OF DEMOCRACY.
WHEN MARTIN WAS RELEASED FROM JAIL FOUR DAYS LATER, HE AND THE SCLC STARTED PLANNING A MASSIVE DEMONSTRATION.
WE WILL MARCH FROM SELMA TO THE STATE CAPITOL OF MONTGOMERY.
SET FOR SUNDAY, MARCH 7, THE MARCH ROUTE WAS TO BE FIFTY-FOUR MILES LONG.

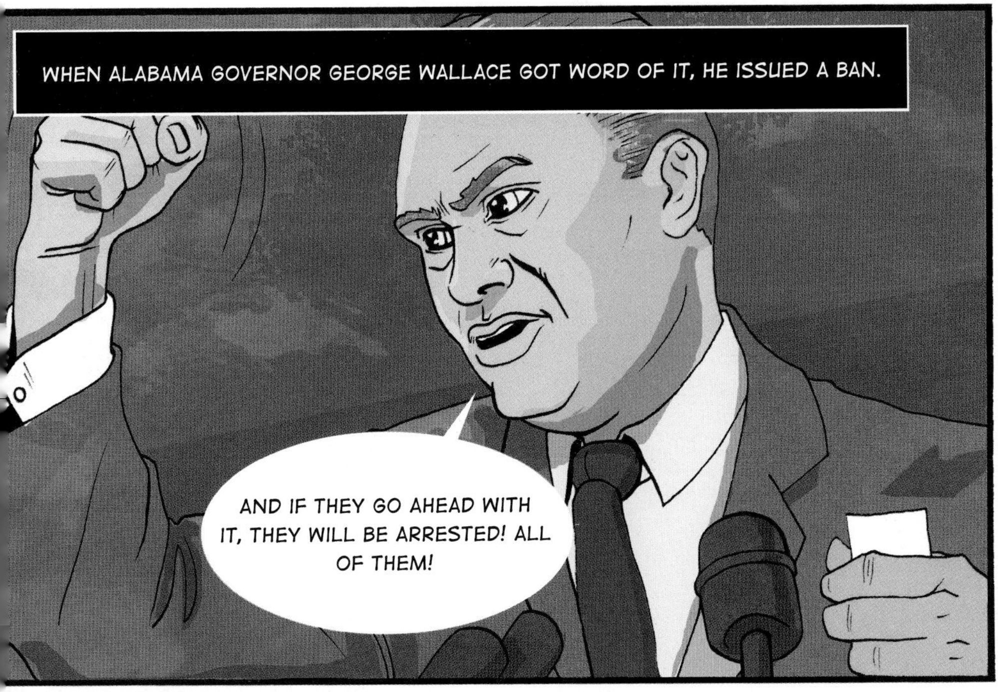
WHEN ALABAMA GOVERNOR GEORGE WALLACE GOT WORD OF IT, HE ISSUED A BAN.
AND IF THEY GO AHEAD WITH IT, THEY WILL BE ARRESTED! ALL OF THEM!

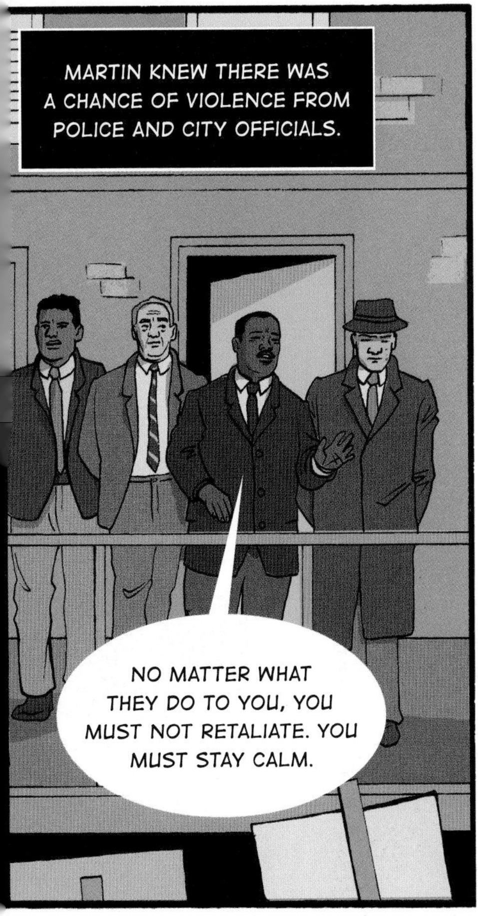
MARTIN KNEW THERE WAS A CHANCE OF VIOLENCE FROM POLICE AND CITY OFFICIALS.
NO MATTER WHAT THEY DO TO YOU, YOU MUST NOT RETALIATE. YOU MUST STAY CALM.

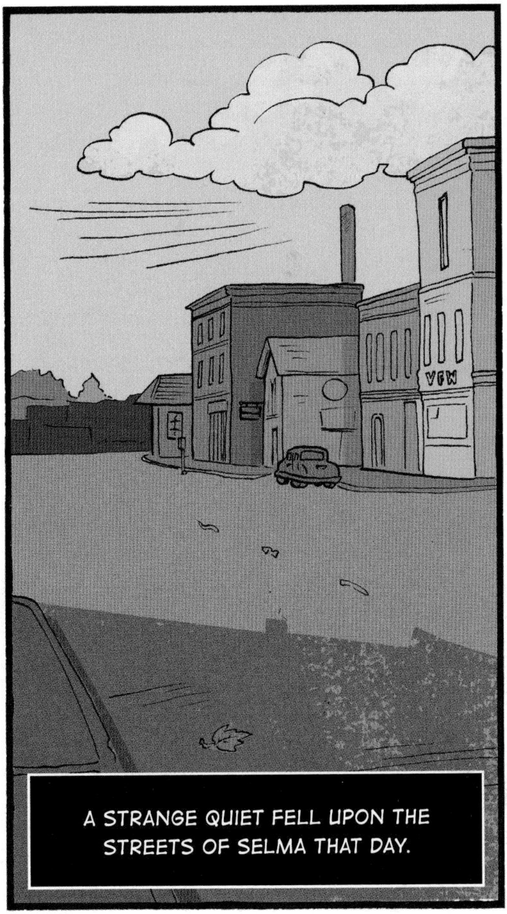
VFW
A STRANGE QUIET FELL UPON THE STREETS OF SELMA THAT DAY.

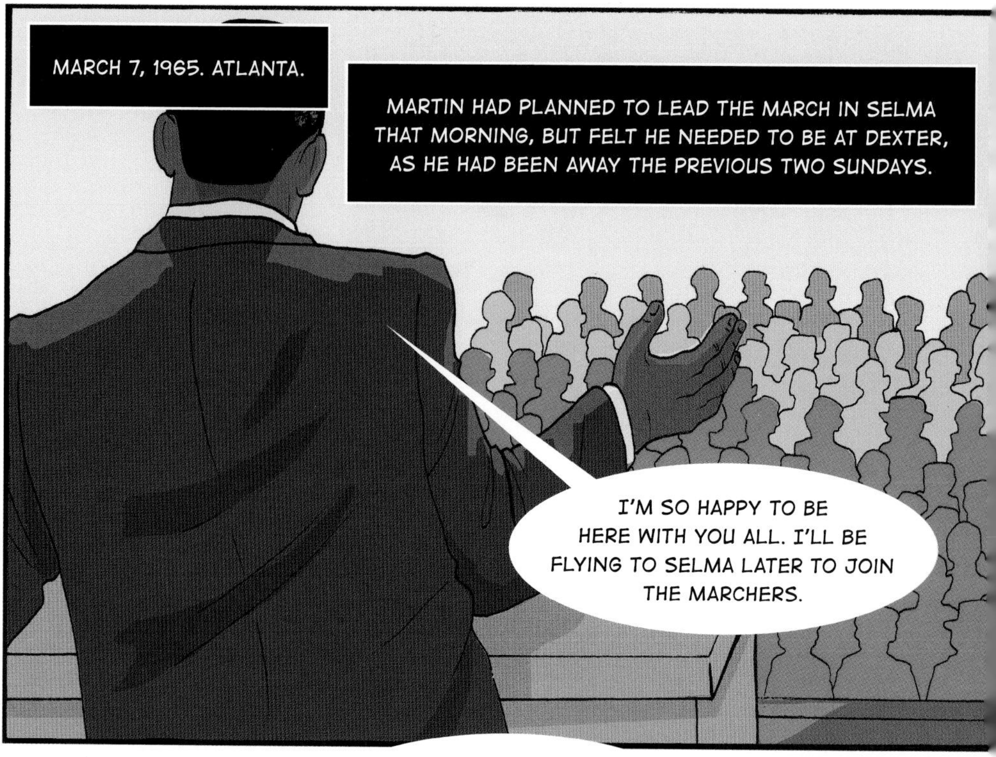
MARCH 7, 1965. ATLANTA.
MARTIN HAD PLANNED TO LEAD THE MARCH IN SELMA THAT MORNING, BUT FELT HE NEEDED TO BE AT DEXTER, AS HE HAD BEEN AWAY THE PREVIOUS TWO SUNDAYS.
I'M SO HAPPY TO BE HERE WITH YOU ALL. I'LL BE FLYING TO SELMA LATER TO JOIN THE MARCHERS.

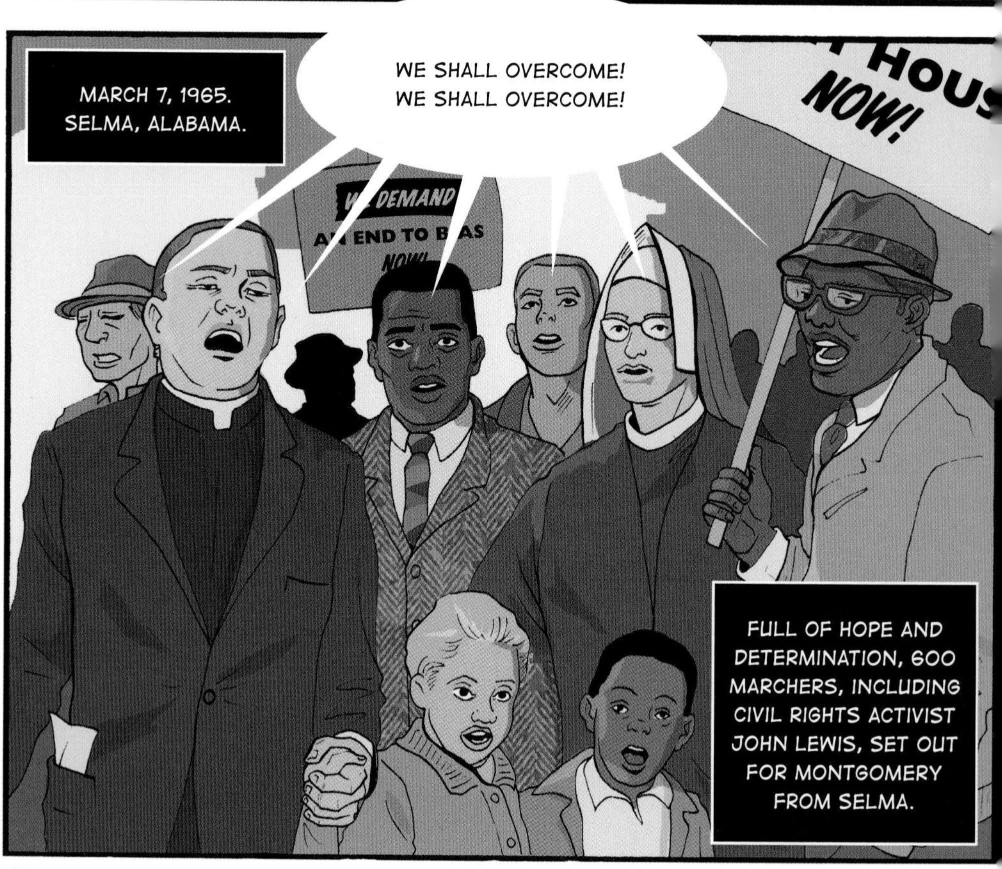
MARCH 7, 1965. SELMA, ALABAMA.
WE SHALL OVERCOME! WE SHALL OVERCOME!
NOW!
FULL OF HOPE AND DETERMINATION, 600 MARCHERS, INCLUDING CIVIL RIGHTS ACTIVIST JOHN LEWIS, SET OUT FOR MONTGOMERY FROM SELMA.

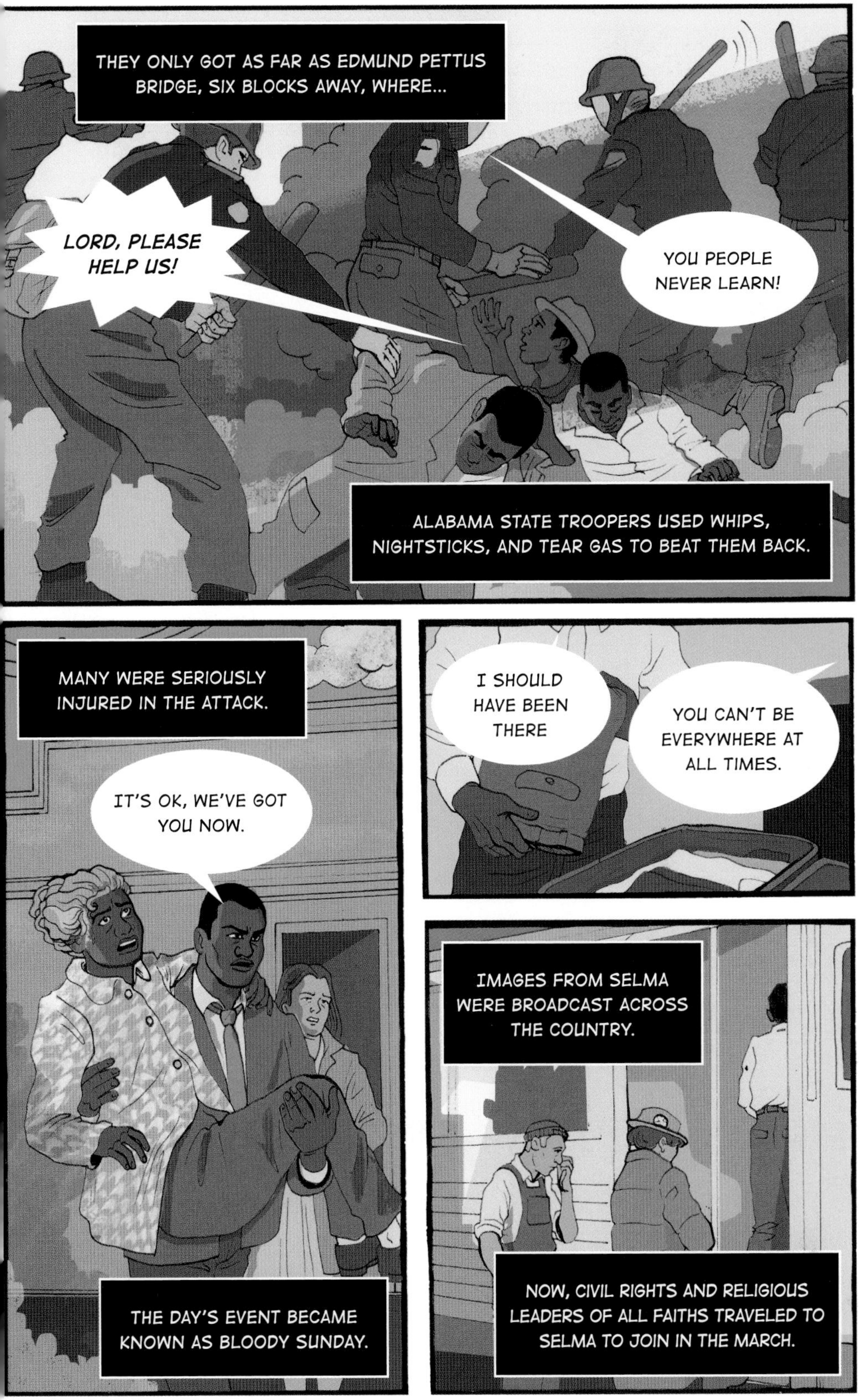
THEY ONLY GOT AS FAR AS EDMUND PETTUS BRIDGE, SIX BLOCKS AWAY, WHERE...
LORD, PLEASE HELP US!
YOU PEOPLE NEVER LEARN!
ALABAMA STATE TROOPERS USED WHIPS, NIGHTSTICKS, AND TEAR GAS TO BEAT THEM BACK.
MANY WERE SERIOUSLY INJURED IN THE ATTACK.
IT'S OK, WE'VE GOT YOU NOW.
THE DAY'S EVENT BECAME KNOWN AS BLOODY SUNDAY.
I SHOULD HAVE BEEN THERE
YOU CAN'T BE EVERYWHERE AT ALL TIMES.
IMAGES FROM SELMA WERE BROADCAST ACROSS THE COUNTRY.
NOW, CIVIL RIGHTS AND RELIGIOUS LEADERS OF ALL FAITHS TRAVELED TO SELMA TO JOIN IN THE MARCH.

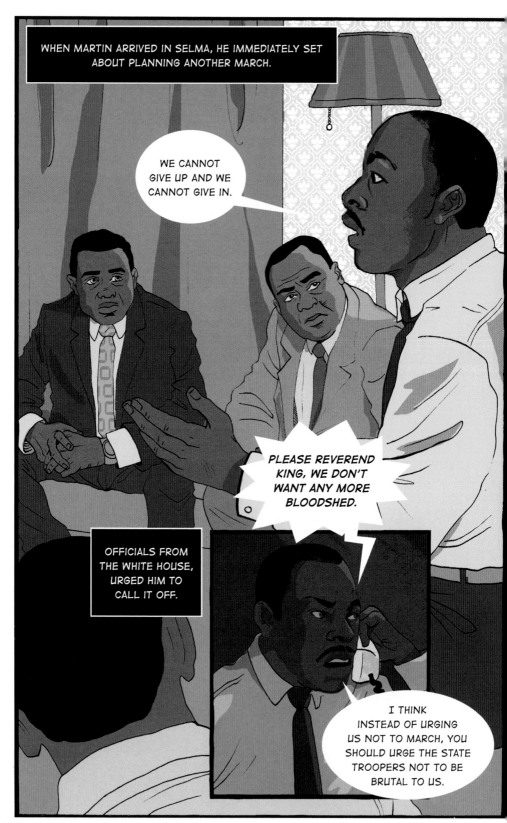

WHEN MARTIN ARRIVED IN SELMA, HE IMMEDIATELY SET ABOUT PLANNING ANOTHER MARCH.

WE CANNOT GIVE UP AND WE CANNOT GIVE IN.

PLEASE REVEREND KING, WE DON'T WANT ANY MORE BLOODSHED.

OFFICIALS FROM THE WHITE HOUSE, URGED HIM TO CALL IT OFF.

I THINK INSTEAD OF URGING US NOT TO MARCH, YOU SHOULD URGE THE STATE TROOPERS NOT TO BE BRUTAL TO US.

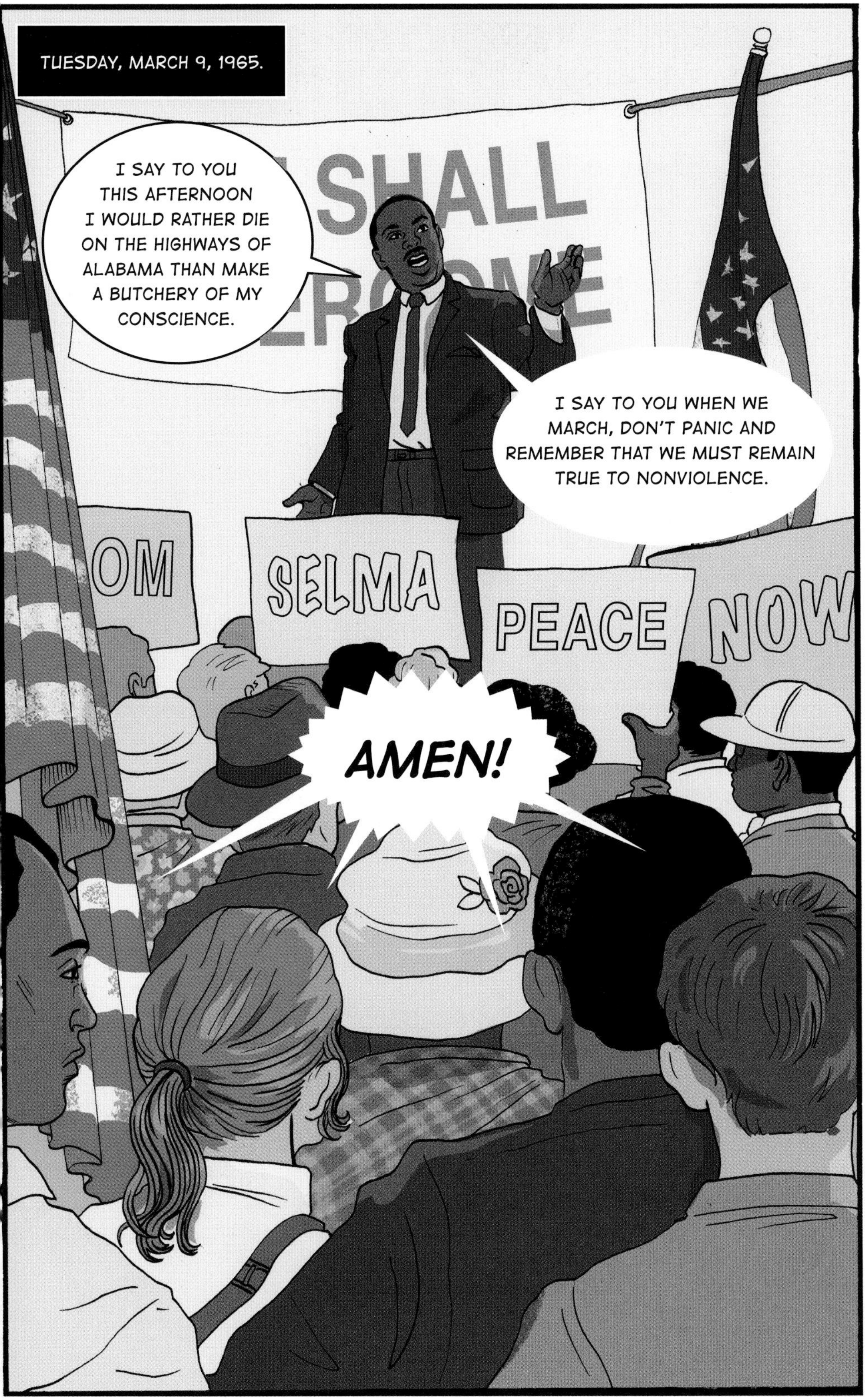
TUESDAY, MARCH 9, 1965.
SHALL
I SAY TO YOU THIS AFTERNOON I WOULD RATHER DIE ON THE HIGHWAYS OF ALABAMA THAN MAKE A BUTCHERY OF MY CONSCIENCE.
I SAY TO YOU WHEN WE MARCH, DON'T PANIC AND REMEMBER THAT WE MUST REMAIN TRUE TO NONVIOLENCE.
OM
SELMA
PEACE
NOW
AMEN!

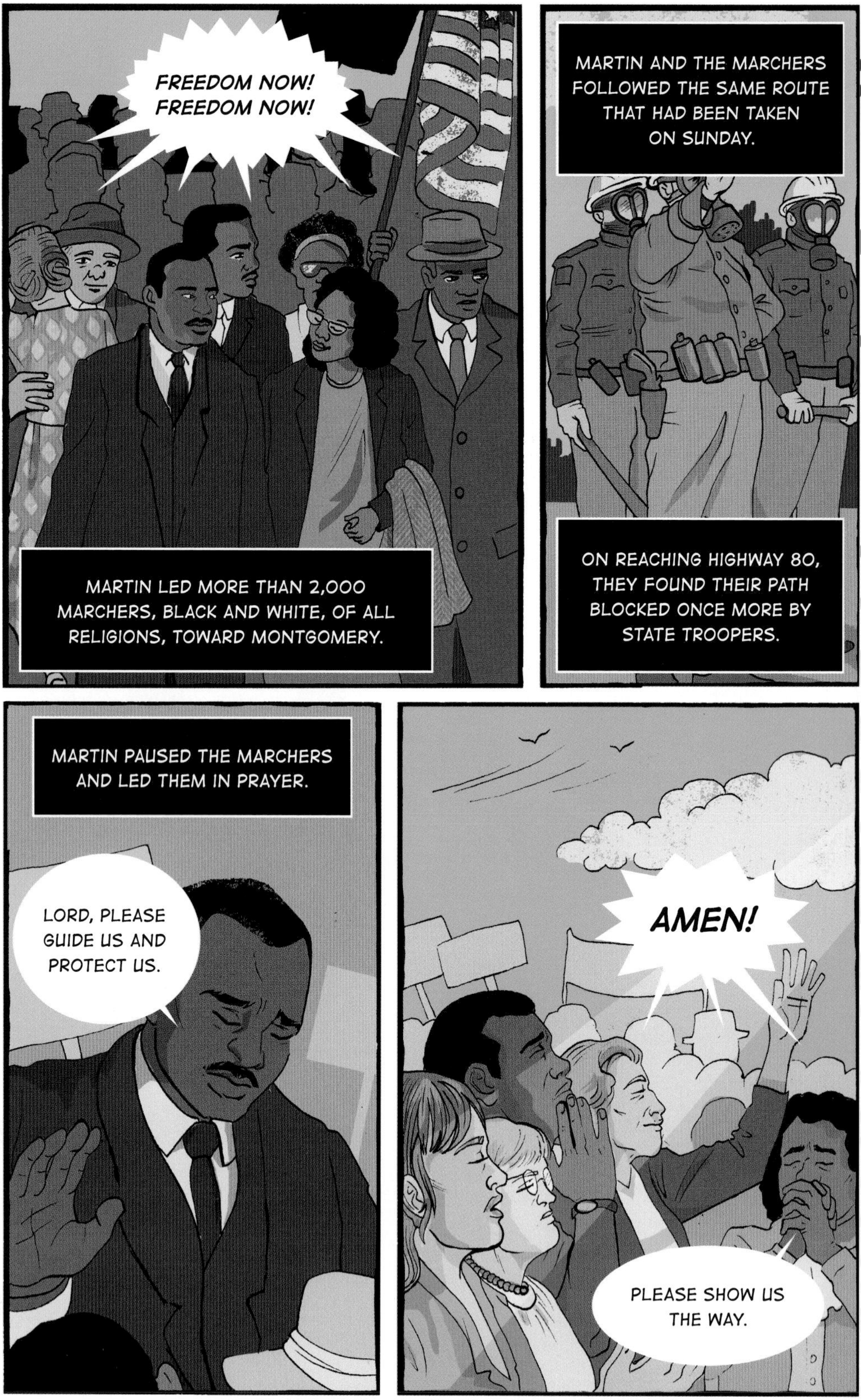
FREEDOM NOW!
FREEDOM NOW!
MARTIN LED MORE THAN 2,000 MARCHERS, BLACK AND WHITE, OF ALL RELIGIONS, TOWARD MONTGOMERY.
MARTIN AND THE MARCHERS FOLLOWED THE SAME ROUTE THAT HAD BEEN TAKEN ON SUNDAY.
ON REACHING HIGHWAY 80, THEY FOUND THEIR PATH BLOCKED ONCE MORE BY STATE TROOPERS.
MARTIN PAUSED THE MARCHERS AND LED THEM IN PRAYER.
LORD, PLEASE GUIDE US AND PROTECT US.
AMEN!
PLEASE SHOW US THE WAY.

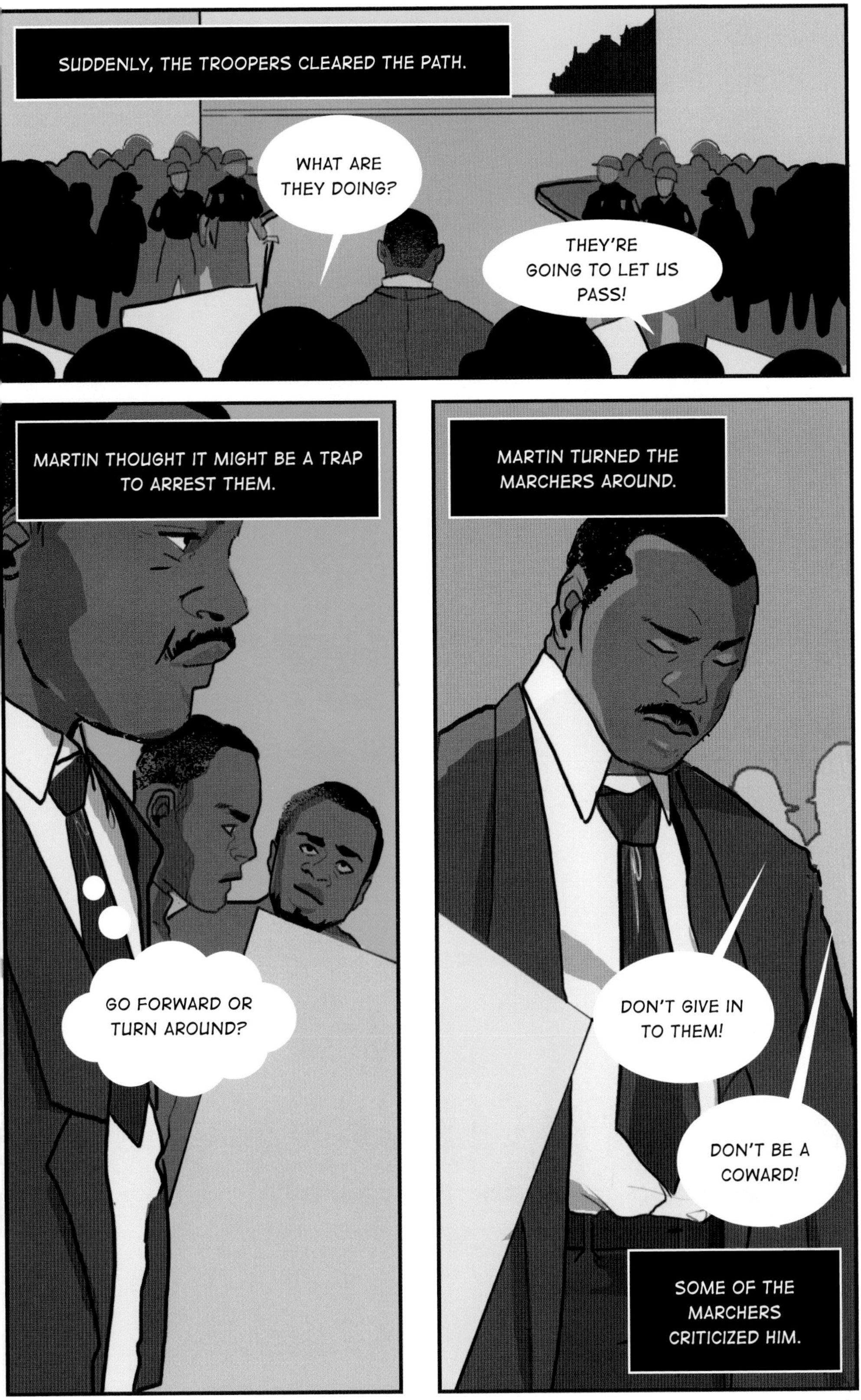
SUDDENLY, THE TROOPERS CLEARED THE PATH.
WHAT ARE THEY DOING?
THEY'RE GOING TO LET US PASS!
MARTIN THOUGHT IT MIGHT BE A TRAP TO ARREST THEM.
GO FORWARD OR TURN AROUND?
MARTIN TURNED THE MARCHERS AROUND.
DON'T GIVE IN TO THEM!
DON'T BE A COWARD!
SOME OF THE MARCHERS CRITICIZED HIM.

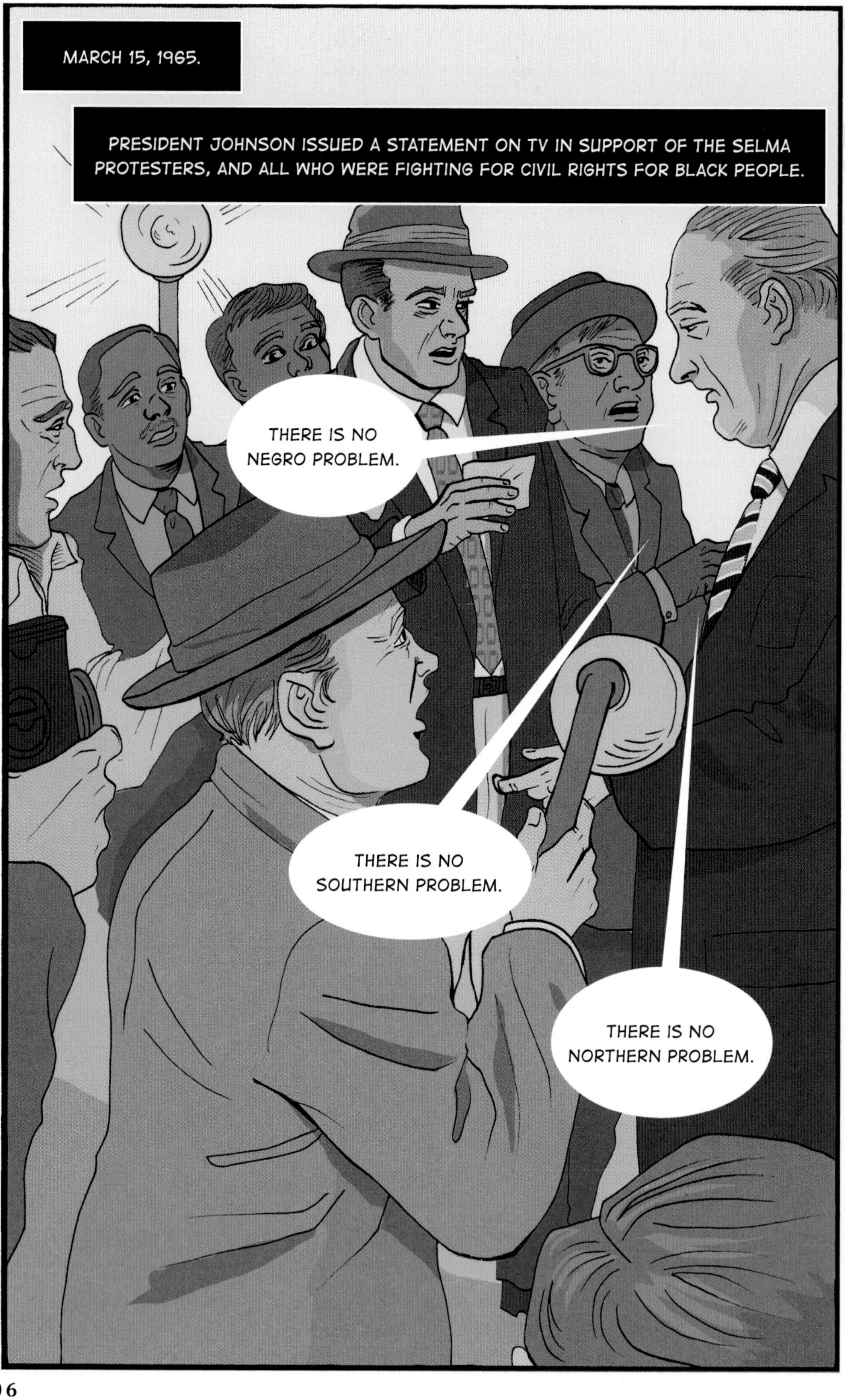
MARCH 15, 1965.
PRESIDENT JOHNSON ISSUED A STATEMENT ON TV IN SUPPORT OF THE SELMA PROTESTERS, AND ALL WHO WERE FIGHTING FOR CIVIL RIGHTS FOR BLACK PEOPLE.
THERE IS NO NEGRO PROBLEM.
THERE IS NO SOUTHERN PROBLEM.
THERE IS NO NORTHERN PROBLEM.

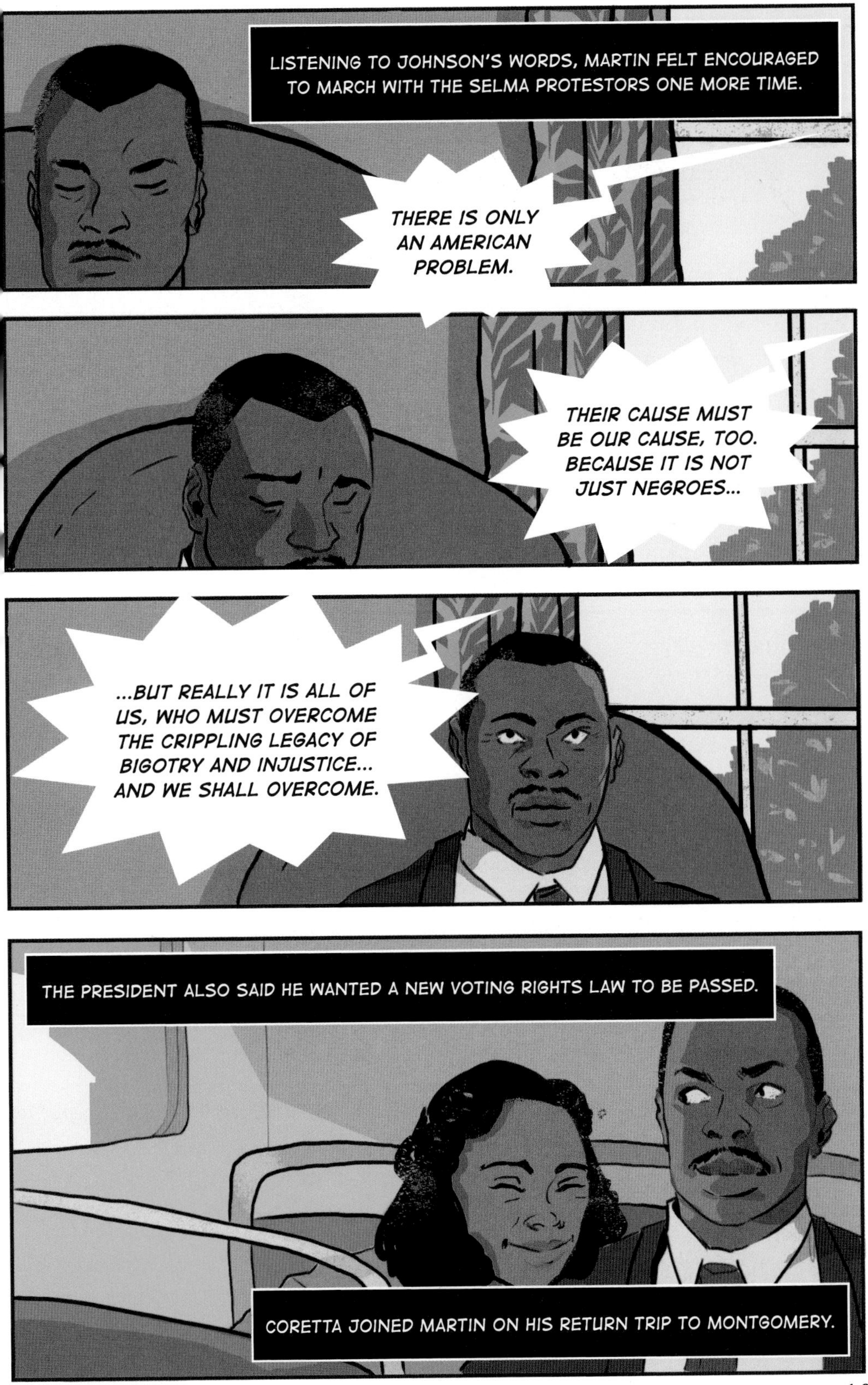
LISTENING TO JOHNSON'S WORDS, MARTIN FELT ENCOURAGED TO MARCH WITH THE SELMA PROTESTORS ONE MORE TIME.
THERE IS ONLY AN AMERICAN PROBLEM.
THEIR CAUSE MUST BE OUR CAUSE, TOO. BECAUSE IT IS NOT JUST NEGROES...
...BUT REALLY IT IS ALL OF US, WHO MUST OVERCOME THE CRIPPLING LEGACY OF BIGOTRY AND INJUSTICE... AND WE SHALL OVERCOME.
THE PRESIDENT ALSO SAID HE WANTED A NEW VOTING RIGHTS LAW TO BE PASSED.
CORETTA JOINED MARTIN ON HIS RETURN TRIP TO MONTGOMERY.

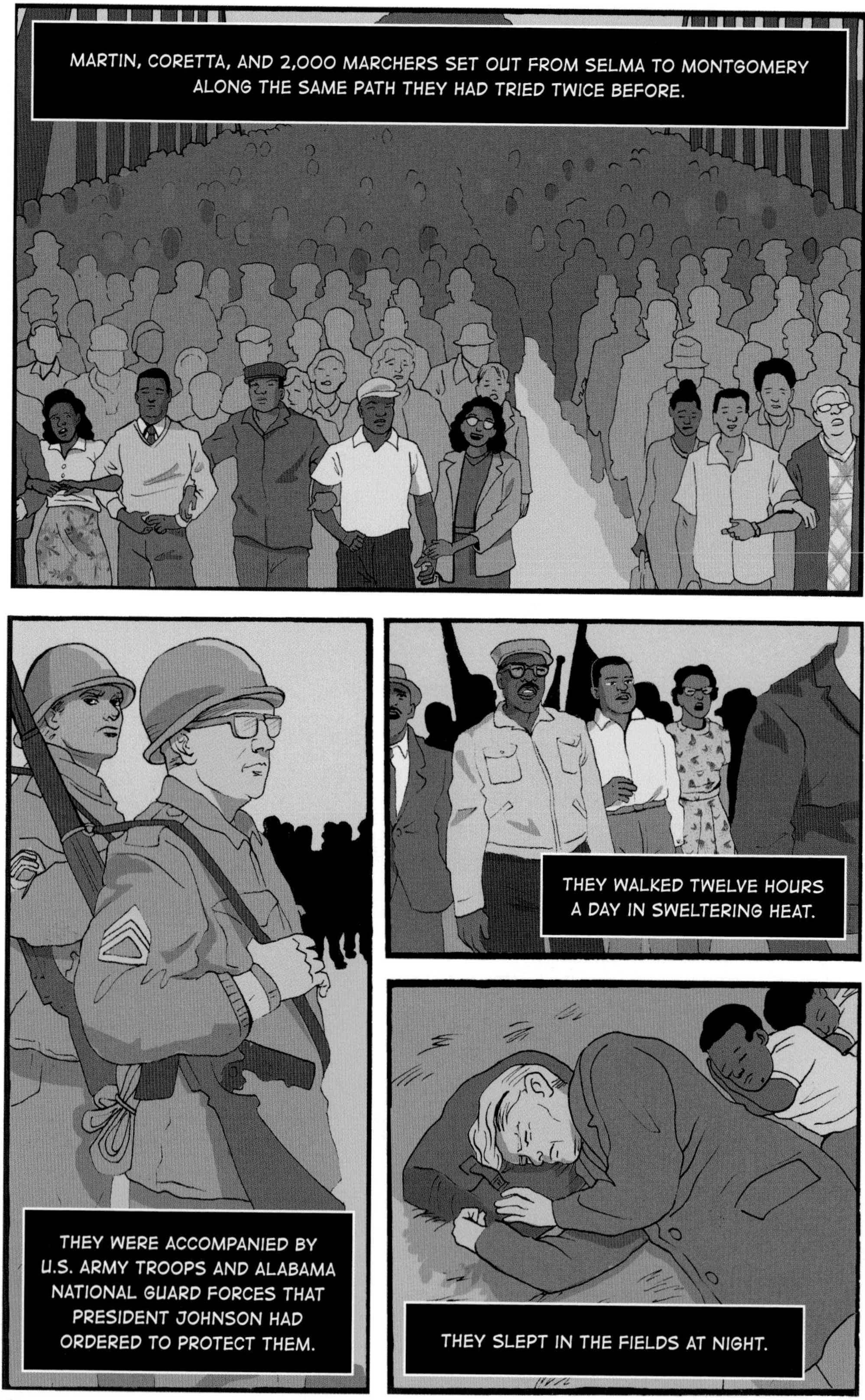
MARTIN, CORETTA, AND 2,000 MARCHERS SET OUT FROM SELMA TO MONTGOMERY ALONG THE SAME PATH THEY HAD TRIED TWICE BEFORE.
THEY WERE ACCOMPANIED BY U.S. ARMY TROOPS AND ALABAMA NATIONAL GUARD FORCES THAT PRESIDENT JOHNSON HAD ORDERED TO PROTECT THEM.
THEY WALKED TWELVE HOURS A DAY IN SWELTERING HEAT.
THEY SLEPT IN THE FIELDS AT NIGHT.

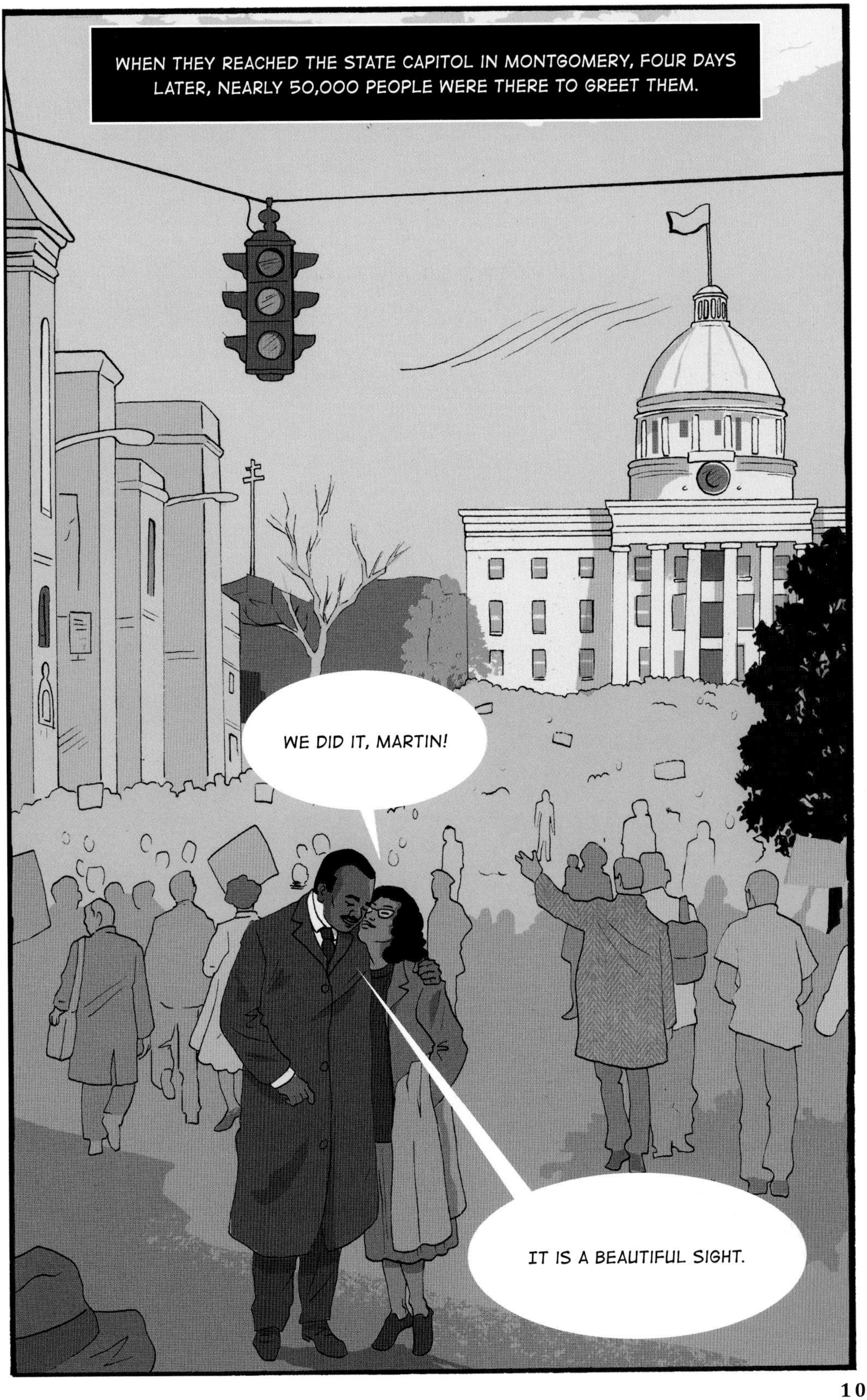
WHEN THEY REACHED THE STATE CAPITOL IN MONTGOMERY, FOUR DAYS LATER, NEARLY 50,000 PEOPLE WERE THERE TO GREET THEM.
WE DID IT, MARTIN!
IT IS A BEAUTIFUL SIGHT.

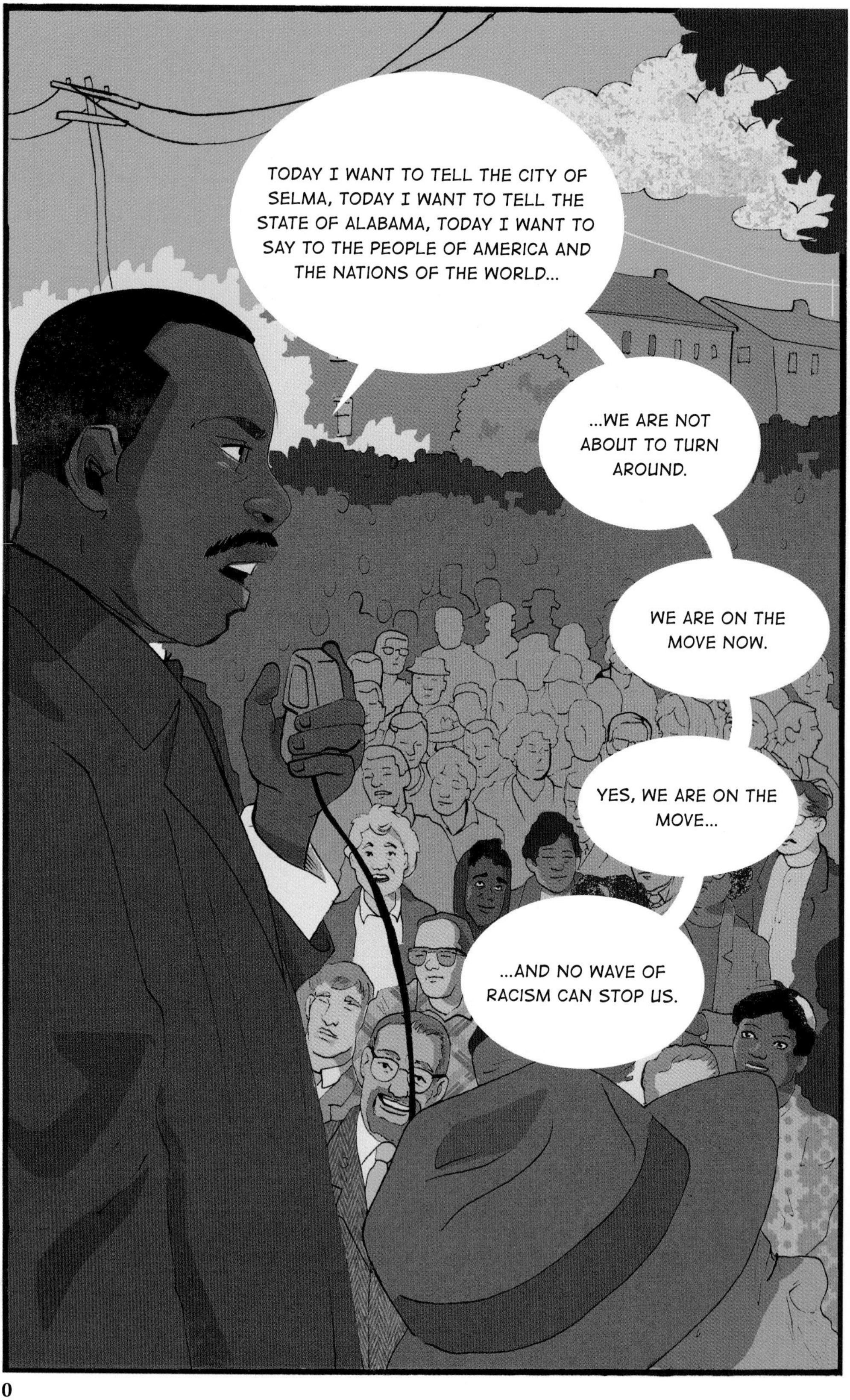
TODAY I WANT TO TELL THE CITY OF SELMA, TODAY I WANT TO TELL THE STATE OF ALABAMA, TODAY I WANT TO SAY TO THE PEOPLE OF AMERICA AND THE NATIONS OF THE WORLD...
...WE ARE NOT ABOUT TO TURN AROUND.
WE ARE ON THE MOVE NOW.
YES, WE ARE ON THE MOVE...
...AND NO WAVE OF RACISM CAN STOP US.

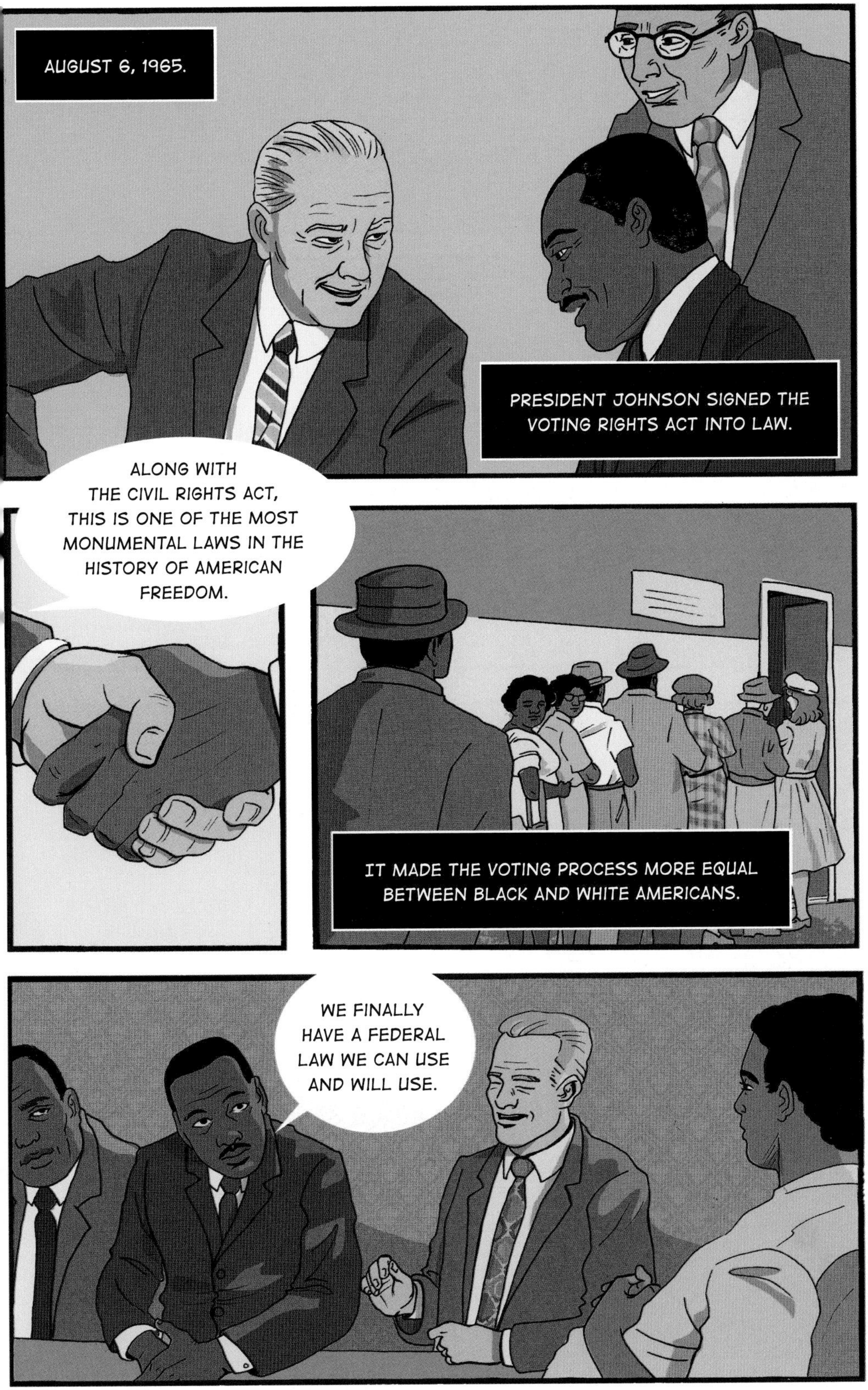
AUGUST 6, 1965.
PRESIDENT JOHNSON SIGNED THE VOTING RIGHTS ACT INTO LAW.
ALONG WITH THE CIVIL RIGHTS ACT, THIS IS ONE OF THE MOST MONUMENTAL LAWS IN THE HISTORY OF AMERICAN FREEDOM.
IT MADE THE VOTING PROCESS MORE EQUAL BETWEEN BLACK AND WHITE AMERICANS.
WE FINALLY HAVE A FEDERAL LAW WE CAN USE AND WILL USE.

CHAPTER 9

THE FINAL DAYS: MEMPHIS

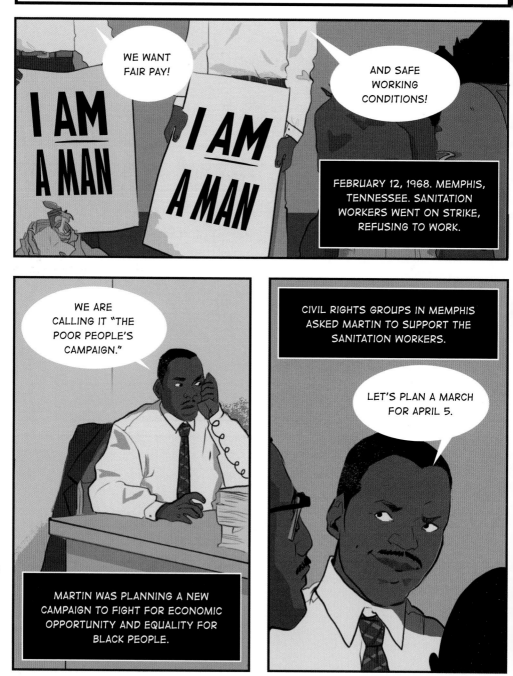

WE WANT FAIR PAY!

AND SAFE WORKING CONDITIONS!

I AM A MAN

I AM A MAN

FEBRUARY 12, 1968. MEMPHIS, TENNESSEE. SANITATION WORKERS WENT ON STRIKE, REFUSING TO WORK.

WE ARE CALLING IT "THE POOR PEOPLE'S CAMPAIGN."

MARTIN WAS PLANNING A NEW CAMPAIGN TO FIGHT FOR ECONOMIC OPPORTUNITY AND EQUALITY FOR BLACK PEOPLE.

CIVIL RIGHTS GROUPS IN MEMPHIS ASKED MARTIN TO SUPPORT THE SANITATION WORKERS.

LET'S PLAN A MARCH FOR APRIL 5.

IN THE DAYS THAT FOLLOWED, REV. RALPH ABERNATHY BEGAN TO WORRY ABOUT HIS FRIEND.

YOU OK, MARTIN?

MARTIN HAD BECOME SERIOUS AND SOMBER OF LATE.

HE HAD DEDICATED HIS LIFE TO FIGHTING FOR CIVIL RIGHTS FOR THE PAST THIRTEEN YEARS, AND WAS BEGINNING TO FEEL EXHAUSTED.

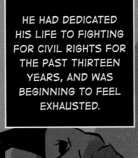

A COUPLE DAYS BEFORE THE MARCH, MARTIN WAS ASKED TO GIVE A SERMON AT MASON TEMPLE, HEADQUARTERS OF THE CHURCH OF GOD IN CHRIST IN MEMPHIS, TENNESSEE.

GOOD EVENING. AND THANK YOU FOR WELCOMING ME TO MEMPHIS.

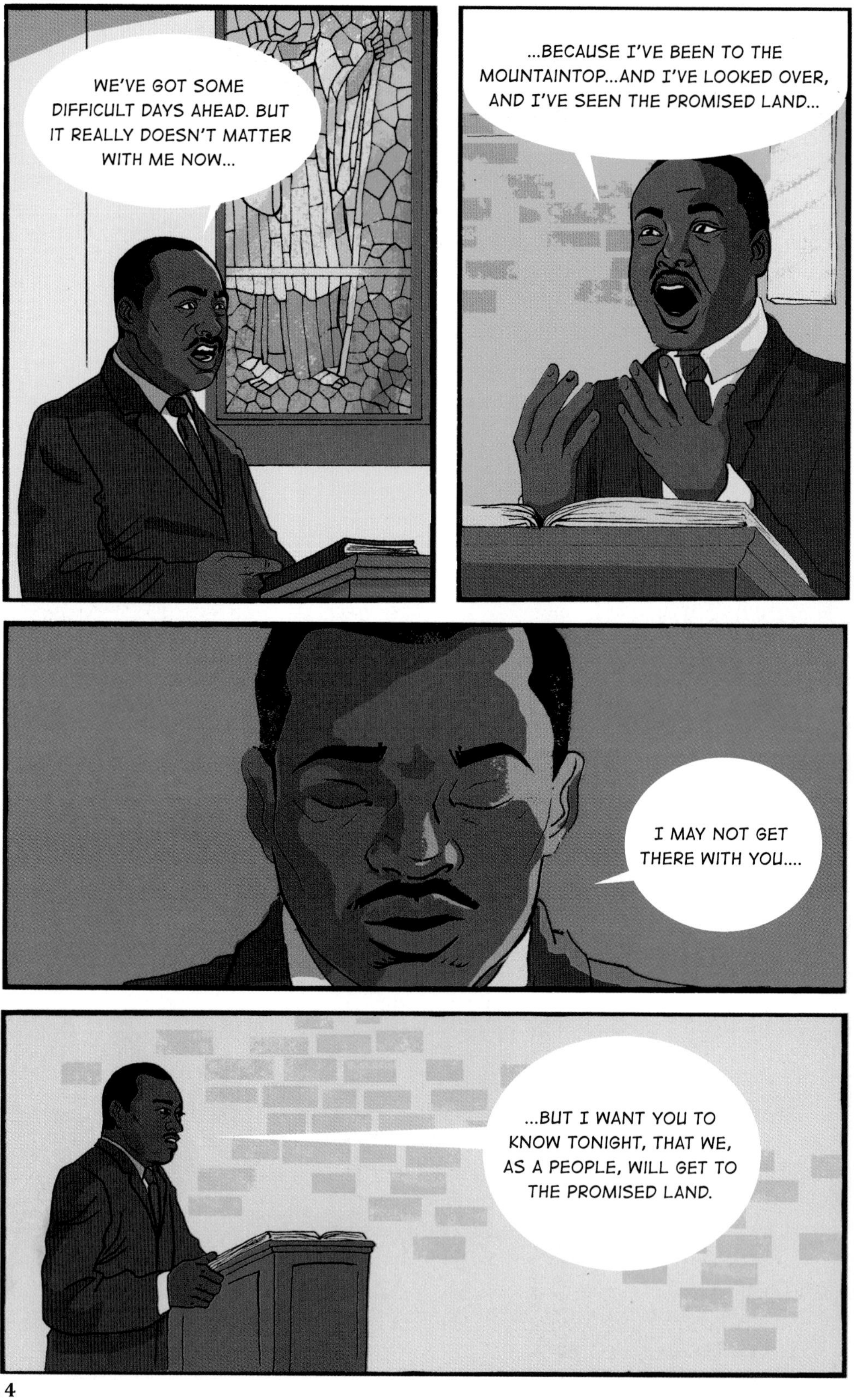
WE'VE GOT SOME DIFFICULT DAYS AHEAD. BUT IT REALLY DOESN'T MATTER WITH ME NOW...
...BECAUSE I'VE BEEN TO THE MOUNTAINTOP...AND I'VE LOOKED OVER, AND I'VE SEEN THE PROMISED LAND...
I MAY NOT GET THERE WITH YOU....
...BUT I WANT YOU TO KNOW TONIGHT, THAT WE, AS A PEOPLE, WILL GET TO THE PROMISED LAND.

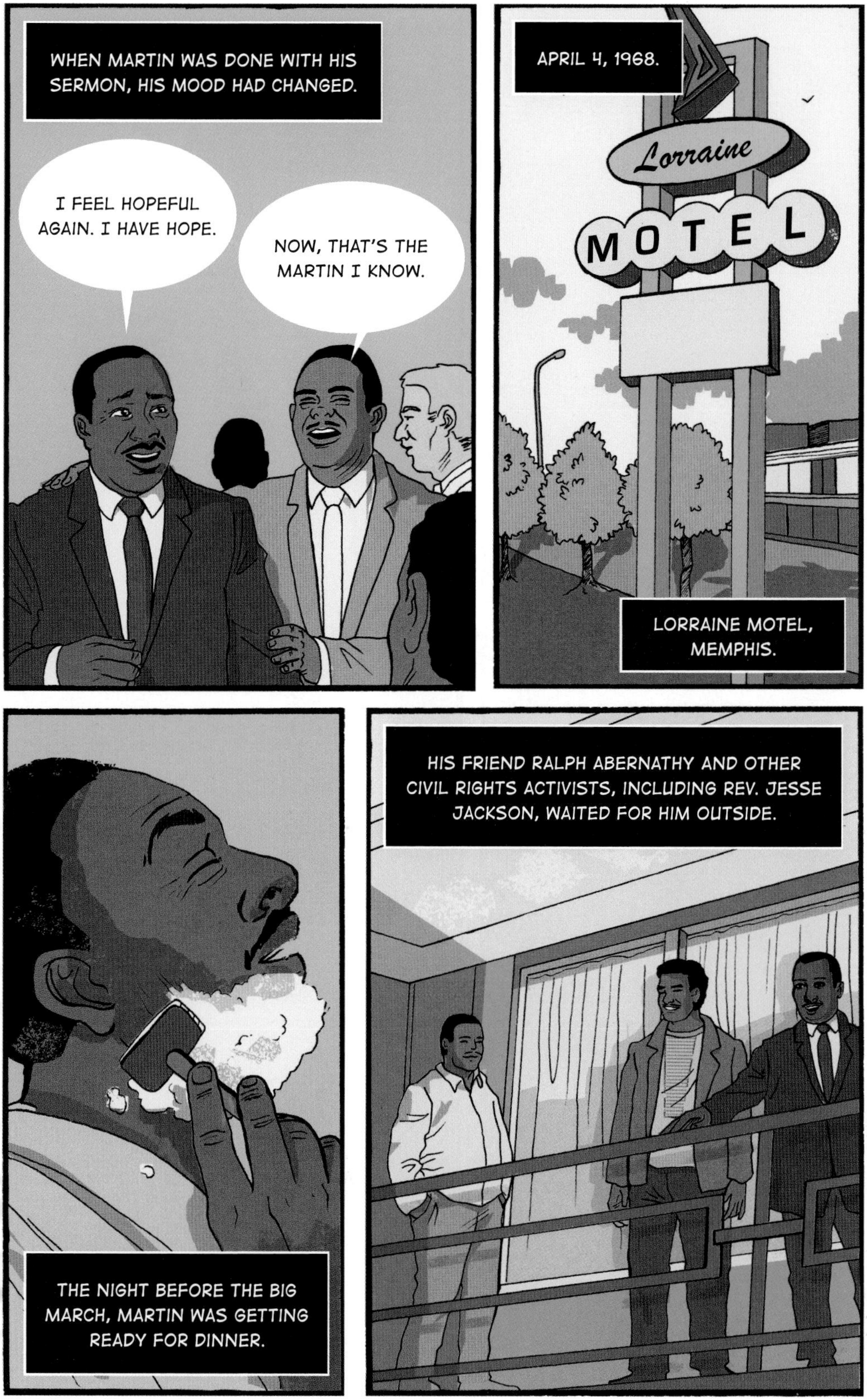
WHEN MARTIN WAS DONE WITH HIS SERMON, HIS MOOD HAD CHANGED.
I FEEL HOPEFUL AGAIN. I HAVE HOPE.
NOW, THAT'S THE MARTIN I KNOW.
APRIL 4, 1968.
Lorraine
MOTEL
LORRAINE MOTEL, MEMPHIS.
THE NIGHT BEFORE THE BIG MARCH, MARTIN WAS GETTING READY FOR DINNER.
HIS FRIEND RALPH ABERNATHY AND OTHER CIVIL RIGHTS ACTIVISTS, INCLUDING REV. JESSE JACKSON, WAITED FOR HIM OUTSIDE.

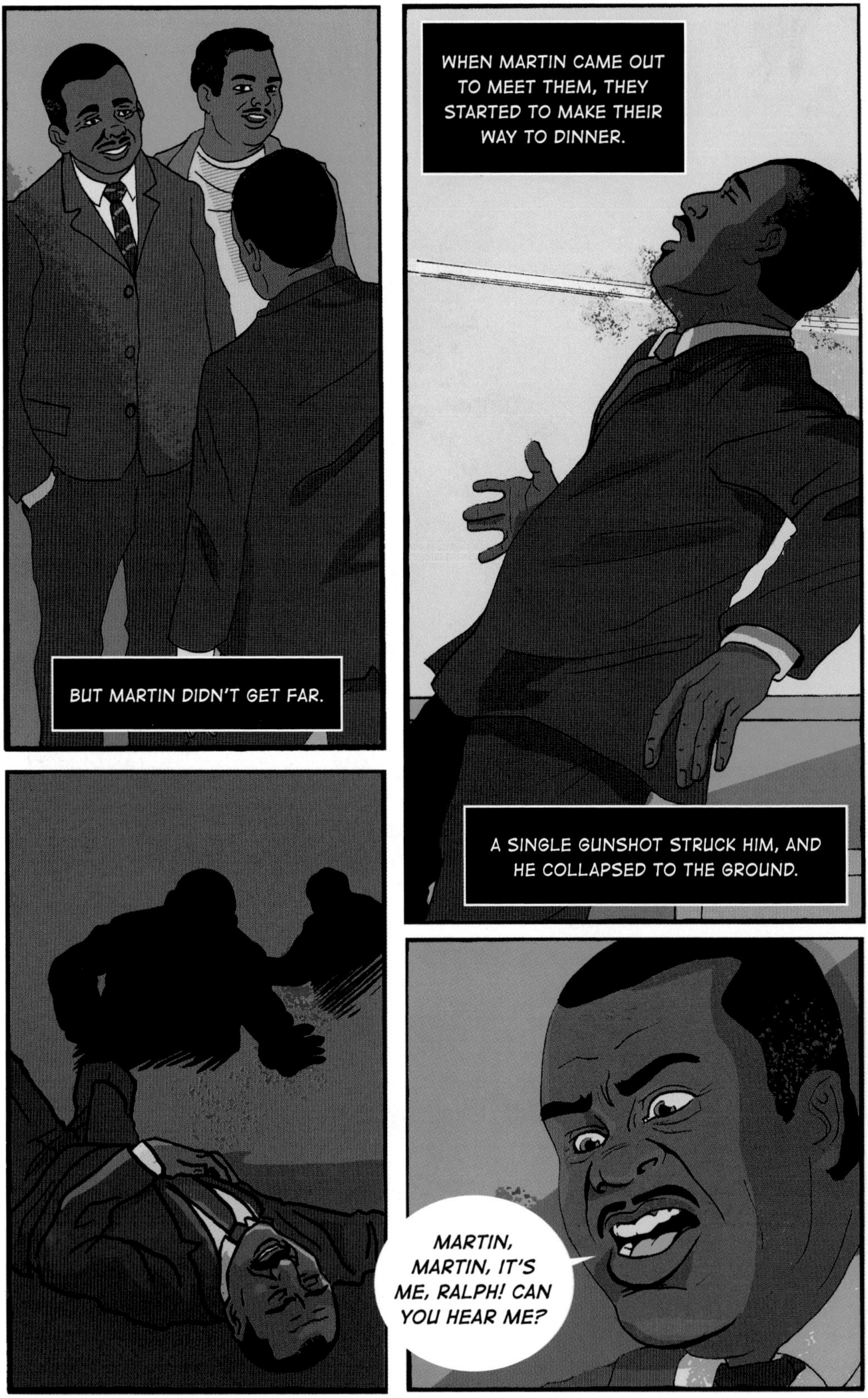
BUT MARTIN DIDN'T GET FAR.
WHEN MARTIN CAME OUT TO MEET THEM, THEY STARTED TO MAKE THEIR WAY TO DINNER.
A SINGLE GUNSHOT STRUCK HIM, AND HE COLLAPSED TO THE GROUND.
MARTIN, MARTIN, IT'S ME, RALPH! CAN YOU HEAR ME?

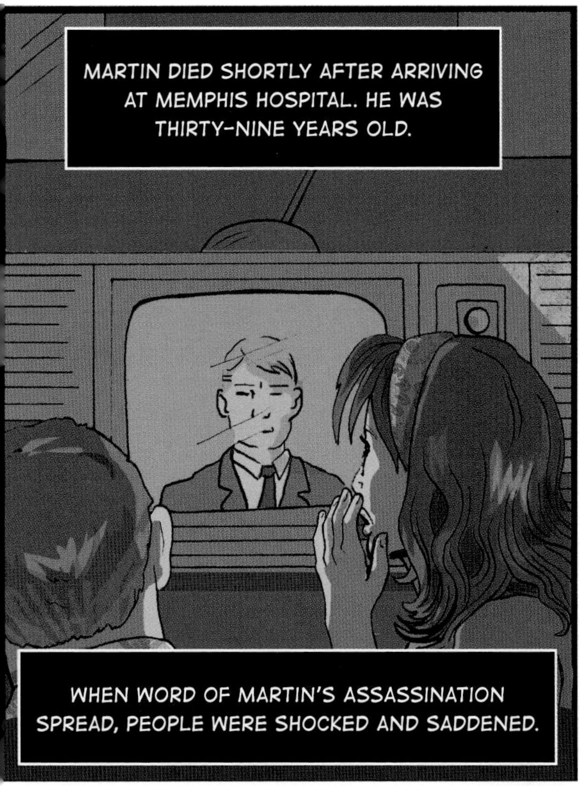
MARTIN DIED SHORTLY AFTER ARRIVING AT MEMPHIS HOSPITAL. HE WAS THIRTY-NINE YEARS OLD.
WHEN WORD OF MARTIN'S ASSASSINATION SPREAD, PEOPLE WERE SHOCKED AND SADDENED.

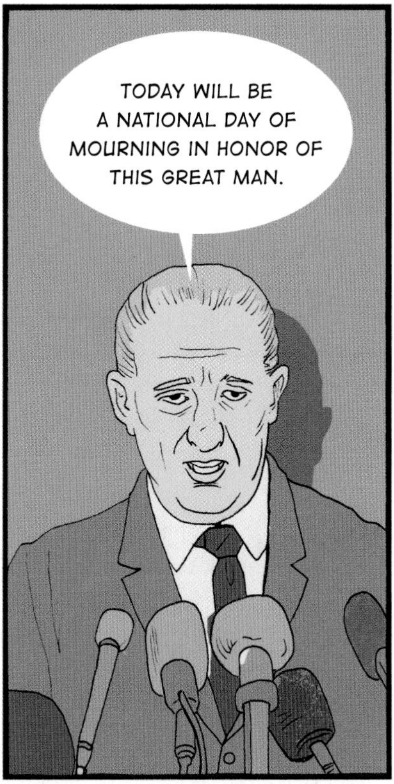
TODAY WILL BE A NATIONAL DAY OF MOURNING IN HONOR OF THIS GREAT MAN.

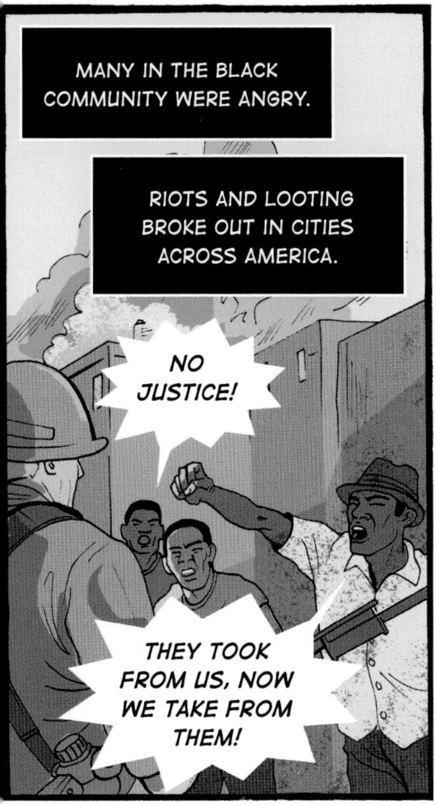
MANY IN THE BLACK COMMUNITY WERE ANGRY.
RIOTS AND LOOTING BROKE OUT IN CITIES ACROSS AMERICA.
NO JUSTICE!
THEY TOOK FROM US, NOW WE TAKE FROM THEM!

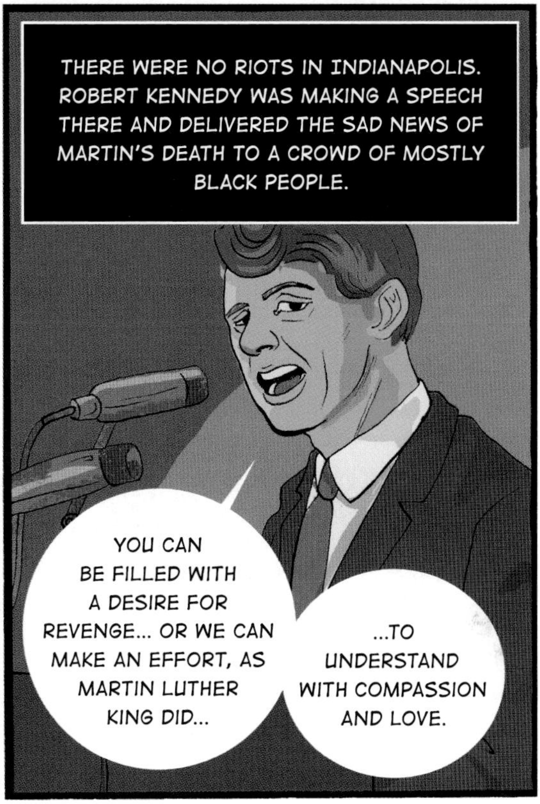
THERE WERE NO RIOTS IN INDIANAPOLIS. ROBERT KENNEDY WAS MAKING A SPEECH THERE AND DELIVERED THE SAD NEWS OF MARTIN'S DEATH TO A CROWD OF MOSTLY BLACK PEOPLE.
YOU CAN BE FILLED WITH A DESIRE FOR REVENGE... OR WE CAN MAKE AN EFFORT, AS MARTIN LUTHER KING DID...
...TO UNDERSTAND WITH COMPASSION AND LOVE.

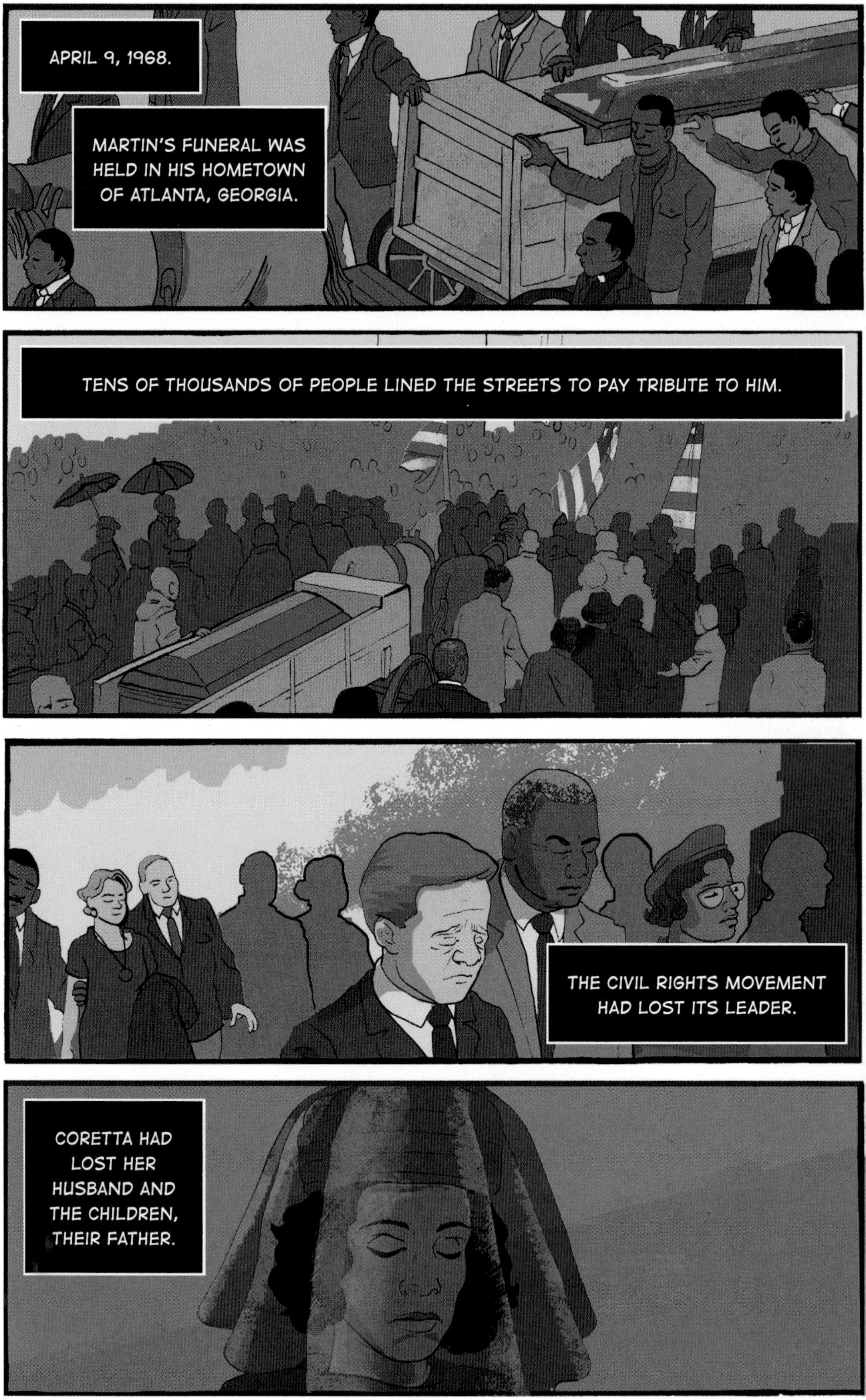
APRIL 9, 1968.
MARTIN'S FUNERAL WAS HELD IN HIS HOMETOWN OF ATLANTA, GEORGIA.
TENS OF THOUSANDS OF PEOPLE LINED THE STREETS TO PAY TRIBUTE TO HIM.
THE CIVIL RIGHTS MOVEMENT HAD LOST ITS LEADER.
CORETTA HAD LOST HER HUSBAND AND THE CHILDREN, THEIR FATHER.

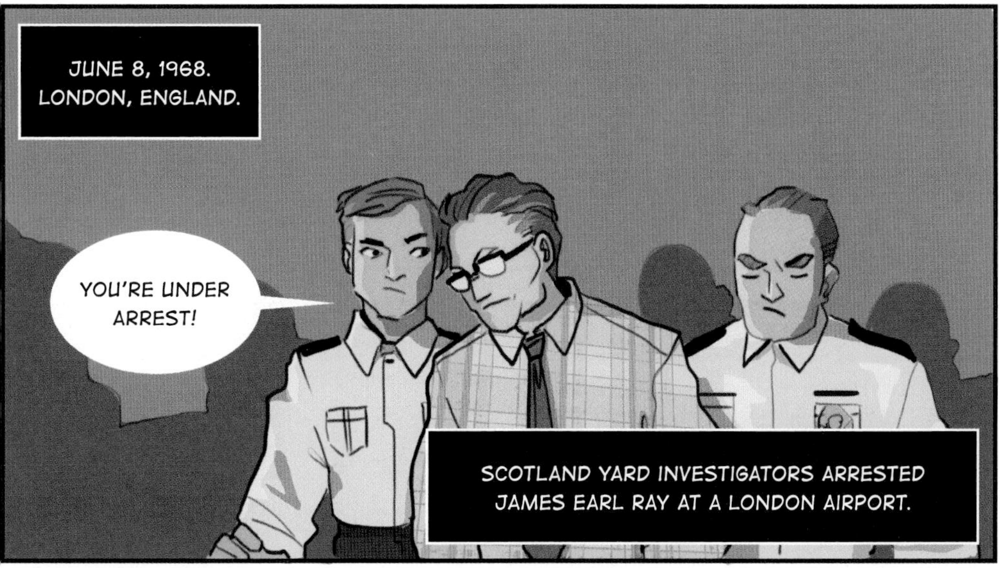
JUNE 8, 1968.
LONDON, ENGLAND.
YOU'RE UNDER ARREST!
SCOTLAND YARD INVESTIGATORS ARRESTED JAMES EARL RAY AT A LONDON AIRPORT.

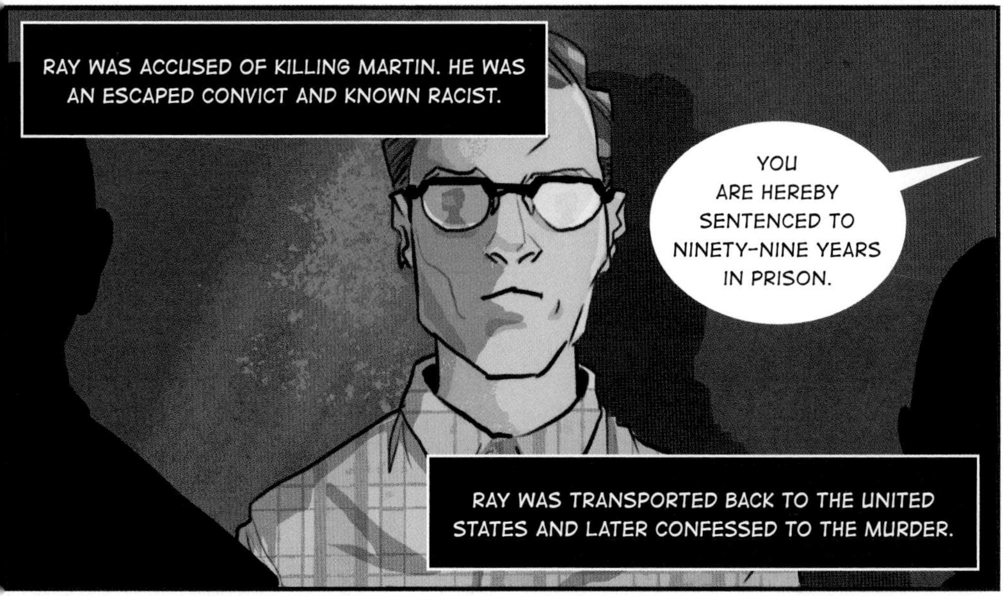
RAY WAS ACCUSED OF KILLING MARTIN. HE WAS AN ESCAPED CONVICT AND KNOWN RACIST.
YOU ARE HEREBY SENTENCED TO NINETY-NINE YEARS IN PRISON.
RAY WAS TRANSPORTED BACK TO THE UNITED STATES AND LATER CONFESSED TO THE MURDER.

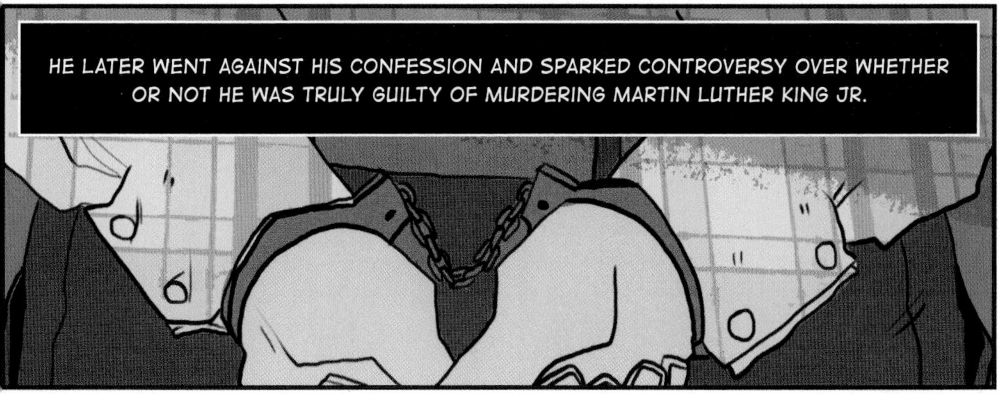
HE LATER WENT AGAINST HIS CONFESSION AND SPARKED CONTROVERSY OVER WHETHER OR NOT HE WAS TRULY GUILTY OF MURDERING MARTIN LUTHER KING JR.

CHAPTER 10

MARTIN LUTHER KING JR. REMEMBERED

AFTER MARTIN'S DEATH, REV. RALPH ABERNATHY TOOK OVER AS LEADER OF THE SCLC...

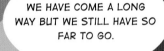

WE HAVE COME A LONG WAY BUT WE STILL HAVE SO FAR TO GO.

...AND CORETTA CARRIED ON MARTIN'S WORK IN THE CIVIL RIGHTS MOVEMENT.

IN 1968, CORETTA ESTABLISHED THE MARTIN LUTHER KING JR. CENTER IN ATLANTA, GA., FOR NONVIOLENT SOCIAL CHANGE.

THE CENTER SITS INSIDE A NATIONAL HISTORIC PARK, ALONG WITH MARTIN'S CHILDHOOD HOME, AND HIS GRAVESITE. IT HOSTS MORE THAN ONE MILLION VISITORS EACH YEAR.

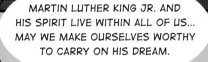

NOVEMBER 2, 1983. THE WHITE HOUSE.

MARTIN LUTHER KING JR. AND HIS SPIRIT LIVE WITHIN ALL OF US... MAY WE MAKE OURSELVES WORTHY TO CARRY ON HIS DREAM.

PRESIDENT RONALD REAGAN SIGNED A BILL DECLARING EVERY THIRD MONDAY IN JANUARY WOULD BE A FEDERAL HOLIDAY: MARTIN LUTHER KING JR. DAY.

THANK YOU, MR. PRESIDENT.

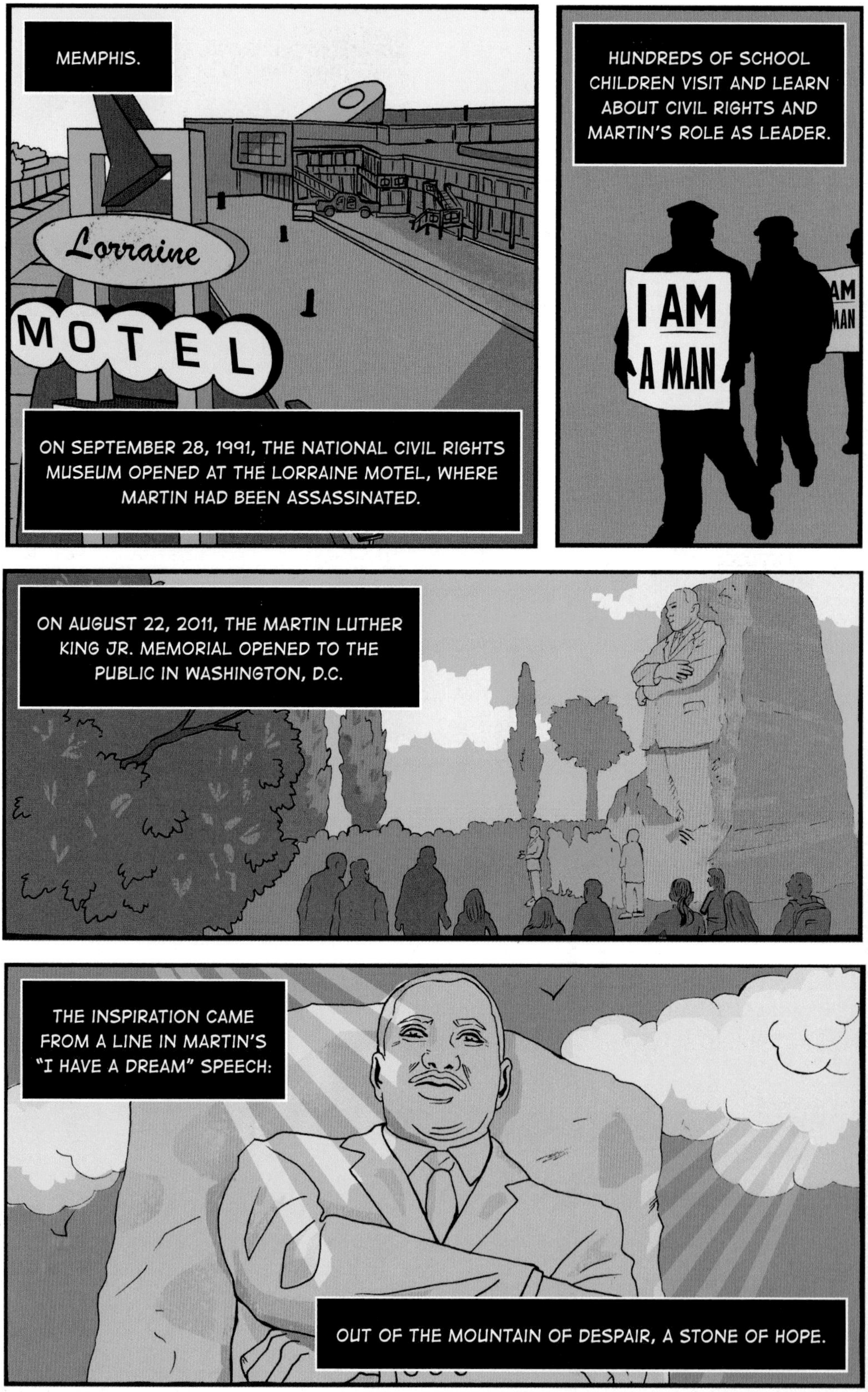
MEMPHIS.
Lorraine
MOTEL
ON SEPTEMBER 28, 1991, THE NATIONAL CIVIL RIGHTS MUSEUM OPENED AT THE LORRAINE MOTEL, WHERE MARTIN HAD BEEN ASSASSINATED.
HUNDREDS OF SCHOOL CHILDREN VISIT AND LEARN ABOUT CIVIL RIGHTS AND MARTIN'S ROLE AS LEADER.
I AM A MAN
ON AUGUST 22, 2011, THE MARTIN LUTHER KING JR. MEMORIAL OPENED TO THE PUBLIC IN WASHINGTON, D.C.
THE INSPIRATION CAME FROM A LINE IN MARTIN'S "I HAVE A DREAM" SPEECH:
OUT OF THE MOUNTAIN OF DESPAIR, A STONE OF HOPE.

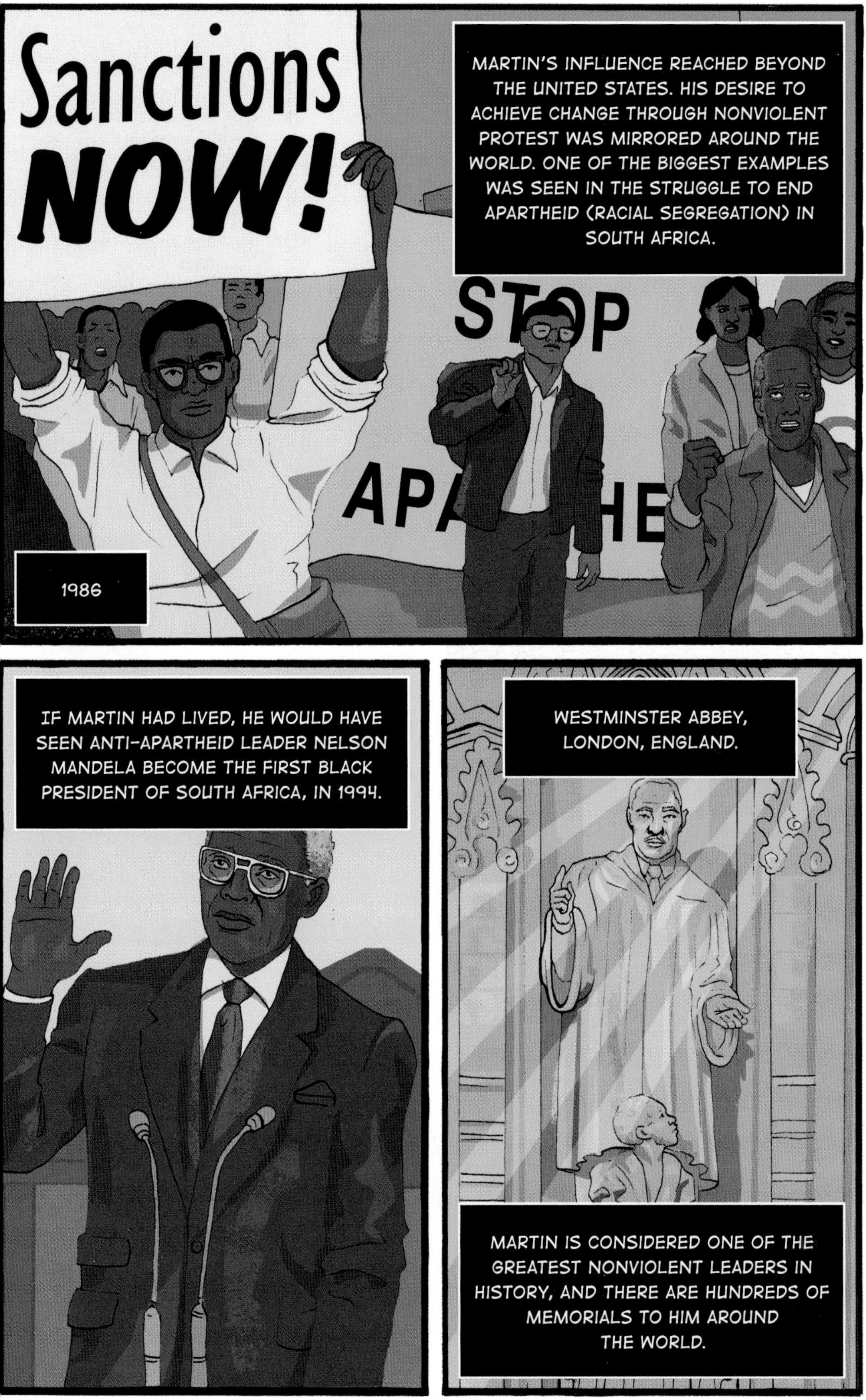
Sanctions NOW!
MARTIN'S INFLUENCE REACHED BEYOND THE UNITED STATES. HIS DESIRE TO ACHIEVE CHANGE THROUGH NONVIOLENT PROTEST WAS MIRRORED AROUND THE WORLD. ONE OF THE BIGGEST EXAMPLES WAS SEEN IN THE STRUGGLE TO END APARTHEID (RACIAL SEGREGATION) IN SOUTH AFRICA.
1986
IF MARTIN HAD LIVED, HE WOULD HAVE SEEN ANTI-APARTHEID LEADER NELSON MANDELA BECOME THE FIRST BLACK PRESIDENT OF SOUTH AFRICA, IN 1994.
WESTMINSTER ABBEY, LONDON, ENGLAND.
MARTIN IS CONSIDERED ONE OF THE GREATEST NONVIOLENT LEADERS IN HISTORY, AND THERE ARE HUNDREDS OF MEMORIALS TO HIM AROUND THE WORLD.

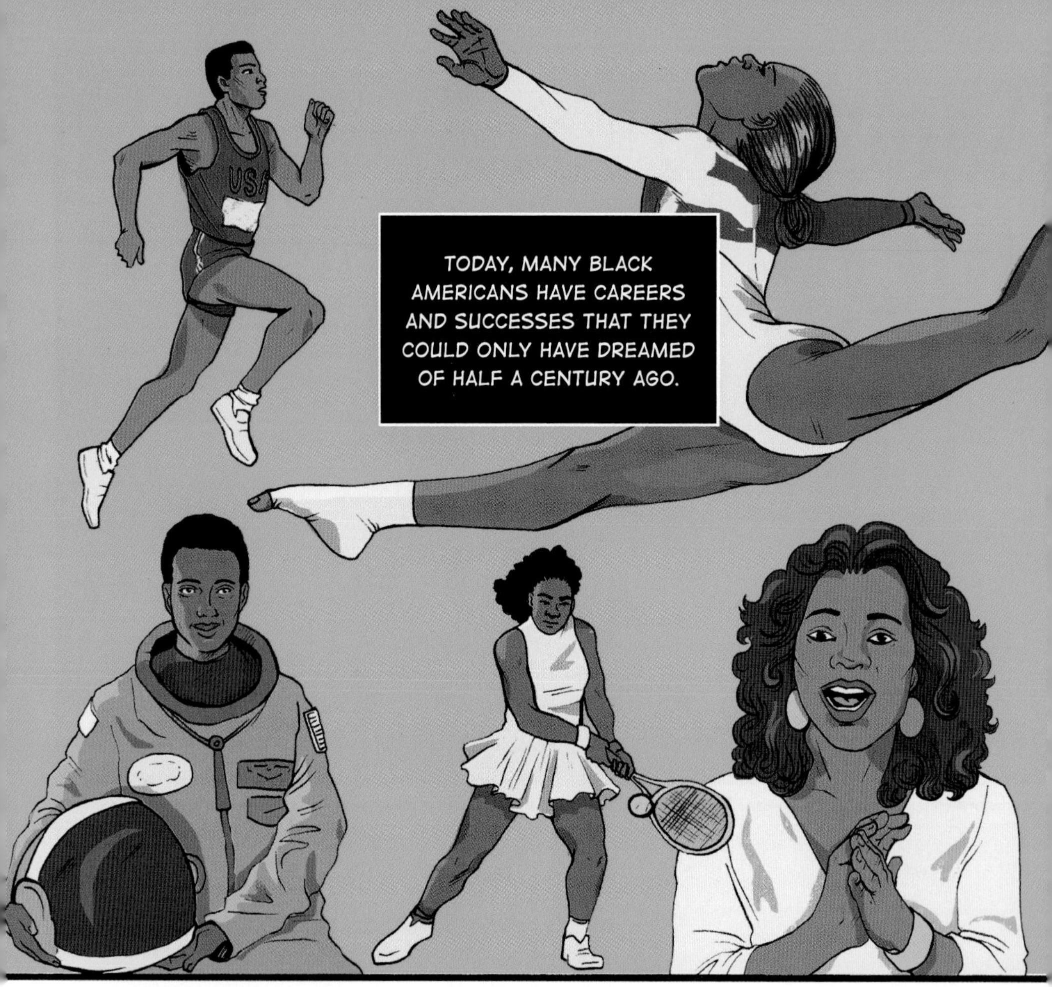
TODAY, MANY BLACK AMERICANS HAVE CAREERS AND SUCCESSES THAT THEY COULD ONLY HAVE DREAMED OF HALF A CENTURY AGO.

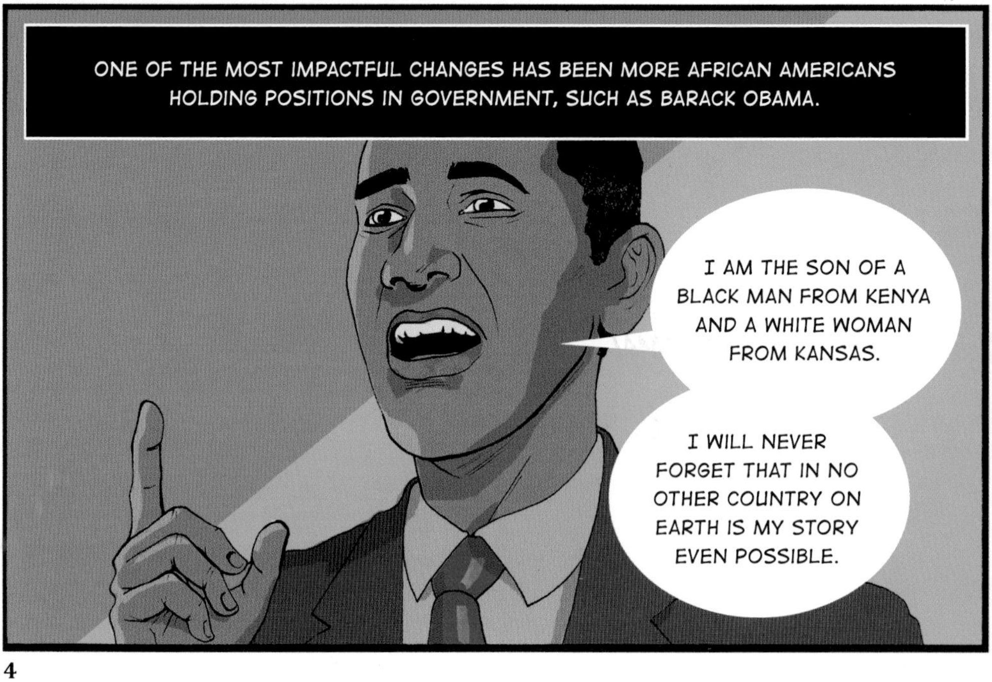
ONE OF THE MOST IMPACTFUL CHANGES HAS BEEN MORE AFRICAN AMERICANS HOLDING POSITIONS IN GOVERNMENT, SUCH AS BARACK OBAMA.
I AM THE SON OF A BLACK MAN FROM KENYA AND A WHITE WOMAN FROM KANSAS.
I WILL NEVER FORGET THAT IN NO OTHER COUNTRY ON EARTH IS MY STORY EVEN POSSIBLE.

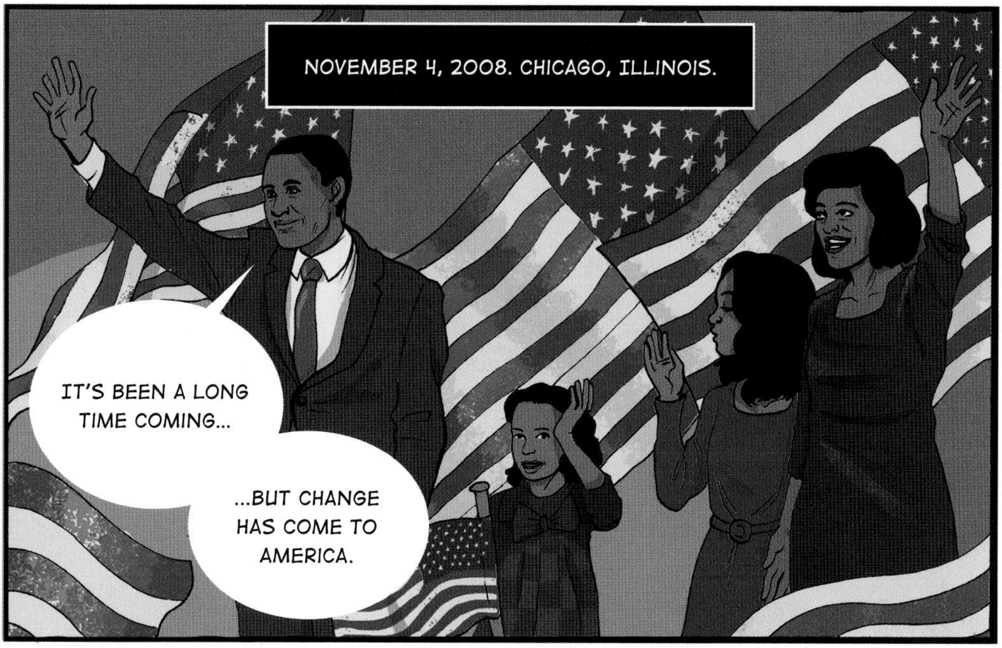
NOVEMBER 4, 2008. CHICAGO, ILLINOIS.
IT'S BEEN A LONG TIME COMING...
...BUT CHANGE HAS COME TO AMERICA.

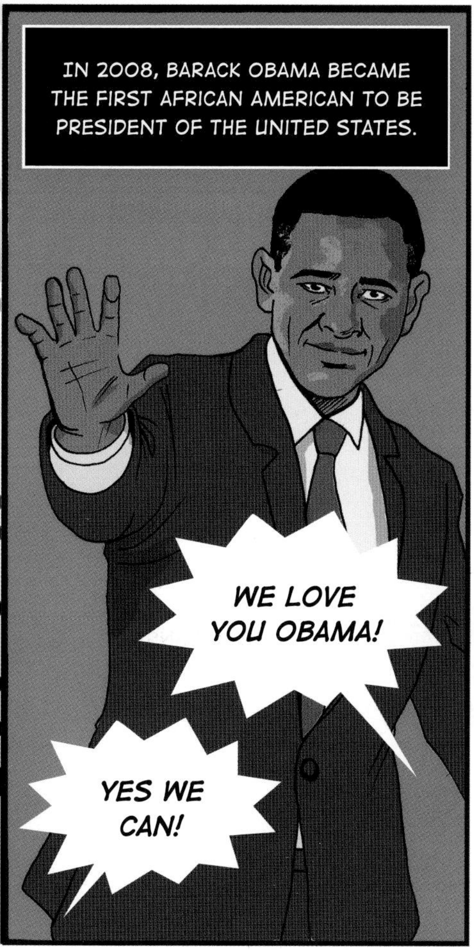
IN 2008, BARACK OBAMA BECAME THE FIRST AFRICAN AMERICAN TO BE PRESIDENT OF THE UNITED STATES.
WE LOVE YOU OBAMA!
YES WE CAN!

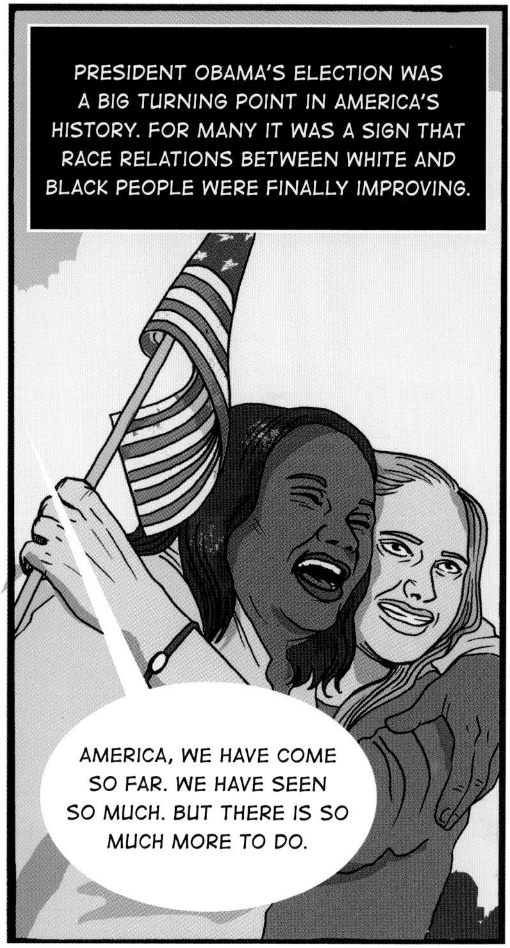
PRESIDENT OBAMA'S ELECTION WAS A BIG TURNING POINT IN AMERICA'S HISTORY. FOR MANY IT WAS A SIGN THAT RACE RELATIONS BETWEEN WHITE AND BLACK PEOPLE WERE FINALLY IMPROVING.
AMERICA, WE HAVE COME SO FAR. WE HAVE SEEN SO MUCH. BUT THERE IS SO MUCH MORE TO DO.

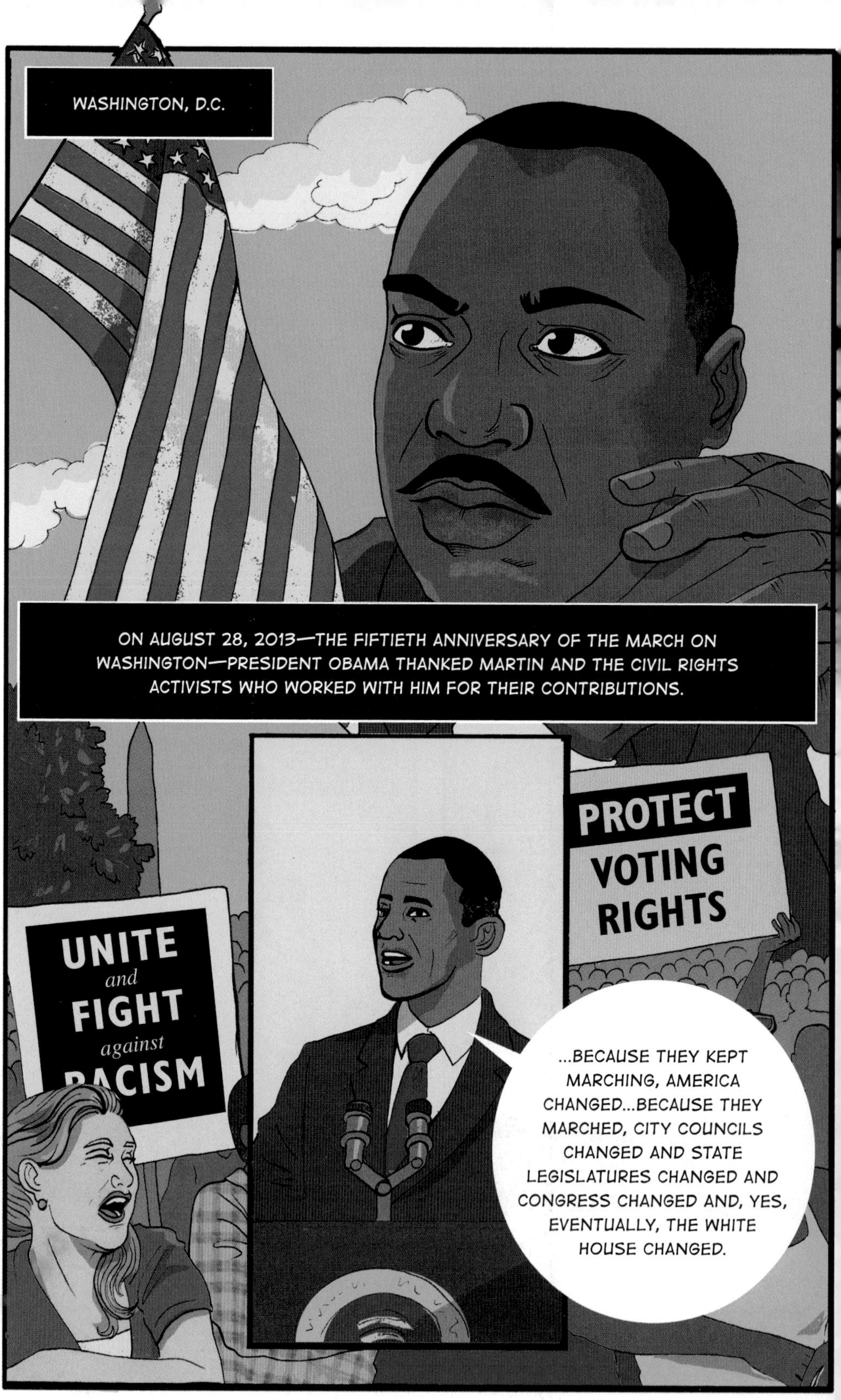
WASHINGTON, D.C.
ON AUGUST 28, 2013—THE FIFTIETH ANNIVERSARY OF THE MARCH ON WASHINGTON—PRESIDENT OBAMA THANKED MARTIN AND THE CIVIL RIGHTS ACTIVISTS WHO WORKED WITH HIM FOR THEIR CONTRIBUTIONS.
UNITE and FIGHT against RACISM
PROTECT VOTING RIGHTS
...BECAUSE THEY KEPT MARCHING, AMERICA CHANGED...BECAUSE THEY MARCHED, CITY COUNCILS CHANGED AND STATE LEGISLATURES CHANGED AND CONGRESS CHANGED AND, YES, EVENTUALLY, THE WHITE HOUSE CHANGED.